Prison Life in
Popular Culture

Prison Life
in Popular
Culture

From *The Big House* to
Orange Is the New Black

Dawn K. Cecil

LYNNE
RIENNER
PUBLISHERS

BOULDER
LONDON

Published in the United States of America in 2015 by
Lynne Rienner Publishers, Inc.
1800 30th Street, Boulder, Colorado 80301
www.rienner.com

and in the United Kingdom by
Lynne Rienner Publishers, Inc.
3 Henrietta Street, Covent Garden, London WC2E 8LU

Library of Congress Cataloging-in-Publication Data
Cecil, Dawn K.
Prison life in popular culture : from the big house to orange is the new black /
Dawn K. Cecil.
    pages cm
    Includes bibliographical references and index.
    ISBN 978-1-62637-279-5 (hc : alk. paper)
    1. Prisoners in popular culture—United States. 2. Prisoners—United States.
3. Prisons—United States. 4. Prisons in mass media. 5. Mass media and
criminal justice—United States. 6. Criminal justice, Administration of—
United States. I. Title.
    HV9466.C43 2015
    365'.60973—dc23

                                                              2015011661

British Cataloguing in Publication Data
A Cataloguing in Publication record for this book
is available from the British Library.

Printed and bound in the United States of America

The paper used in this publication meets the requirements
of the American National Standard for Permanence of
Paper for Printed Library Materials Z39.48-1992.

5 4 3 2 1

Contents

Tables and Figures

Tables

Figure

Acknowledgments

RESEARCHING AND WRITING THIS BOOK HAS BEEN A JOURNEY, during which my greatest supporter was my mother. Though she is no longer here to see the finished product, I am forever grateful for her encouragement and support. I must also thank my family, friends, and especially, Rick for being there when I needed them the most and for listening to me talk endlessly about prisons.

My interest in prisons can be traced back to the very first criminal justice class I took as an undergraduate. It was my professor's enthusiasm for the subject that convinced me to change my major, so I must thank Lois Guyon for starting me on this journey all those years ago. I would also like to thank those who helped me to develop my research and ideas on prison imagery, including my students at the University of South Florida St. Petersburg, especially Jennifer Leitner, who assisted in some of the early stages of my research on prison documentaries. I also thank Andrew Berzanskis of Lynne Rienner Publishers for guiding me through the process and Ray Surette and an anonymous reader, whose reviews and comments were helpful in the development of this work.

—*D. K. C.*

1

History of Prisons and Prison Imagery

Like candy to cavities, a diet heavy on popular culture will rot one's perceptions of reality.
—*Ray Surette, "Prologue: Some Unpopular Thoughts About Popular Culture"*

BAD GUYS MAKE GOOD ENTERTAINMENT. FROM EARLY DIME NOVels and comic books to films and television programs, Americans have always been enchanted with tales of the good guys catching outlaws. The final satisfaction is often provided by the echo of cell doors slamming, reassuring us that criminals are being punished. While many are simply entertained by these crime tales, others rely on these stories to learn about the criminal justice system. Most of these stories offer assurance that the system is effective and justice is achievable, but often the story is much more complicated, especially when it comes to punishment.

People have always been fascinated with punishment. In the past, they would gather in the town square to watch as wrongdoers were punished; however, in the late eighteenth century, most punishment moved behind prison walls. What took place there was a mystery to most. In the modern era, people often turn to the media and popular culture to feed their curiosity about this social institution. The prison film genre developed early in the history of moviemaking (Rafter 2006). Many of these films have a special place in US culture. *The Shawshank Redemption,* which is perhaps the most beloved prison film of all time, celebrated its twentieth anniversary in 2014 with a weekend of events, including a cocktail party at the prison. In 2013, the cable station TNT

1

devoted 151 of its programming hours to airing the movie (Schulz 2014). That same year more than 18,000 people visited the county in which this movie was filmed, exploring the Ohio State Reformatory and other filming sites (Schulz 2014). This prison is not the only one that people tour; on average, 4,000 people per day take the ferry across San Francisco Bay to tour Alcatraz (National Parks Conservation Association 2010). People who do not travel to one of these institutions can get their fix by turning on the television to watch marathons of the prison documentary series *Lockup* on the cable news station MSNBC or by binge-watching *Orange Is the New Black* on Netflix. We may not make punishment as visible today as in the past, but there are ample opportunities to satisfy people's curiosity.

In the twenty-first century, people have instantaneous access to many different types of crime-related imagery. With the flick of a switch, click of a mouse, or a swipe on a tablet, they can watch criminals plotting and executing their crimes, law enforcement in pursuit and making arrests, attorneys arguing in court, judges pronouncing sentences, and ultimately justice being achieved through punishment or death. Some of these are fictional representations while others are reality based. One could live off of a diet of crime-related media. While engrossed in these images, some viewers become armchair criminologists; by ingesting all of the information fed via the mass media, they become "experts" on the inner workings of the criminal justice system and the causes of criminal behavior.

People also learn about crime and justice through their own experiences. Personal knowledge trumps symbolic awareness such as that obtained by gorging on crime-related media. If someone has prior experience with the criminal justice system, then he or she is less likely to rely on the media (Pickett et al. 2014). Comparatively speaking, the United States has high crime rates (despite the fact that these rates have been decreasing since the mid-1990s), but in reality most people do not have experience with the entire criminal justice system. They observe police on a daily basis and at times have interactions with these law enforcement officers. They may even go to court for jury duty or to fight a traffic ticket. In all likelihood, however, they have never experienced the system of punishment. If they have, it was most likely community based, such as probation, which is the most common sanction given. They may have even spent a night in jail. Prisons, however, are far removed from the daily lives of most people. These institutions are closed; access to them is strictly controlled. Unless one works, visits, or is incarcerated in a prison, opportunities for experiencing it firsthand are extremely limited. When personal experiences are absent, people turn to the media to gain knowledge of social issues (Krczmar and Strizhakoa 2009). The end result is an overreliance on media imagery as a source of information about prison. The problem is that the media are known for presenting an inaccurate depiction of crime and punishment (Dorfman and Schiraldi 2001). While some portrayals may be more accurate than others, it is not possible for the media to offer a complete representation. Limited personal experience mixed with a reliance on imprecise or incomplete information is a dangerous combination, particularly in a nation in which imprisonment plays such a large role. In this book, I set out to uncover how we as a culture have come to understand prisons through media imagery and the implications of this process.

While we do not know the exact extent to which media representations of crime shape people's perceptions, we do know that they do have an effect. Even college students studying criminal justice are not immune to the power of popular representations. In one of my criminology courses, students are asked to read articles about the drop in crime, look at current crime statistics, and discuss the ongoing decreases in the crime rate. During multiple semesters, a surprising number of students denied that there had been a drop in crime at all, often citing how much crime they saw every day in the media. Even when presented with factual information, the power of popular representations overrode the truth for many of these students. Relying on popular constructions of crime and justice can, to some extent, create a false understanding of the issues at hand. While this is just one example, research has found that people who rely on the mass media are less knowledgeable about punishment (Pickett et al. 2014). We will never be able to stop people from ingesting the endless information on crime and punishment provided by the media; thus, we cannot prevent this imagery from shaping people's perceptions of the issues. But there is a growing understanding of how this imagery impacts these perceptions, which could be used to combat common misconceptions. Prisons are a costly and at times detrimental social institution; therefore, it is important to identify any misrepresentations and messages contained within modern depictions. For much of the existence of the prison system, there was only limited availability of media images of life behind the walls of these institutions. Now, the choices are seemingly endless. Prisons have become ingrained in both society and popular culture.

Imprisonment Rates and Penal Populism

Imprisonment is a critical social issue in modern US society. The government spends billions of dollars each year on the prison system. The

United States currently incarcerates more than 2 million people, making it the world's leader in incarceration (Carson and Sabol 2012). Of these prisoners, 1.5 million are locked up in state and federal prisons (Carson and Golinelli 2013, 1). There are signs that the trend is shifting, ever so slightly. In 2012, the number of people in state and federal prisons declined for the third year in a row (Carson and Golinelli 2013, 1). But how did we get to the point of incarcerating 1 out of every 108 American adults (Glaze and Heberman 2013, 2)?

Until the 1970s the United States's incarceration rate was not much higher than elsewhere in the world, but, since then, it has transformed into one of the most punitive countries (Tonry 2004). During that time we began what James Austin and John Irwin (2012) term the "imprisonment binge." Just like binge-drinking or -eating, we began to incarcerate more people than is healthy for our well-being. Michael Lynch (2007, 3) defines it as "the tendency for America's prison population to continue to expand." In 1973 the rate at which we incarcerated people began to increase more quickly than the US population (Lynch 2007), marking the beginning of the imprisonment binge. To understand where we are today and how prison growth coincides with increases in prison imagery, let us take a brief look at the changes that took place between 1973 and 2009.

In *Big Prisons, Big Dreams: Crime and the Failure of America's Penal System,* Lynch conducts a comprehensive analysis of the United States's changing incarceration trends. In 1930 there were 129,453 people incarcerated in prisons across the country, and by the end of the twentieth century there were approximately 1.3 million (Lynch 2007). Most of this growth occurred during the imprisonment binge. Between 1930 and 1976 the incarceration rate increased by approximately 15 percent, or less than 1 percent per year; however, once the imprisonment binge began, the average annual increase was 15 percent. The modern prison system is ten times larger than what it was at the start of this binge (Lynch 2007). The binge began shortly after the government declared a war on crime and continued to grow under Republican and Democratic administrations. In the 1990s there were unprecedented changes to crime control policies, making punishment harsher than ever before. States introduced three strikes and truth-in-sentencing laws as well as zero-tolerance policies, culminating in more people in prison serving longer sentences (Tonry 2004). The effects are still being felt today. Representatives of both political parties are considering the next step—how to dig themselves out of the hole caused by this reliance on imprisonment. The recent decreases are mainly attributed to changes in

California's prison population (Carson and Golinelli 2013). The state was mandated by the Supreme Court to decrease the prison population to 137.5 percent of capacity. In response, California passed the Public Safety Realignment Act of 2011, which transferred the responsibility of low-level offenders to the county and shifting some inmates from prisons to jails (California Department of Corrections and Rehabilitation 2013). California is not alone in its quest to decrease the state's reliance on prisons. Many other states are now considering how to proceed before their prison systems lead them to bankruptcy or supervision by the federal government.

Many factors come into play when explaining why the United States relies so much on imprisonment. According to Lynch (2007), these include imprisonment as a response to crime, public demands for a solution to crime and the political responses to their requests, the perceived failure of the system, and the age structure of society. Lynch himself takes a materialistic approach when explaining the US reliance on imprisonment. For the purpose of the discussion at hand, the demands of the public and the responses of politicians are the most relevant. For an in-depth explanation of the other factors, please refer to Lynch's discussion. For now, I turn to the idea of penal populism.

Imprisonment policies are enacted by politicians. Since they are elected officials, they are not immune to pressure from public and private entities. Some of the changes to imprisonment polices can be attributed to pressure from campaign contributors, lobbyists, and other private sector entities (Lynch 2007). There is big money in incarceration; thus, increasing its use benefits some organizations. The idea behind penal populism, however, focuses on public pressure. It suggests that strict imprisonment policies are enacted in response to this type of demand, whether perceived or real, rather than on the basis of effectiveness (Roberts et al. 2003; Pratt 2007). Populist pressure cannot explain all of the changes contributing to the imprisonment binge (Roberts et al. 2003), but it is a large part of the equation. The 1970s ushered in a more conservative mindset among the US public. By the 1980s, there were increasing crime rates and a collective concern about crime as a major social issue. The public demanded that officials get tough—the response was imprisonment. Rehabilitation was perceived by many to be a failure; thus, prison needed to be used for incapacitation and deterrence, translating into longer sentences. The end result was unprecedented incarceration rates that ultimately surpassed every other country in the world. Our place as a prison nation was firmly established.

US Media Culture and Prison Imagery

Not only is the United States a prison nation, it is a media culture. It is one in which "images, sounds, and spectacles help produce the fabric of everyday life, dominating leisure time, shaping political views and social behavior, and providing materials out of which people forge their very identities" (Kellner 1995, 1). In the latter part of the twentieth century, people's reliance on media grew exponentially, and it has become an overwhelming force in the lives of many Americans. We went from daily newspapers and network television to cable television and instantaneous access to all sorts of media representations on the Internet. According to Douglas Kellner (1995, 2), "In a contemporary media culture the dominant media of information and entertainment are a profound and often misperceived source of culture pedagogy: they contribute to educating us how to behave and what to think, feel, believe, fear, and desire and what not to." While providing lessons on proper behavior, it teaches us the consequences of breaking societal rules. People learn that failure to conform often results in death or imprisonment (Kellner 1995).

People turn to the media for a variety of reasons. For many, there is an expectation that the media will entertain and educate. The lessons and entertainment provided by crime-related tales is undeniable. As imprisonment rates increased, so too did the amount of television programming devoted to crime and justice. *Cops* and *Law and Order,* which debuted in 1989 and 1991 respectively, mark changes in the representation of crime on television. Both offered viewers "real" lessons on the criminal justice system—*Cops* by relying on actual footage and *Law and Order* by ripping its stories from the headlines. From televised news magazines to dozens of copycat programs of *Cops,* infotainment television programming became more prevalent. However, the blending of entertainment and education can be troublesome because the former typically overshadows any pedagogy. Americans are simultaneously fascinated and troubled by the media depictions of crime and justice that they crave. Despite the fact that the great US drop in crime started in the mid-1990s, many people remain under the misconception that crime is worse than ever before, just like the criminal justice students above. The reliance on violence as a form of entertainment is partially responsible for this misunderstanding that contributes to fear and feeds punitive attitudes. Reinforcing the need for a harsh system are many of the prison images consumed by US society.

By the end of the twentieth century, the United States was officially in the midst of an imprisonment binge, and images of these institutions started to become more plentiful and popular. Instead of imagining the inner workings of these institutions, avid consumers could now consider themselves extremely knowledgeable about imprisonment in the United States. Prison has become so ingrained in the culture that people are familiar with strip searches, snitches, shanks, striped uniforms, and Secure Housing Units (SHUs) without ever setting foot in a prison. Many of these elements have become clichés, and misunderstandings are abundant. For example, some people cannot differentiate between prisons and jails precisely because the mass media commonly use these terms interchangeably. Regardless of the specific source, each image of prison has the potential to reinforce preexisting stereotypes and send specific messages about the use of incarceration in US society.

A brief note before I continue this exploration of prisons in the media and popular culture. Prisons and jails are distinctly different institutions. Both are used for incarceration; however, they serve different functions in the criminal justice system. We rely on *jails* to house people awaiting trial and those serving short sentences, as well as those awaiting transfer to other institutions. These institutions serve a greater purpose than just punishing offenders. *Prisons,* however, hold those sentenced to longer periods of incarceration—anywhere from 1 year to life. Their overriding purpose is to carry out the punishment dictated by the state. Each type of institution has its own set of issues. The effects of the imprisonment binge have been felt in both prisons and jails, but in the long term they have placed significantly greater pressure on the prison system. While media representations of jails also influence people's social construction of imprisonment, the purpose of this inquiry is to look exclusively at prison imagery.

Prison Imagery and Social Constructionism

A simple equation underlies my examination of prison images—the further a subject is removed from the public eye, the more influential images become in shaping people's perceptions. Most people will never encounter a real prison; therefore, they must rely on prison tales to become informed. Prisons, by design, are removed from our daily lives. This exclusion is a vast change from punishment in the colonial era, which was highly visible and a part of community life. Punishment such as the stocks, pillories, other forms of corporal punishment, and the gallows were a public spectacle. However, the invention of the penitentiary in the late eighteenth century changed the face of punishment. Prisons were designed to keep people locked away from the community. When prisons were created, isolation was considered the key to reformation, so much so that solitary confinement and silence were the norm. The massive walls surrounding these prisons provided further seclusion as well as a veil of mystery. Not knowing what was taking place behind the walls of these structures also served as warning to the masses. While removed from the public eye by design, the walls were not impenetrable to all. As early as 1839 several prisons, including Eastern State Penitentiary and Auburn Prison, opened their gates to tourists who could pay the admission price (Cox 2009), but it was a luxury that many could not afford.

Over the centuries, since the birth of the penitentiary, there have been major developments in corrections and in media representations (see Table 1.1). Modern prisons are surrounded by fences instead of solid stone walls, yet they are removed from most people's day-to-day lives. This isolation is both physical and symbolic. According to Peter Y. Sussman (2002, 258), "Prisons are surrounded by high walls—walls of con-

Table 1.1 History of Prisons and Prison Imagery

■ **1790–1890s**

The penitentiary system was born in 1790 when a wing of the Walnut Street Jail in Philadelphia was converted to hold prisoners as punishment. Eastern State Penitentiary, which opened in 1829, is considered the quintessential penitentiary. Solitude, silence, and reflection were cornerstones of this system, and work was eventually added. Over the next hundred years, the system grew and transformed. Reformatories eventually developed, focusing on education and vocational training as well as allowing inmates to earn release for good behavior.

Prison Imagery

Popular prison imagery was almost nonexistent, although people could buy penny postcards depicting sketch drawings of these institutions.

■ **1900–1950s**

The prison population increased and work replaced education and training, transforming penitentiaries into big houses. In the 1930s, the Federal Bureau of Prisons was created and its flagship prison, United States Penitentiary (USP) Alcatraz, opened. Eventually, the medical model was adopted and rehabilitation became the foundation of the prison system.

Prison Imagery

Prison films emerged at the beginning of the twentieth century, and by the 1930s enjoyed their golden days. Throughout this period of time, these films were the most common form of prison imagery.

continues

Table 1.1 continued

■ **1960–1970s**
Problems that had been brewing in the prison system for decades bubbled to the surface. Major abuses were uncovered in the 1960s when prison systems in Arkansas and other states were deemed unconstitutional. The infamous riot at Attica Correctional Facility erupted in 1971. Rehabilitation was deemed a failure when Robert Martinson (1974) released his "What Works" article. On a positive note, the courts abandoned their hands-off policy for dealing with prison issues, thus affording prisoners certain rights. The war on crime was waged, contributing to the beginning of the imprisonment binge.

Prison Imagery
Prison films were less common. Those that were made depicted a more violent prisoner population than films of the past. Advances in documentary filmmaking set the stage for prison documentaries to emerge.

■ **1980–2000**
The United States returned to the use of solitary confinement with the development of supermax units and prisons. USP Marion became the first to receive this designation in the early 1980s and was replaced by Administrative Maximum Facility (ADX) Florence in the 1990s. Get-tough attitudes were signified by changes to drugs laws, the creation of zero-tolerance policies, mandatory minimums, and three strikes policies, which contributed to a skyrocketing prison population.

Prison Imagery
Crime-related television changed considerably during this time. Prison documentaries became more sensationalistic and the first US TV prison drama was aired.

■ **2000–present**
Trends that started in the latter part of the twentieth century continued. The use of solitary confinement became more prevalent and the prison population increased through 2009, after which California was court ordered to decrease its prison population and other states began closing institutions due to budgetary concerns. Policymakers began to question the use of solitary confinement.

Prison Imagery
The televised prison documentary series became popular, independent documentaries became more easily accessible, and prison films continued to become less common.

crete and razor wire, of course, but also walls of secrecy and stereotype." Prisons are located in rural areas, many times sustaining entire communities while being far away from most. Prison tours still exist but, with the exception of educational tours, the public can visit only historic relics that are no longer in use. Most people must rely on the media to tell them about what is taking place in these institutions. Some media representations are littered with prison stereotypes while others offer incomplete information due to limited access to these institutions.

Developing an understanding of all the factors involved in shaping the public's opinion about imprisonment is a complex task. One critical factor that influences people's perceptions is the media images that they consume (Roberts et al., 2003; Surette 2011). Historically, people relied on one another to gain information about social issues; however, in post-modern society, they must gather this information from less personal sources, such as the media (Giddens 1990). In this day and age, the media have become the main source of what many people know about crime (Wright 1985). The same can be said about their knowledge of prison.

For thousands of years, people have debated the processes involved in the development of human's beliefs about themselves and the world around them. Empiricists, such as John Locke, argued that all knowledge comes from personal experience while rationalists, such as Plato and Immanuel Kant, believed that our mental processes shape what we know (Gergen 2009). This book is based on social constructionist ideas about reality and knowledge. Reality is a social construction (Berger and Luckman 1967) that is created through a combination of personal experiences or experienced reality and information gained from other sources or symbolic reality (Surette 2011). The latter is thought to be particularly powerful for matters far removed from our personal lives and, thus, our experiences.

In 1922, Walter Lippmann began laying the groundwork of the social constructionist ideas that underlie the basis of my examination of prison images. He stated that, instead of defining things for ourselves, "we pick out what our culture has already defined for us, and we tend to perceive that which we have picked out in the form stereotyped for us by our culture" (Lippmann 1922, 54). The implications of this idea are vast. For instance, if the media are constantly telling people that prisons are an effective crime-fighting tool, they may begin to define them as such, especially if they have no other knowledge. Lippmann's statement was written decades before one of the most powerful forms of media entered our daily lives—television, which brings images of strange and unknown things into the comfort of our homes (Yousman 2009). Television's effects are powerful due to the cumulative nature of exposure to these images (Gerbner et al. 1994). Given the placement of prison in our society and the current nature of prison-related television programming and films, it is undeniable that the images produced will have a profound effect on people's perceptions of these social institutions.

The potential sources of symbolic reality of prison extend beyond these mass media images. People choose when they prefer to see prisons and under what conditions, whether by watching a film, going on a prison tour, or tuning into the latest reality-based television program about imprisonment (Brown 2009). In this sense, "popular culture presents us with the most powerful place in which the practice of imprisonment has been reenacted to the largest audience" (Brown 2009, 54). Popular culture is "culture by the people for the people," elements of which are likely to be entertaining and recreational (Danesi 2012, 4). It is a part of the larger culture of society. Today popular culture is a mass culture that reaches multitudes through the media and communication technologies (Danesi 2012). The mainstream media are a part of popular culture, but they extend beyond these representations. Crime and justice are ingrained in other aspects of US popular culture. One can find crime and justice, including prison, represented in virtually everything from films, music, and cartoons to games and merchandise.

Exactly how media images influence people's perceptions is a subject of debate. In general, there is an agreement that substantial exposure persuades "consumers that the symbolic reality presented in the media is an accurate reflection of objective social conditions" (R. L. Fox, Van Sickel, and Steiger 2007, 8). Various media effects models exist, which can help explain how images of prison can influence people's perceptions of this social institution. The direct effects model argues that the content of the media has an immediate and consistent effect on consumers (Perse 2001). The audience is viewed as passive; they simply take in the information that they are fed. According to this model, if media images consistently support mass imprisonment to deal with crime, those who ingest this information will take it at face value. However, it is likely that the effect of prison images is more complicated than the direct effects model suggests.

Rather than viewing the consumer as a passive part of the equation, the conditional effects model proposes that media effects are dependent on the individual who is consuming the images. People choose what they want to watch and react differently based on their own experiences and knowledge. They are selective in what they choose, usually picking images that match their already existing beliefs. For many, this means that their opinions will be reinforced, although it also argues that, depending on the person, these views could be altered (Perse 2001). Various types of prison images are available to consumers, and this model can explain fluctuations in people's desire to see prison images as well as the type of images they prefer.

Regardless of the specific images that someone decides to indulge in, there typically is overlap in the content displayed. The cumulative effects model focuses on the repetitiveness of media content. Seeing similar messages time and time again typically culminates in viewers adopting the media's construction of the issue (Perse 2001). The crime-related messages inherent in much of prison imagery are similar to those already disseminated in other crime-related images. If one is an avid consumer of crime-related media, the repetitive messaging culminates in the belief that crime is rampant and incarceration is the answer. Essential elements of the cumulative model are agenda setting and cultivation. *Agenda setting* is the proposition that, over time, the media has the ability to direct attention toward specific issues (Perse 2001). The traditional saying about the news media is that "if it bleeds, it leads." This statement holds true of most news broadcasts, thus viewers are persuaded to think about crime and violence in society. *Cultivation* posits that the more television that people watch, the more likely they are to adopt the recurrent views and messages about the world sent via these images (Morgan, Shanahan, and Signorielli 2008). Thus, someone who rarely consumes these images is less likely to adopt these mainstream views. Cultivation looks at what people absorb, not what they think about it. Cultivation is "a continual, dynamic, ongoing process of interaction among messages, audiences, and contexts" (Morgan, Shanahan, and Signorielli 2008, 38). Several decades of research have demonstrated that heavy viewers of television see more violence, which in turn leads to exaggerated ideas about the prevalence of crime in our society as well as other misconceptions about crime and justice (Gerbner et al. 1979, 1980; Shanahan and Morgan 1999; Holbert, Shah, and Kwak 2004; Holbrook and Hill 2005; Goidel, Freeman, and Procopio 2006). Together, these culminate in more punitive attitudes.

Each of these models suggests that both mass media and popular culture have the potential to influence people's perceptions. There is no doubt that the media focus a lot of attention on crime and justice. Even when not focusing on prison per se, the inherent messages are highly supportive of current incarceration policies in the United States. Whether through direct, conditional, or cumulative effects, or a combination of these models, media images of prison have the possibility to shape social constructions of this institution and, thus, opinions. My examination of prison imagery does not set out to determine which of these models is in play. Instead, I focus on what people take away from this mediated experience.

Uncovering Media Frames and Messages

In today's media culture, people can turn to a vast variety of sources in their quest for knowledge and entertainment. Each of these sources has its own way of conveying information, and each has the potential to send different messages about the prison system. There are various ways that one can begin to dissect the information presented in these media images. One can begin by describing how films, television programs, and documentaries depict prison to their audiences. These descriptions uncover the particular aspects of imprisonment detailed in these stories. For example, a commonly used scene is a new inmate being processed into the institution. This image is familiar to people; yet alone, it does not send any particular message about prison. Initially it taught viewers about the process, later it was used to set the stage. Looking at the bigger picture, there is much more to prison imagery than just these descriptions.

To truly uncover the meaning of prison imagery in our culture, we need to identify the underlying messages and determine how the issue of imprisonment is framed. The cumulative messages are created by visual images and the words and sounds that accompany them. In general, crime-related media are known for conveying messages about crime control and due process. The crime control message shows people that the goal of the criminal justice system is deterrence and punishment (Surette 2011). It does not matter how you get to that point—the boundaries can be pushed as long as there is punishment. In essence, the end justifies the means. *Dirty Harry* (1971) is an early and quintessential example of this type of messaging. The audience did not mind that Detective Harry Callahan took matters into his own hands in order to catch the Scorpio Killer. He did what he had to in order to keep people safe. The crime control message has become popular in many of the popular crime shows on television. The police are often depicted as bending the rules to get the bad guys. The due process message is not as common, but it does exist. The due process model focuses on protecting individuals' rights. It is the government's job to follow the rules that are in place before exacting punishment (Surette 2011). The means that one uses to get to the punishment phase are critical. Media imagery that send a due process message highlight the importance of these procedures in the quest for justice. It is most often the underlying message in courtroom films and TV shows. Viewers watch the attorneys follow a strict set of rules in order to ensure the achievement of justice. The crime control and due process messages are just two examples. Crime-related media representations can send a variety of messages about crime, its causes, and its possible solutions. Prison imagery sends some of these same messages. However, there are also unique messages that are crucial to our understanding of what people are taking away from all of these representations of life behind bars.

Underlying messages are affected by the way that the issue is framed; therefore, to understand any media representation it is critical to look at the frames used by the creator. Frames "are the focus, a parameter or boundary, for discussing a particular event. Frames focus on what will be discussed, how it will be discussed, and above all, how it will not be discussed" (Altheide 1997, 651). A frame determines what topics will be included and how they will be covered. Frames are shaped by the media organization itself as well as by previously used frames, history, and ideology (Tuchman 1978). Media representations of crime often use violence to frame the issue. Time and time again consumers view images of violent criminals, thereby ignoring the most common types of offenders. Media images of prison are also known for using the violence frame, but there are other ways the issue is framed that affect information gleaned from these sources. The specific content, messages, and frames used in modern prison imagery come together to form the larger picture of prison life, and it is these elements that can ultimately shape people's social construction of prison.

Modern Prison Imagery

Exploring prison imagery is not a new endeavor; others have examined prisons in films, television programming, and the news. While my discussion draws from this literature, its uniqueness lies in the consideration of the new media images popularized in the twenty-first century. By considering the cumulative messages about prison presented in popular media and culture, we can begin to understand how prison is constructed in the eyes of many Americans.

Today, there is an endless variety of imagery available to those who are curious about the world behind prison walls. There are many commonalities in the ways that prison is presented, yet there is also variation depending on the source. Each genre that I explore in this book has unique qualities. Creating nonfictional representations has more boundaries than developing fictional accounts of prison life. Furthermore, there are different factors that come into play when trying to entice people to pay for a movie ticket versus trying to sustain television viewers' attention for years on end. To best understand the variations in this imagery, as well as its development, I examine prison imagery genre by genre.

To begin, in Chapter 2 I briefly look at where representations of prison are found in US culture. The most obvious place is the news media, which has been known for not paying a lot of attention to prison issues. After looking at the role of the news media in the social construction of prison, I explore other aspects of US popular culture that have embraced imprisonment. Today, both children and adults catch glimpses of prison in the most unexpected places—from cartoons to alcoholic beverages. While these are not the most influential sources of information on prison life, they serve as examples of how prison has become ingrained in many aspects of our culture.

In Chapter 3, I delve into the most enduring prison imagery—the prison film. For generations, people relied on films to peek into the mysterious world behind prison walls. Early on, many of these films were a form of propaganda that highlighted the need to reform the system. A standard formula was immediately devised, and elements of it remain intact today. In the twenty-first century, however, the importance of the prison film has waned. Pure prison films are rare, but those that exist contain lessons on modern prison life.

The seeds of sensationalistic prison imagery can be found in the development of televised prison dramas, which I examine in Chapter 4. US television has been slow to embrace dramas about prisons, instead relying on the investigative side of the system to provide entertainment. In the midst of the imprisonment binge, however, prison dramas appeared. Given the serial nature of these programs, more context can be provided on inmates and life inside; however, these dramas tend to rely on emotional manipulation, negative imagery, and violence to entertain viewers. And in the long run, this type of fictional prison drama failed to develop beyond the initial stages.

While the dramatized images presented in films certainly contribute to people's perceptions, it stands to reason that viewers will have more faith in nonfiction accounts. Since news reports are limited, it is left to documentarians to provide a more complete look at prison. Documentary films on prison life were slow to develop, but now are plentiful and easily accessible. In Chapter 5, I explore the development of documentary films in general as well as those that were made about prison life. Some of these films took a historical look at infamous institutions such as Alcatraz while others investigated the system or attempted to deter viewers from a life of crime. By the 1990s, documentarians began to record the stories of maximum security life. While there are some hints of humanity in these films, many have focused on violent inmates out of control behind bars, thus laying the groundwork for the spectacle to come.

At the turn of the century, people's appetites for reality-based television and infotainment grew. So too did the number of prison documentaries, which placed a heavy emphasis on sensationalism to attract viewers. In Chapter 6, I examine popular cable television documentary series as well as independent documentary films made in the twenty-first century. As the genre developed, the imagery became more complex but still provided a spectacle at which viewers could gawk. Some of the old documentary tradition was maintained, but these are not the most prevalent or popular sources of prison tales today. Instead, it is the infotainment genre of televised documentaries that people seem to crave.

Latent lessons about masculinity are contained within nearly every type of prison imagery. Viewers are also exposed to strong messages about proper female behavior and femininity in films, television shows, and documentaries about women in prison. In general, all media images are gendered and present specific messages about masculinity and femininity. Stories about life behind bars are no different. Men make up most of the prison population; thus, the dominant depiction is based on the male perspective. Given that men and women experience imprisonment in their own ways, the differences in the imagery are an important consideration. The next two chapters focus on the ways in which the female prison population is depicted. In Chapter 7, I examine fictional representations of women behind bars, beginning with melodramatic films of the 1930s through the newest women in prison dramedy *Orange Is the New Black*. In Chapter 8, I cover the way that this correctional population is depicted in documentaries. Some of these documentaries appear to borrow elements from their Hollywood predecessors while others are better able to reflect the reality of these women's lives by focusing on unique prison programs, motherhood, and abuse. Taken together, both fictional and nonfictional representations send powerful messages about proper female behavior in US society.

While most of the book focuses on the visual images provided in films and on television, in Chapter 9 I take a look at prisons in music and comedy, which both offer a variety of takes on imprisonment. One might brush off these types of images as trivial and unimportant; however, the degree to which prison is embedded in US popular culture demonstrates that this is truly an incarceration nation.

After taking an in-depth look at prisons in all of these facets of US media and popular culture, I conclude by tying the vast representations together. Across the genres there are mainstream and alternative images, each presenting their own view of prisons in the United States. In their own way, both have the potential to distort people's perceptions of prison, but mainstream imagery is more likely to reinforce punitive attitudes. Yet today people can chose the type of imagery that they are most interested in. Ray Surette (1998) believes that too much popular culture results in the rotting of perceptions. If we can begin to understand the specific sources of this decay, we can understand why so many people have been reluctant to question the use of incarceration in the United States.

2

Prisons in Headlines, Prisons in Unexpected Places

FOR MORE THAN TWO CENTURIES AFTER THE INVENTION OF THE prison system, imagery of these institutions was almost nonexistent. The mysteries of prison life were basically contained behind the prison walls. Today, nothing could be further from the truth. In the current media culture, people have instantaneous access to fictional and nonfictional representations of prison life. Prisons are represented in the most and the least expected areas of media and popular culture. I begin this discussion with the most expected representations found in the news media and end with some of the least expected—prison in children's stories and as a marketing tool. None of these are the most prevalent sources of prison imagery, but each has the potential to be a part of someone's mediated experience of prison. Together, they tell us something about how people think of imprisonment in the United States and also serve as an indication of how ingrained prisons have become in the culture.

Prisons as News

The news media would seem to be the most logical and widely available source of penal knowledge. They serve as the forefront of current issues. People can turn to a variety of news sources to obtain information on events and trends. And while they used to have to wait for their news to be verified, in today's media culture news often breaks before we even know if there is an actual story worth telling. For the most part, prison has never been considered a vital news story. From time to time the general public has been able to catch a glimpse of the reality of prison life from news stories, whether through newsreels in the theaters during the early twentieth century or through modern newspaper articles, Internet news, and news broadcasts. While the news media provide realistic images, their coverage of the correctional system is limited in frequency and breadth. Newsworthy prison events, such as riots and escapes, are few and far between (Chermak 1998; Lipschultz and Hilt 2002). Furthermore, prison administrators have historically restricted media access to these institutions for the sake of security (Sussman 2002). Combined, these factors mean that prisons are rarely the focus of news stories, especially in comparison to other parts of the criminal justice system (Chermak 1998; Yousman 2009). This trend has continued throughout the imprisonment binge.

When the news media cover prison stories, the information given within the structure of the news format is limited. Bill Yousman (2009) notes that prison-related stories are episodic, not thematic. Episodic news focuses on single events (Iyengar 1991), relies on easily accessible information, and forms stories that contain only the most essential information. What this type of coverage does not allow for is an in-depth look at the issues surrounding incarceration in the United States (Yousman 2009). Over time, these stories have become commodified and "reduced to certain presumably crowd-pleasing categories that serve as easily digestible substitutes for uncomfortable realities and soothing anesthetics for fears of social dislocation" (Sussman 2002, 273). By focusing on stories of escapes, riots, and horrible prisoners behind bars, the news presents the public with the same type of stimulation that they get from action films (Sussman 2002). Thus, even when presented with real prison images via news coverage, the audience remains unaware of most issues surrounding this isolated world. These overwhelmingly negative stories, absent of context, send viewers specific messages about incarceration without offering a true understanding of the subject.

One area of the prison system that has often been off-limits to many journalists is supermax housing units, commonly referred to as Secure Housing Units. In these, the prison system has returned to its origins with a reliance on complete isolation for certain inmates. This practice is one regularly debated among academics and policymakers. James Ridgeway (2013) believes that most people are unaware of the real conditions of these housing units and the long-term effects of such confinement. To tell stories about solitary confinement in the United States, most journalists must rely exclusively on public records and letters written by inmates. One of several stories about solitary confinement on NPR reported that the Federal Bureau of Prisons refused to allow an interview on the issue (NPR 2013c). Some journalists have been able to gain access to SHUs and create critical stories that have contributed to changes such as Illinois's shutting down of Tamms Prison (Ridgeway 2013). "The stories have been effective. But their scarcity also suggests that the lack of press access to these sites around the nation has stifled public debate on a significant issue of policy and human rights" (Ridgeway 2013, par. 13). If more journalists were able to tell detailed stories about solitary confinement, perhaps we would not be to the point of holding US Senate hearings on the issue.

Recent newsworthy events have begun to change news stories on solitary confinement in US prisons. Some states are investigating ways to reform their use of isolation, which has brought about more news coverage. In 2013, the media reported on a two-month hunger strike held by more than 30,000 prisoners in California who were protesting the use of solitary confinement (see, for example, Caldwell and Harkinson 2013; Devereaux 2013; Medina 2013). In 2014, the *New York Times* published a series of articles and editorials on the practice (see, for example, Kysel 2014; Raemisch 2014). It is promising to see an increased interest in prison-related news stories; however, the news format limits its ability to make its target audience completely knowledgeable about the subject. More important, the news about solitary confinement does focus on a detrimental practice, but one that affects only a small portion of the prison population. The larger issues that grab less attention remain on the back burner.

Today's news exists in a "user-controlled" media universe (Rehm 2014). Consumers decide what type of news they are interested in and from which sources to get that news. They rely on some sources for their sports news and, perhaps, other sources for world events (Rehm 2014). This type of media universe can also explain the lack of news coverage on prison issues. One cannot forget that news organizations are businesses and, in today's media culture, there is a lot of competition. These organizations are driven partially by the demands of their market. If they think people are not interested in a subject, it is not considered newsworthy. Yet there are indications that some people are interested in prison issues. The *Huffington Post,* which is an online news aggregator and blog, is an example. Its format allows it to cover more topics and to feed the interests of its target audience. Similar to other news organizations, the *Huffington Post* has a section devoted to crime. But unlike others, it also has a section devoted to prison news.

Some of the stories are sensationalistic, but many of the reports pertain to current issues including the nation's incarceration rate, imprisoning the poor, and how the crime rate is affected by having fewer prisoners. While still limited in the details given, interested parties can use links provided in these stories to follow up on the issues, including reading reports on which the information is based. The possibilities for educating the US public on prisons in this way are endless—but first, they have to care enough to click on the links.

Prisons as a Children's Story

While children were once incarcerated in institutions with adults, that practice was abandoned long ago and there has been an attempt to shield them from the horrors of prison life. The imprisonment binge has brought the issue closer to the lives of many innocent children in the United States. It is estimated that there are more than 2.7 million children with an incarcerated parent (Reilly 2013). Books have been written to help children understand where their parent has gone, including *The Prison Alphabet: An Educational Coloring Book for Children of Incarcerated Parents* (Muhammad and Muhammad 2014) and *The Night Dad Went to Jail: What to Expect When Someone You Love Goes to Jail* (Higgins and Kirwan 2011). These books have a specific audience and are not well known. The topic, however, has been incorporated into popular culture.

Perhaps nothing says more about the integration of prison into US culture than introducing children to imprisonment via *Sesame Street*. Erik Ortiz (2013) explains, "*Sesame Street* is teaching kids about bedtime, bath time and jail time." *Last Week Tonight*'s host John Oliver (2014) comments that "so many people are incarcerated in America right now that it has become one of the things that *Sesame Street* has to explain to children. . . . Just think about that. We now need adorable singing puppets to explain prison to children in the same way they explain the number seven or what the moon is." How has this famous children's television show broached the subject of parental incarceration?

Joining Big Bird and the other *Sesame Street* characters is Alex, a boy whose father is in prison. Alex is featured in "Little Children, Big Challenges: Incarceration," a multimedia project, including a smartphone application, to help children deal with having an incarcerated parent. The *Sesame Street* website provides resources for service providers and caregivers, such as activities to do with children and a variety of tips. One tip advises the adults: "Answer Honestly: When explaining where an incarcerated parent is, you can say, 'Daddy is in a place called prison (or jail) for a while. Grown-ups sometimes go to prison when they break a rule called a law'" ("Little Children, Big Challenges: Incarceration" 2013). For the child audience, there is a series of videos to watch, some of which include real children with a parent in prison as well as their caregivers. Alex, along with an adult named Sophia, teach children what incarceration is, why adults go there, how to deal with their feelings, and, perhaps most important, that there are other kids out there who are having the same experience. Often when children see references to prison in other television shows, it is with a comedic twist, such as Bugs Bunny and Daffy being sent to an Alcatraz-type prison in the *Looney Toons Show* "Jail Bird, Jail Bunny" (Brandt et al. 2011). But *Sesame Street,* while using cute puppets, takes a more serious look at the issue.

When *Sesame Street* debuted in 1969 with the purpose of preparing kids for preschool, one could not have imagined that prison would be a topic of interest in what would become the world's most popular children's program. But that was before the United States became a prison nation. People are now talking about the number of children affected by the imprisonment binge. The current media culture also supports *Sesame Street*'s decision to tackle this subject and other sensitive ones. It allows the creators to address these issues and reach their targeted audience. While incarceration is not tackled in any episodes aired on PBS, the resource is on the website to help teach the children who are in need of help. According to Oliver (2014), "At least *Sesame Street* is talking about prison. The rest of us are much happier completely ignoring it."

Prisons as a Marketing Tool

Popular culture encompasses a variety of areas, including art, music, dance, merchandise, and even social media. Spectacle and nostalgia are commonly used elements of popular culture. Entertainment is provided through spectacle. Nostalgia is the emotional connection that it provides, which allows specific pop culture references to endure (Danesi 2012). Each of these factors is seen in many representations of prison life. In the United States, popular culture is directly related to consumer culture, and, for many Americans, consuming is a way of life (Goodman

2003). "Every public space, every occasion for public gathering, every creative expression is seen as an opportunity to encourage more consumption" (Goodman 2003, 4). Merchandising has become the norm. But what people may not immediately think of is how prison is incorporated into goods and services. Several businesses have capitalized on prison to find their niche in their respective markets, using both spectacle and nostalgia to attract consumers.

Ohio's Richmond County has capitalized off prison imagery and marketing in the twenty years since *The Shawshank Redemption* was filmed at the Ohio State Reformatory and other locations throughout the county. In 2013, visitors specifically seeking a *Shawshank* experience brought $3 million to the county's economy (Schulz 2014, para. 5). Small businesses in the area have been cashing in by tying their products to the popular prison film. Visitors sip on Redemption IPA, Reformatory Red Wines, Jail House Java, or Prison Break Soda while eating Redemption Pizza or a Shawshank Bundt Cake (Schulz 2014). When the filmmakers first came to their town more than two decades ago, the citizens probably had no idea that there would be enduring benefits for the economy. But they soon became successful at using prison to their advantage.

Reformatory Red Wines and Redemption IPA are not the only prison-themed adult beverages for sale. For the past two decades, the wine market in the United States has grown every year and, with this growth, has come intense competition for consumers (Wine Institute 2013). Today's wine labels are like book covers, geared to catching shoppers' eyes as they peruse the unique names and illustrations on the shelves at a wine store. The craft beer industry is similar. There has been tremendous growth in craft breweries, with an average of one new brewery opening every day (Brewers Association 2013). Some stores sell literally thousands of different beers and wines. If one looks closely at the shelves, there are references to prison life.

In California, near the Soledad Correctional Training Facility and Salinas Valley State Prison, is a winery that is aptly called Big House Wine Company. The description at its website demonstrates the company's take on the theme:

As The Warden, Georgetta Dane, it is one of my responsibilities to inform you about The Big House! Big House Winery in Soledad, CA (Monterey County) is a mere ankle iron's toss from the Soledad State Correctional Facility, a.k.a. "the Big House," "The Clink," "The Slammer," which explains the recurring prison theme depicted on the labels. The brand's cornerstone is a rebellious New World winemaking

style blending Mediterranean varieties. Big House wines unshackle
consumers from ball and chain wine choices and rules, creating criminally exhilarating everyday wines. (Big House Wine Company n.d.)

As mentioned in the description, each variety of wine has a prison-
related name and label such as Big House Red, Big House White,
Unchained, The Usual Suspect, The Slammer, and Birdman. Each label
colorfully depicts scenes commonly associated with prison life. Mim-
icking the ever popular prison escape, Big House Red and Big House
White have sketches of the outside of a prison on the front and, if you
look closely, there are sheets hanging down outside of a cell's window
and a getaway car speeding away. Unchained's bottle features prisoners
in striped uniforms working on a railroad. The names and labels are caricatures of a more romanticized time in prison history—the big house
era that is commonly depicted in old prison films. The winery is capital-
izing on its location and perhaps even people's love of old prison films.
Its cartoonish labels and funny names allows it to stand out in a compet-
itive market.

Similar to the Big House Wine Company, Jailhouse Brewing Company, outside of Atlanta, has capitalized on its location with an entire
line of prison- and jail-inspired beers. The brewery is located in the old
jailhouse of Hampton. During "visitation," costumers taste a variety of
beers including The Slammer Wheat, Breakout Stout, Conjugal Visit,
Last Request, Midnight Special, Hop Riot, Hard Time Barley Wine, and
Prison Camp Pils. Other prison-inspired breweries include Lockdown
Brewing Company and Alcatraz Brewing Company in California and
Prison Brews in Missouri. Santa Fe Brewing Company has one prison-
inspired beer, State Pen Porter, with the label featuring the top of the
prison walls and the guard tower looming over it. Each of these companies has capitalized on people's fascination with prison to make their
products unique in a vast marketplace. This attraction and the US consumer culture ensure that people will buy these products.

The prison theme extends to other businesses as well, the most well
known being prison tour companies. As a *USA Today* article about these
tours begins, "There's new glamour in the slammer" (Wisely and Creagar 2012). The most popular tour takes place on Alcatraz Island. It is
estimated that more than 1.4 million people visit the prison annually
(National Parks Conservation Association 2010). Eastern State Penitentiary has seen a significant growth in the number of visitors over the
past decade, now receiving about a quarter of a million visitors each
year (Wisely and Creagar 2012). Visitors can also tour West Virginia

Penitentiary, Missouri State Penitentiary, Ohio State Reformatory, and Prison of Southern Michigan, among others. In addition to touring actual institutions, there are prison museums such as those at Angola and Folsom Prisons. Most of these tours and museums also sell a wide variety of souvenirs—consumerism at its best. Visitors walk back into the free world with coffee mugs, shot glasses, clothing, magnets, and knickknacks of all kinds.

People who are interested in a longer prison stay can book a room in former prisons and jails that have been converted into hotels and hostels. These hotels can be found around the world. In the United States, there are a few hotels in old jails. The Liberty Hotel is housed in an old jail in Boston. It is a luxury hotel that houses a restaurant called Clink, with the old cells creating nooks for dining. Located on the original catwalk of the jail is a bar, aptly called Catwalk, and an outside event area is called The Yard. Other bars and restaurants also have taken on the prison theme. Chicago is home to Lockdown Bar and Grill, and Salem, Massachusetts, to the Great Escape Restaurant, the latter of which is located in an old jail. On the other hand, Lockdown Bar and Grill describes itself as a virtual concert venue with large screens streaming rock concerts. The owners are heavily influenced by the bands that they listened to growing up, which makes the prison-inspired decoration and menu perplexing. When asked why they decided on a prison theme, David Jacobs, one of the owners, explained, "We were just looking to be different and have an interesting theme. Chicago has enough Irish style pubs and trendy spots. It gave us lots of names and a lot of fun for people." (personal communication, January 17, 2013). Their burgers have names such as the Lockdown Warden, Conjugal Visit, Punk Bitch, and The Big House. In the appetizer section of their menu, called Juvenile Delinquents, they offer items such as Chain Gang, Prison Shank, and The Prison Yard. These hotels and restaurants are similar to the breweries and wineries; by drawing on their historic locations or prison stereotypes, they offer consumers unique experiences.

Given the current role of imprisonment in US society, it is not surprising that prison has been incorporated into consumer culture. None of these products offer any lessons on modern prison life; each is a reflection of the past, and many are caricatures reminiscent of old prison films. What makes a person want to buy prison wine, visit a prison, or stay in a prison hotel? The wine, beer, and souvenirs are novelties to entertain and, perhaps to some extent, the same could be said of prison hotels and restaurants.

Prison tours, on the other hand, hold deeper meanings and potential implications. Michelle Brown (2009) discusses prison tourism extensively in her book *The Culture of Punishment: Prison, Society, and Spectacle*. This form of "dark tourism" is similar to visiting concentration camps or war battlegrounds—it takes a culturally prohibited space and opens it to the public. People go to these places because they happen to be there, they are curious, or the tourism industry has sold it as a place to go (Brown 2009). Not everyone tours a prison to learn about institutional history and consider the role of prisons in US society. Many of these prisons open their doors not only to provide historical tours, but also for ghost tours and haunted houses, for art exhibits, and even as venues for weddings and other events. Regardless of why visitors initially set foot in the institution, they walk in with preconceived notions. These expectations are likely drawn from prison films and other media representations. Given that, in order to be profitable, the tours feed into those beliefs. According to Brown (2009), visitors will enjoy a tour if it meets their expectations, and what ultimately results is a hybrid museum theme park. The day-to-day monotony of prison life is made more exciting with stories of violence, escapes, and (in)famous inmates.

Conclusion

Prison imagery ranges from the expected news reports to the unexpected images on bottles of wine. Each type of imagery gives us an indication of what we think of prisons in our culture. The news seeks to inform, but its coverage of prisons is limited even during the current imprisonment binge. The issue of prisons is truly too large for a two-minute spot on the nightly news; yet the right stories can work toward raising interest. Ultimately, the news media still serve as the frontline of prison-related issues in the United States; however, to obtain more complete coverage of the topic, one must turn to other sources.

Sesame Street gives us an indication of how far prison has crept into US culture. In general, this program seeks to use entertainment to teach kids the alphabet, the importance of brushing their teeth, sharing, and many other things. In today's prison nation, this includes dealing with the loss of a parent to incarceration. While other children's programming has included references to prisons, but only just enough for children to learn that this type of place exists. Luckily, we have found a way to address a very real issue that affects millions of children while leaving the true lessons about prison life to adult-oriented representations.

Last but not least is the marketing power of prison. Prisons themselves are big businesses, but, in this case, they are used to sell goods and services. Prisons have become a part of the US consumer culture. While some of this serves to educate, much of it is a marketing gimmick. Visitors to Eastern State Penitentiary and Alcatraz can learn a lot about the history of imprisonment, thereby gaining an educational experience. But even these tours rely on the spectacle and nostalgia incorporated in the popular culture (Danesi 2012). The spectacle of infamous gangsters and murderers locked up on the Rock provides entertainment. The tours also offer an emotional connection through the nostalgia of the big house. It could be either spectacle or nostalgia that influences the visitors to walk away with all sorts of souvenirs of their time behind bars. Prison knickknacks are not a new invention. Early in the history of prisons, there were some tours and these institutions marketed themselves with postcards and memorabilia such as collectable plates depicting some of the most quintessential big houses (Cox 2009). Of course, now we can sit in the comfort of our own homes and sip on a glass of wine that we were lured into buying by the nostalgic representations on the label—consumerism at its best.

Nothing could seem more different than the news, a children's program, tours, and merchandise—yet, together, they say something important about prisons in US culture today. Although millions of adults are behind bars with incredible financial and social costs to society, the topic is not seen as particularly newsworthy, despite the fact that we must use *Sesame Street* to teach young children about prison. And all the while, many people are content reflecting back to the golden days of prison, to a time way before the imprisonment binge, by touring institutions and purchasing memorabilia and drinks. None of these examples serve as the main basis of the social construction of prison, but they are a part of the equation. People are most likely to draw from the moving images found on the big screen and the small screen as the primary sources of symbolic knowledge of prison life. It is to these sources that I now turn.

3

The Big House on the Big Screen

THE MYSTERIOUS PRISON—EVEN THE VISUAL NATURE OF THESE foreboding structures is likely to conjure up frightful visions of life behind the massive stone walls. Before prison films, there were few visual images available; the technology simply did not exist to disseminate pictures to the masses. It was not until the late nineteenth century that newspapers gained the capability to print photographs. But given the scarcity of prison-related news items, it is unlikely that the public saw pictures taken behind prison walls. Finally, at the dawn of the twentieth century, the ability to capture moving images on film unveiled some secrets of prison life to ordinary people. For many, the silver screen provided their first glimpse at prison life. Given the availability of prison films and their enduring quality, for generations these films have played a pivotal role in shaping views of prison. In today's media landscape, however, one might question whether prison films remain influential. We can now turn on the television or computer and be inundated with countless real-life images of these institutions. Therefore, are fictional depictions still an important source in the social construction of prison life? And if so, what do modern prison films say about incarceration in the twenty-first century? To consider the role that the movie industry plays in shaping people's perceptions, it is important to take a step back and touch on earlier influential prison films before delving into those released in the new millennium.

A Historical Look at Prison Films

Movies about prison are nearly as old as film itself. *Prison Bars* (1901) was the first, released during the silent film era. Overall, more than 350

29

films were produced in the twentieth century (Mason 2006). A substantial body of literature has explored the history of these films as well as their plots and characters. According to Brian Jarvis (2004, 167), "The prison film is a repeat offender on the counts of character, plot and mise en scène." While the context of prison stories has changed over time, at the core they are replicas of early productions. To understand modern prison films and their place in people's social construction of prisons, it is important to first look at the development of these films. My discussion borrows the chronological approach used by Derral Cheatwood (1998) to connect the evolution of prison movies to actual variations in prison policies in the United States.

The Golden Age

The prison film genre was established in the 1930s, which was the golden age of prison films (Mason 2006; Nellis 1988; Rafter 2006; Wilson and O'Sullivan 2004). In all more than sixty prison films were released during this decade (Gonthier 2006), including *The Big House* (1930), *Numbered Men* (1930), *The Criminal Code* (1931), *20,000 Years in Sing Sing* (1933), *San Quentin* (1937), *Behind Prison Gates* (1939), and *Mutiny in the Big House* (1939). Cheatwood (1998) refers to this time period as the depression era. The moviegoing audience was enamored by images that they had never before seen. Audiences found themselves rooting for the inmate protagonist who is framed as a hero in his fight against injustice. He is either a victim of the system or a not-so-innocent gangster who redeems himself. During a time of great strife, these films provided people with an escape from their daily concerns (Rafter 2006). The entertainment came from watching the inmate hero fight against the oppressive prison regime, with justice restored through a riot or escape. This story line became the template for most prison films.

Of the many prison films released during the 1930s, David Gonthier (2006, 33) considers *The Big House* to be the "real 'granddaddy' of prison movies." *The Big House* depicts the story of new inmate, Kent Marlowe, who is sent to prison for killing someone while driving intoxicated. Despite being a convicted criminal, he is unfamiliar with and uncomfortable in the prison system. Viewers watch Marlowe's journey into a harsh repressive system. This story is an example of realism, reform, and transformation in early prison films.

Although prison films are fantasies, movie audiences turned to them to catch a glimpse of life behind bars (Rafter 2006). To represent prison with some accuracy, filmmakers consulted with wardens. The early twentieth century was marked by increasing prison populations and over-crowded institutions. The wardens witnessed firsthand the effects of this massive influx of prisoners. They were adamant about reforming the sys-tem (Wilson and O'Sullivan 2004), which was reflected in these films. A standard character is the paternalistic warden who is in sharp contrast to other prison workers who either support punishment or are simply out-right cruel. The paternalistic warden routinely expresses the need for change, even when no one else agrees. In *The Big House,* this is Warden Adams. The warden and some of his staff know that there are problems with the system, but their hands are tied. When Marlowe enters the prison, Warden Adams has no other choice, because of overcrowding, but to place him in a cell with one of the most notorious inmates, "Machine Gun" Butch. Warden Adams tells a guard, "I warned them at the last governor's council. We have 3,000 here and cell accommoda-tions for 1,800. They all want to throw people in prison but they don't want to provide for them after they are in. And, you mark my word Pop, someday we are going to pay for this short-sightedness" (*The Big House* 1930). The message is briefly sent that the system is overcrowded and ill-equipped to handle so many inmates. Other images in the film further reinforce this message. Marlowe is brought to a cramped cell, with bunks three beds high, and is victimized by his cellmates. Several scenes in the film contain hundreds of inmates marching in and out of the yard and through the prison. This imagery is successful in reiterating that the institution is filled to the brim. These particular images suggest the inmates are just numbers, which becomes a part of the iconic imagery of the big house presented in these early films (Cox 2009).

Classic prison films not only highlight the need to change the sys-tem, they also illuminate the issue of reforming offenders. Ingrained within the stories is the debate between punishment and reformation and, in many films, the messages are mixed. Wardens typically believe that the men in their institutions can be changed while guards and others are intent on keeping punishment as the purpose of imprisonment. Many of the guards ensure that punishment will be meted out by being harsh. The cruel guard established in these narratives becomes a standard in prison films (see Box 3.1) and is later adopted by other types of prison representations such as televised dramas. Reformation of bad men is reflected in the stories of transformation contained within these films. Several of these are highlighted in *The Big House* (1930). Viewers see Morgan, Marlowe's cellmate, transformed from a typical con to a responsible and moral man. The film also depicts how serving time can

---

Box 3.1 Smug Hacks: Prison Guards in Films

Correctional officers are an integral part of the prison system. People's perceptions of those on the job may be shaped by their portrayal in the media. The most enduring representation can be traced back to early prison films. To depict tales of injustice, a distinction had to be made between the inmate hero and the jailers; thus, the birth of what some refer to as a "smug hack" (e.g., Freeman 2000, 6). To establish injustice within the stories, an antagonist must be presented. The prison regime controlled by sadistic guards becomes what the protagonist must fight against. Over time, this characterization of prison guards has become a media trope. Nearly every fictionalized account incorporates guards who abuse and torture inmates for no reason. Eventually, many wardens were also depicted in this manner. The stereotype of the smug hack has become firmly established in popular culture; it is found in anything from the news to prison comedies.

---

destroy a man who is not a true criminal. Viewers watch Marlowe struggle to survive and eventually come unraveled during a failed escape because he is afraid of what the others will do to him for squealing. Finally, inmates like Machine Gun Butch, who led the attempted prison break, are depicted as unredeemable men who must be kept in prison to protect society. Ultimately, these transformations demonstrate that prisons are part of a utilitarian agenda. To produce the greatest amount of good for society, men like Marlowe are sacrificed so society can be safe from men like Butch.

Depression-era prison films continued until the early 1940s. Overall, these films provide a glimpse into institutional life while questioning the purpose of prisons and proposing needed changes. Ultimately, these films frame prisons as a social necessity (Cox 2009). This message is reiterated time and again in prison films to come, with even more justification provided by the vilification of the men behind bars.

Development of the Genre, 1940s–1970s

In no other decade were prison films as prevalent as during the 1930s. Despite decreasing in number, the prison film genre continued to develop. Changes in both the movie industry and prison policies influenced the characteristics of these films. In his discussion of prison films, Cheatwood (1998) divides films of the 1940s through the 1970s into two eras—the rehabilitation era (1942–1962) and the confinement era (1963–1980). The changes to prison films during these four decades are subtle—the main developments come in the form of violence and the causal factors involved.

Institutional violence has always been an integral part of prison films. There is abuse at the hands of cruel guards and inmates rioting against the prison regime as well as vicious inmates terrorizing weaker prisoners. Films of the 1930s blame the system itself for this behavior. But the rehabilitation era of prison films, which began in the 1940s, shifts the blame to the individuals (Cheatwood 1998). These films were a reflection of changes to the philosophy adopted by the system: we entered a period of individualized justice when the system adopted the medical model, which posits that the cause of criminal behavior can be diagnosed and a cure prescribed.

Films of the rehabilitation era include *Men of San Quentin* (1942), *You Can't Beat the Law* (also known as *Prison Mutiny*) (1943), *Brute Force* (1947), *Inside the Walls of Folsom Prison* (1951), *My Six Convicts* (1952), *Duffy of San Quentin* (1954), *Riot in Cellblock 11* (1954), and, perhaps the most well-known, *Birdman of Alcatraz* (1962). These films follow similar story arcs, but contain even more violence and a focus on how to fix the inmates. Reflecting rehabilitative beliefs that were popular at the time, a new character became prominent in prison films—the prison doctor or psychiatrist (Wilson and O'Sullivan 2004).

The movie *Men of San Quentin,* with its tagline "Slaughter in the Slammer," serves as a good example of a rehabilitation era film. The film is dedicated to San Quentin's warden Clinton T. Duffy. It opens with a paragraph briefly describing the history of the institution and where the story begins. It informs viewers that an institution was needed to house outlaws who invaded the state during the gold rush, "and thus San Quentin Prison began its bloody history. Riots, escapes, and murders were frequent. Our story opens with the fearful tranquility that follows the slaying of a guard. Solitary cells are jammed with inmates, the guards restless and a political upheaval impending." Violence is highlighted with murders and suicide. Rehabilitation is reflected through changes made by a new warden, who institutes classes that culminate in a prison variety show. While *Men of San Quentin* begins as a seemingly hopeless story, it is a propaganda film at heart. In the end, it demonstrates that rehabilitation programs are needed to reform the men behind bars.

The 1960s ushered in another shift in the underlying messages contained in prison films. Some truly classic films were released between 1963 and 1980, including *Cool Hand Luke* (1967), *The Longest Yard* (1974), *Midnight Express* (1978), *Escape from Alcatraz* (1979), and *Brubaker* (1980). As mentioned above, Cheatwood (1998) refers to this prison film time period as the confinement era. Changes in societal beliefs, which included turning a more critical eye toward the justice system, are reflected in these films. The underlying message is that inmates deserve to be locked up and there is nothing that the system can do to reform them (Cheatwood 1998).

During this prison film era, the level and type of violence continued to change. David Wilson and Sean S. O'Sullivan (2004) cite *Riot* (1969) as the most pivotal film of this era in large part because of its use of violence. It was filmed at the Arizona State Prison, with the warden and a group of inmates playing themselves to provide a sense of realism. The film depicts the story of a group of inmates, led by Big Red, digging an escape tunnel. Their plans go awry, hostages are taken, and a standoff begins; in the meantime, Big Red and the others continue plotting and digging. While the film's title alludes to a riot as a major part of the story line, there is not much of a riot in this film. The events that unfold over the course of the standoff show a very different, much more brutal, side of inmate culture than was seen in previous prison films (Wilson and O'Sullivan 2004). The inmates make vats of raisin jack (alcohol), drink in excess, and pass out all over the prison. On "Queen's Row," cross-dressing inmates open a brothel. These scenes are supplemented with a series of violent, out-of-control inmates who want to kill the guards and any inmates who get in their way.

It is these types of images that lead Wilson and O'Sullivan (2004) to conclude that *Riot* was the first to present a predatory prison environment, yet they do not speculate as to what brought about these changes. Considering society and events of the time, there are some possible explanations for this shift. Inmate disturbances were erupting, the country was turning its focus from the Cold War to law and order, and a new era of conservatism was being ushered in. It is in this same environment that *Dirty Harry* (1971) was embraced. "Dirty" Harry Callahan is depicted as the ideal, albeit rogue, cop who does anything to get the bad guy. Scenes in the movie that show predatory offenders locked up reinforce the crime control message that was becoming more popular at the time. These decades marked a turbulent time in the history of US prisons, from prison scandals and abuses to significant disturbances and riots. On one hand, the courts began to recognize the ways that the system was mistreating inmates. On the other hand, everyone was questioning rehabilitation and ultimately abandoned this idea in favor of deterrence- and incapacitation-based strategies. Filmmakers were influenced at least in part by these factors in their creation of a more brutal prison environment, a tradition that continued for decades to come.

The Diminishing Prison Film, 1980s–2000

Over the decades, it became increasingly difficult to craft unique prison tales. As Cheatwood's (1998) administrative era began in 1980, prison films had been around for a half-century. Generations of viewers had seen these images repeated time and time again, and filmmakers borrowed heavily from early prison films. It is within this era that *The Shawshank Redemption* (1994) was released, but it is not indicative of most movies during this time. Other prison films of this era include *Weeds* (1988), *Lock Up* (1989), *American Me* (1992), and *Murder in the First* (1995). These examples are vastly different from one another, ranging from inmates putting on a play in San Quentin to dealing with abuse in one of the most infamous institutions in the United States; however, even seemingly different films still have commonalities. Caster (2010, 112) demonstrates this in his comparison of *The Shawshank Redemption* (1994) and *American History X* (1998): "Both describe prison as a violent setting of sexual predation, vicious inmates, and cruel corrections officers, a hellish place that paradoxically proves transformative, man-making, and redemptive for the charismatic central characters." According to Caster, in their own way, each of these films reinforces the system of punishment in place.

The administrative era of prison films coincides with additional changes to the prison system. Having abandoned the rehabilitative ideal in the 1970s, the ushering in of deterrence-based policies marked the beginning of the imprisonment binge. The consequences of mass incarceration, however, are reflected only in science fiction—in *Escape from New York* (1981) and *Escape from L.A.* (1996). Other science fiction films address the future of imprisonment but, since they are not pure prison films, these movies are out of context with my discussion (refer to Nellis 2006).

In the administrative era, the prison film splintered off into other movie genres, making the prison story less prominent and the pure prison film a rarity. Cheatwood (1998) ends his examination of prison films in 1995; however, the administrative era continued until at least the turn of the century. Between 1995 and 2000, few prison films were released and even fewer were pure prison films. Instead, there were comedies, such as *Life* (1999), and action films, including *Con Air* (1997). The "going-to-prison" film (Wilson and O'Sullivan 2004, 170), such as *Slam* (1998), emerged. Entering into the twenty-first century, shifts in television programming and the new media created changes in the film industry.

Modern Prison Films

While Gonthier (2006, 189) believes that "the prison film continues to evolve, transform, and mutate," the popularity of this type of film peaked long ago. Prison films emerged at a time when other images were scarce while modern prison films exist in a world of instantaneous imagery. With the click of a button, individuals can watch anything from old films to real-life images of prison life. Where does this change leave prison films? Since 2000, fewer than fifty prison films have been released. The prison films of the twenty-first century continue the tradition of the administrative era in that these movies run the gamut from slapstick comedies to sports and science fiction films. True prison films remain an anomaly.

   The types of films in the modern film era are not distinct from those of the twentieth century. In general, there are nonincarceration films and incarceration-related films. The most prevalent type of prison film is one that takes place in prison, but is not about incarceration—these stories are about anything from romance to revenge. Two of the most popular and highest-grossing prison films released since 2000 are examples. *Monster's Ball* (2001) and *The Longest Yard* (2005) are not about prison life; instead, they are a romantic drama and a sports film, respectively, and each could just as easily be told in another environment. Other examples include *Doing Hard Time* (2004), *Stone* (2010), and *I Love You Phillip Morris* (2009). Prison films featuring boxing and mixed martial arts have also become popular in the twenty-first century, including *Locked Down* (2010), *Ring of Death* (2008), and *Undisputed* (2002) and its three sequels. The popularity of science fiction and futuristic films has continued, including *Death Race* (2008) and its sequels as well as *Lockout* (2012). The images depicted in these movies are typical representations used throughout the history of prison films. The complexities of prison life and the imprisonment binge are absent from their narratives in favor of other story lines (see Box 3.2).

Pure prison films or films about incarceration are the second category of prison movies. It is these films that have the potential to offer the truest, albeit fictional or fictionalized, representation of imprisonment in the United States. Therefore, it is these types of films that are the focus of my discussion. Most of these films repeat the tale of injustice that has been recycled for decades; however, they are shaped by media trends and prison policies. At the turn of the century, the justice system was rooted heavily in "get tough" incarceration-based policies. Many people appeared to wholeheartedly embrace this technique for dealing with crime. Furthermore, this same population had an appetite for a dose of reality in their entertainment. These films use realism to depict tales of imprisonment in maximum security prisons.

Box 3.2 Revenge: *Doing Hard Time*

Doing Hard Time (2004) is an example of a film that uses prison as the backdrop for the story line. The title suggests that this movie is about serving time in prison, but close examination demonstrates that it is not. The protagonist is Michael Mitchell, whose son is accidently killed during a gang shootout. The two men responsible for his son's death, Durty Curt and Razor, are found not guilty of murder but are still sent to prison on drug convictions. This part of the plot sets the stage for the real purpose of this story—revenge. The first part of the film features action outside of the prison, from the shooting to the trial and Mitchell's grieving process that ultimately leads him to plan and prepare to be purposefully sent to prison. Scenes of Durty Curt and Razor in prison are juxtaposed with Mitchell's experiences on the outside. *Doing Hard Time* combines elements typical of prison films with those found in revenge films. Viewers see inmates being processed into the prison and introduced to their cellmates. There are corrupt guards, shower scenes, drug smuggling, stabbings, and rape. Before Mitchell is brought to the prison, Durty Curt and Razor fight, resulting in Razor's death. Once Mitchell is processed in, he sets out to kill Durty Curt, which he nearly does with the help of a corrupt guard. Revenge is a common theme in countless movies over the decades and, with the exception of the setting, this film is no different from other revenge films.

Purporting to reveal secrets of life behind bars is one of the lures of prison films. From telling true stories to consulting with wardens and filming at actual prisons, filmmakers have injected realism into prison films since their beginning. However, advances in filmmaking have increased the ability to present more realistic-looking imagery. One example of realism in these films is *Animal Factory* (2000). Similar to many other prison films, it depicts the journey of a new inmate, Ron Decker, who is sent to prison on a drug conviction. Immediately, this quiet young man gains the sympathy of the audience, particularly once he is seen in contrast to the other inmates. Ron's transformation begins when he meets Earl, an old con who is in the mix. Viewers see standard prison images of cross-dressing inmates, attacks in the yard and in the bathroom, solitary confinement, a riot, and eventually an escape. While borrowing heavily from the formula used in many prison movies before it, the style of filmmaking employed by Steve Buscemi reflects a change. The film has a documentary-like quality that was likely influenced by the popularity of reality TV programming (Gonthier 2006). Adding to the realism provided by the filming techniques is the setting—it was filmed at a prison, using inmates as extras. It is the combination of an actual institution, with the documentary-like style and the present-day setting, that may make audiences buy into the reality of prison life presented in *Animal Factory*.

Another way to inject realism into the story is to draw from real-life events. Ric Roman Waugh's *Felon* (2008) is a good example. While still relying on tales of injustice and an inmate hero, *Felon* also tackles current prison issues. Waugh describes his film as a horror flick. There are no insane serial killers on the loose or ghosts terrifying people; instead, his film explores what would happen to an innocent man thrust into the prison jungle. The end result is one of the few pure prison films released since the turn of the century that addresses issues such as the effects of incarceration on the family, prison gangs, and Secure Housing Units. Part of the story line is similar to events that took place in the California prison system when several correctional officers were indicted by the federal courts on charges of violating inmates' civil rights by staging gladiator fights between inmates (Arax 2000). Film critic Stephen Holden (2008) tells readers to forget *Oz*'s claims of reality: "The high security men's prison in *Felon* is the real thing" (par. 1). He continues that this film is "one of the most realistic prison films ever made" (par. 2). But we must ask, How much realism could possibly be in this fictional depiction of prison life? The story is drawn from true events but, to make it entertaining, it must fit viewers' expectations by providing standard prison film elements.

Felon (2008) depicts the story of Wade Porter, a family man, who accidentally kills a burglar. The film follows Wade as he is brought to jail and through court appearances that ultimately land him in prison to serve a three-year sentence. He has no prior convictions, a family, and owns a business, but he is sent to serve his time in a maximum security institution. To make matters worse, when an inmate is stabbed on the transport bus, Wade is immediately sent to administrative segregation. After his disciplinary hearing, he is transferred to an SHU. During his transfer to the unit, the film incorporates images of inmates attacking one another, yelling, and working out, with the Certified Emergency Response Team in action to establish the intensity of the setting. As Wade is placed in his cell, a correctional officer tells him, "We are hands on here. You'll receive no warning shots" (*Felon* 2008). Wade is surrounded by monsters, in the form of inmates and guards; the horror has truly begun.

SHUs are a reality in prisons today. Typically used for high-risk inmates who have caused problems within the system, they are often described as the "prison within the prison" (Brown, Camber, and Agha 2011). California has historically used its SHUs to separate gang members. These inmates are kept in isolation for more than twenty-three hours per day and, when allowed to exercise, it is within a one-person pen. Technically speaking, if this reality was reflected in the film, the audience would be bored; thus, *Felon*'s story line is made more exciting by allowing for regular human interactions. Soon after being placed in the SHU, Wade is given a cellmate, John Smith, an old con serving a life sentence. Both men spend a considerable amount of time outside of the cell and in the company of others. During recreation time, they are placed in a small exercise yard, surrounded by high walls and filled with other prisoners of all races. A group of correctional officers watches with weapons, armed and ready. It is within this environment that prison politics becomes clear to viewers. The lines are quickly drawn, with various facets of the prison population constantly at odds with one another. Wade must navigate his way through this new world.

While tackling the issue of what it takes to survive in prison, like many films before it, *Felon* (2008) weaves stories of transformation. Viewers watch Wade go through the prisonization process as he is forced to participate in the gladiator fights to survive. He is no longer the innocent man who entered prison—the brutality of the institution has changed him. They also watch how the experience changes his fiancée. She goes from being completely supportive of Wade to being shocked by his physical and mental changes, to struggling on the outside with finances and writing him a Dear John letter. She eventually takes Wade back when their son keeps asking about his father. John changes as he witnesses Wade's transformation and eventually sacrifices himself to save his cellmate. A rookie correctional officer stops himself from becoming one of the cruel guards that are mentoring him by becoming a part of the plan to stop these officers' cruelty. Each of these transformations is a part of the "justice achieved" story line. Wade almost loses his life and John sacrifices his to expose the smug hacks. Like many classic prison films, Wade is released into the arms of his loving fiancée. In a further attempt to legitimize the story, the film ends with a 2008 statistic indicating that there are more than 2.3 million people incarcerated (*Felon* 2008).

Whether its intention or not, *Felon* tackles issues prevalent in the age of imprisonment. Wilson and O'Sullivan (2004) believe that it is important for US prison films to depict stories of supermax institutions (although they recognize that this is more apt to be captured by documentarians). Classic prison films often send characters to solitary only to be released at a certain point in the story line. Some films depict these characters as no worse for the wear while other films show the toll it takes. *Felon* sets itself in a supermax unit without truly representing its reality. Its viewers do not clearly see the toll that years, even decades, in solitary confinement takes on individuals. But that is not what would make it a profitable film. Instead, as predicted by Wilson and O'Sullivan (2004), the topic remains in the realm of documentarians.

Animal Factory and *Felon* are just two of the modern prison films. Few abandon the precedents set decades before in early prison films. Today's movie audiences, however, have different standards of entertainment, which is seen in the realism presented in some of these films. There are two other differences presented in recent prison films. Qualitatively, many offer a slightly different look at life behind bars by the way that violence and race are depicted.

Violence in Modern Prison Films: Animalistic Inmates and Sadistic Guards

Prison film narratives have commonly highlighted riots and cruel guards, violence, and abuse. Today, however, the prison environment is depicted

as being particularly brutal. As previously discussed, *Riot* has been identified as a turning point in the depiction of inmates because the predatory
prisoner entered the narrative (Wilson and O'Sullivan 2004). In the age
of the imprisonment binge, prisoners are depicted as superpredators. Animalistic inmates cannot help but attack one another. Poetic license in fictional storytelling means that filmmakers can get creative in their depiction of inmate violence. The 2004 film *Jailbait* is an example: the entire
movie features a predatory inmate named Jake. *Jailbait* is about twenty-
year-old Randy who is sentenced to twenty-five years for vandalizing
his neighbor's car. He is placed in a cell with Jake, a man serving a life
sentence for killing his wife. Unlike Earl in *Animal Factory* or John in
Felon, Jake is sadistic and cruel as he psychologically and physically
tortures Randy throughout the film. At times Jake appears to be kind,
engaging his cellmate in conversation and offering him advice, but this
is a facade. Every word out of Jake's mouth is to manipulate and torture
his young cellmate. From making Randy tie his shirt like a girl to go to
dinner, to beating him up and forcing him to perform oral sex, Jake is
relentless. *Jailbait* does not have the nonstop violence and chaos of
some other prison films. It is slow paced, yet it establishes the pain of
being imprisoned with a predator.

Typical prison violence is depicted throughout these films, from
stabbings to putting broken glass in another inmate's drink. These violent predators do not stop at these types of physical attacks. Early prison
films may have depicted inmate violence, but they never included
prison rape; only during the past three decades has it been incorporated
(Cox 2009). Now, prison rape is a topic that people expect to be a part
of the story, and films released since 2000 tend to meet that expectation.
For example, there are the sexual assaults in *Jailbait* and *Animal Factory* as well as an inmate who is repeatedly raped in *Lockdown* (2000).
In the film *Doing Hard Time,* an inmate named Cleaver is brutally
attacked and sodomized with a mop handle. In comparison to the other
forms of violence in these films, rape is not the most prominent, but as
noted by Stephen Cox (2009) it is now a typical part of the story line.

Similar to inmate violence, cruelty at the hands of guards has been
a common depiction in prison films since the beginning. In each film
released in the new millennium, smug hacks have been incorporated.
Some simply take bribes to look the other way, but there is also some
extreme cruelty and abuse in these films. The aforementioned film
Felon (2008) highlights gladiator fighting orchestrated by guards—they
force the inmates to battle one another and shoot at them to gain com-
pliance. Another example of extreme abuse by the guards is *The Manns-*

field 12 (2007), which depicts the story of guards torturing a group of inmates to get them to confess to a crime. In *Shackles* (2005), the guards are not just abusive to the inmates: in one scene, the emergency response team brutally attacks the prison teacher, Ben. All of these acts of violence, whether at the hands of inmates or staff, frame the prison environment as a deadly battleground in which predators thrive and, to survive, one must become one of the pack. This representation fits with other popular media portrayals of predatory criminals.

Race in Modern Prison Films: Battle Lines and Representation

Prisons have always held a disproportionate number of minority offenders, yet the racial and ethnic makeup of the prison population typically has been misrepresented in prison films. *Cool Hand Luke* (1967) is the quintessential example. Luke is sentenced to serve time on a Florida chain gang during the 1940s. The inmates in the movie are predominately white. But Southern prisons have had a long history of incarcerating high numbers of African Americans. Prison farms and other camps for prisoners essentially created a workforce that had been lost by the end of slavery. Available data on the racial makeup of prisoners admitted to Florida prisons in the 1940s demonstrates the distortion of the images presented in *Cool Hand Luke*. According to the Bureau of Justice Statistics, more than 50 percent of those sentenced to the Florida Department of Corrections during this era were African American (Langan 1991, 22–25). This reality is not reflected in the film. (See Box 3.3.) This misrepresentation can be partially attributed to the Hollywood of the 1960s, where roles for African American actors were limited. Another film from the same era, *Riot,* did present the audience with a diverse prison population; however, it relied on inmates as extras.

By the 1990s, films generally featured more diverse casts, and prison movies offered a better (albeit not actual) representation of the prison population. Many of these films tackle the issue of race in prison by demonstrating the racial divide. Early in their story lines, the new inmate learns that in order to survive he must associate only with his own kind. This aspect of prison life is carried on into the new millennium. For example, in *Felon* (2008), Wade quickly learns this lesson. On the prison transport bus, an inmate tells him about the Aryan Brotherhood and that he needs to get with his own race when in the yard. And it is within the yard that most of the brutal interactions between white, African American, and Hispanic inmates take place.

Box 3.3 Race, Imprisonment, and Imagery

Early prison imagery, especially in films, presented a mostly white prison population. This representation is due in part to the history of Hollywood filmmaking; however, another important factor to consider is the actual racial and ethnic makeup of the prison population. For much of their history US prisons were filled mainly with white inmates, with 70 percent of the prison population being white until as late as the mid-twentieth century (Wacquant 2001, 96). It was in the latter part of that century that the makeup of the prison population changed and, eventually, so did the way that prison imagery presents the inmate population.

In the 1960s blacks constituted about one-third of the prison population, and by the early 1990s they made up nearly half of those incarcerated (Tonry 2011, 31). Many factors contributed to this dramatic change such as the war on drugs, which included the now infamous "100-to-1" sentencing law (see Tonry 2011, 47–53, for additional factors). Tough punishments for possession or distribution of crack cocaine resulted in a large number of African American drug offenders entering the prison system. In the late 1960s audiences began to see a more diverse prison population in films, although it would be decades before the voices of African American inmates would be prominent in popular prison imagery. These voices emerged in the form of hip-hop, where early message raps highlighted tales of injustice and the pains of imprisonment (see Chapter 9). The first televised drama about prison life, *Oz,* made its debut in the late 1990s and presented a racially and ethnically diverse prison population (see Chapter 4). Despite these developments, at the end of the twentieth century prison imagery still failed to offer a true depiction of the incarcerated.

These trends have continued into the twenty-first century. Imprisonment rates of blacks continue to be five to six times higher than those of whites (Carson 2014, 8); however, the representation of these disparities remains lacking. Black filmmakers began to produce films featuring predominately African American inmates, yet many of these movies remain relatively unknown. Rappers continue to send messages about the discriminatory prison system, but their words are often overshadowed by the glamorization of the gangster lifestyle depicted by others. And while prison documentaries have become popular on television, many of these tend to create a false picture of race and imprisonment in the United States (see Cecil and Leitner 2009).

The most significant change to the representation of race in prison films comes from movies produced or written by African American filmmakers and starring predominately African American actors. African Americans are significantly overrepresented in the prison population and, while historically true, the imprisonment binge has confounded the issue. At the beginning of this binge, African American artists expressed their views through rap music. But these films are another way to bring the issue to the forefront. Black filmmaking took off in the 1990s, when directors like Spike Lee and John Singleton produced more theatrically released films by African Americans than ever before. Some of these films depicted the violent lives of inner-city African American males, making critics fearful that most of these films perpetuated stereotypes of these men as drug-dealing thugs (Film Reference n.d.). Initially the story of how incarceration affects minorities in the United States was largely absent from films. "Texts that are widely or highly regarded (or both) at particular historical moments can be understood as meeting some need, fulfilling some lack or expectation in their representation" (Caster 2008, 5). The rates at which African American men were being incarcerated could no longer be ignored, and at the turn of the twenty-first century these filmmakers began depicting prison life. Films featuring African American inmates include: *Lockdown* (2000), *Unshackled* (2000), *Conviction* (2002), *Prison Song* (2001), *The Visit* (2000), *Undisputed* (2002), *Doing Hard Time* (2004), *Shackles* (2005), *Animal* (2005) and its sequel, *The Mannsfield 12* (2007), and *The Wrath of Cain* (2010). Not all of these films can be considered true prison films and many were not theatrically released, yet the imagery in each has the potential to bring race to the attention of the viewers.

Filmmakers have different ways of telling the story of African American prisoners. *Unshackled* (2000) is a historical look at race in the prison system, depicting the true story of Harold Morris's time in the Georgia State Penitentiary during the 1970s. The prison is racially divided and, following a riot, the warden forces Morris to share a cell with a black inmate. Morris and his cellmate work together to hold the first integrated baseball game behind prison walls. *Shackles* (2005) is very different in that it incorporates elements of traditional prison films (cruel guards, fights in the yard, riots, and hardened inmates) with a story line commonly seen in films about an inspirational teacher in an inner-city school (e.g., *Dangerous Minds* 1995; *Freedom Writers* 2007). A former teacher, Ben Collins, gets a job at a new school located in Shackleton Prison, where he inspires inmates to participate in poetry slams, only to be killed in a riot that erupts during a slam contest.

A final film worth mentioning is *Prison Song* (2001). This film is about more than prison life; it ties incarceration to the context in which it is occurring during the imprisonment binge. It is a commentary on the fate that faces many young African American men from impoverished communities. The film opens with statistics on the number of children with parents in prison as well as the number of male African Americans in juvenile detention and prison (*Prison Song* 2001). These figures set the stage for the story of Elijah. As a young boy, Elijah goes to foster care when both his mother and her boyfriend end up in prison. Despite the odds, he becomes a talented photographer who dreams of going to art school. A series of events result in his conviction for second-degree murder, for what appeared to be an act of self-defense. Once Elijah goes to prison, the scenes that unfold are fairly typical of this type of film (with the exception of the songs that characters sing throughout the movie). The film also tackles the issue of education and work in prison. The classes are depicted as inadequate and underfunded, and eventually they are shut down. The work is demeaning and even dangerous. For example, inmates are forced to demolish an asbestos-infested building without protection. Elijah protests both of these things and first ends up in solitary and, eventually, dead during an attempted escape (*Prison Song* 2001). While borrowing many elements from early prison films, *Prison Song* does not end with justice being served.

Many of the films cited here may not be highly regarded, yet they do in fact tell a story that is of critical importance in the twenty-first century. Is it coincidental that prison films became more brutal when they started to feature more stories about African American inmates? Representations of black men typically rely on a single stereotype of the extremely masculine and, thus, aggressive male figure. Inevitably, he is shown as a criminal and, therefore, a prisoner (Caster 2008). Thus, many films may simply be drawing from the most common representation of these men. Even in rap music created by African American artists, this persona is often depicted and, thus, it is replicated in prison films created by African American filmmakers. Films such as *Shackles* and *Prison Song* do not rely on one-dimensional characters in their attempts to bring the problems with the system to the forefront. In general, however, other prison films are equally as violent. Predatory inmates come from all racial and ethnic backgrounds in these films.

Conclusion

Prison films have been a staple of filmmaking since the golden age of Hollywood films. For the most part, these films continue to be formed from the same mold with inmate heroes, cruel guards, riots, escapes, injustice, and justice. In the twenty-first century, however, films that take place in prison far outnumber those about incarceration. Those that do exist, such as *Animal Factory* and *Felon,* depict the harsh world of maximum security life imprisonment by offering realism through film-making techniques and story lines based on true events. These films borrow elements from classic prison films, but both inmates and guards are more violent. These images coincide with many others that emerged around the turn of the century.

The scarcity of pure prison films in the new millennium is part of the natural evolution that any film genre goes through. When a specific film type emerges, it is a novelty (Mason 2003). Similar to any new product, people are fascinated by images they have never seen before. For prison films, this stage of development occurred in the 1930s. It was the first time that audiences caught a glimpse into the inner work-ings of prisons and the culture within them; thus, their level of interest was high. After a while, however, the audiences became familiar and the films became generic. In this phase, the audience knew what to expect of a prison film (Mason 2003). One might argue that, at this point, these films began to lose their significance—being used to the plots, characters, and images, the audience became more passive. They knew what a prison film was and simply sat back to enjoy the images before them. One might think that this would be the end. However, Paul Mason (2003) believes that, after a significant amount of time, the genre exhausts itself; at this point, these films are too well known and they are no longer taken seriously. This exhaustion could mean that there will be no new stories to tell and the genre might disappear or at the least just repeat old popular formulas. Wilson and O'Sullivan (2004) argue that to think of the genre as being exhausted is too simplistic. As prison films have developed, they have split off into many subgenres and, therefore, continue to develop. Prison films will no doubt continue for decades to come; however, with time, they are becoming less and less about imprisonment.

Prison films are also victims of an ever evolving movie industry. Some of these films have been critically acclaimed and won accolades at film festivals across the nation (e.g., *Animal Factory*); however, there have not been any blockbuster hits. The movie industry in general has changed considerably—if there is not an extraordinary amount of action and franchise and merchandizing capabilities, then studios are less likely to invest time and money in a film. A pure prison film is not likely to ever meet any of these qualifications. For the most part, these films have become relics of the past.

The impact of decades of prison films is undeniable. For many generations, these movies provided the main material for how many people perceived the inner workings of the prison system. What was once exclusively the purview of film producers was adapted for the small screen in the late twentieth century. This transition showed that large screens and surround sound were not required to depict prison tales, and that other vehicles could provide a different and more comprehensive take on prison life. As the availability of other popular, fictional and nonfictional, images of prison life became more prevalent, pure prison films became difficult to find. If people can simply turn on the television or search the Internet to find prison dramas and documentaries, then the lure of true prison films loses its appeal. What began as the primary source of prison tales has faded into the background in a world dominated by real-life imagery.

4

Televised Prison Dramas

AS PRISON FILMS WERE DWINDLING, CRIME-RELATED TELEVISION programming was taking off. Carried over in part from popular radio shows of the 1940s, crime shows emerged when people brought television into their living rooms. For decades, viewers have watched police officers investigate crime, chase bad guys, and almost always apprehend the suspects. Separately, they have watched attorneys on their quests to achieve justice, which means convicting the guilty or acquitting the innocent. Although these are essential parts of the criminal justice system, neither type of drama truly broaches the subject of punishment. Even when *Law and Order* began paying equal attention to the police and courts, each episode essentially ended at the sound of the final gavel. What happened to the offender after that was left to the viewers' imaginations (Rapping 2003). For the most part, viewers were content knowing that the offender was caught and punishment would follow; in essence, for them it was the end of the story. Yet there is more to the tale if the camera follows the convicted offender out of the courtroom to the punishment that awaits him or her.

In the United States, punishment encompasses many options. Viewers, however, may not be fully cognizant of the choices at hand. Given that they tend to overestimate the punishment of media offenders (Raney 2005), it is likely that many assume that these bad guys are going to prison. This thought alone may be enough to satisfy their quest for retribution. Television shows are able to feed this belief from time to time by incorporating scenes that feature prisoners. Images of prisons and inmates have made their way into virtually every genre of television programming (Jewkes 2006). US television viewers can see prisons on soap operas, dramas, fantasy and science fiction shows, and even sit-coms. Each of these contain their own messages or at least innuendos about imprisonment, but to what extent? For example, in the third season of the popular AMC series *The Walking Dead* (2012), a prison serves as the only place of refuge for a former sheriff and his companions in their fight to stay alive. Most of the prisoners have been turned into zombies and even those who have not are painted as untrustworthy and even evil. In the end, the one prisoner who proves to be a good guy is killed off. Surprisingly, this show about dead flesh-eating humans unknowingly sends messages about prisoners similar to other popular constructions of inmates. Prisoners are demonized, quite literally in this case. As far-fetched as a show may appear, by repeating common depictions it has the power to forward ideas about the incarcerated. The more powerful images, however, are found in crime dramas.

When people tune into crime shows they get specific messages about crime and justice. Many shows depict more conservative messages about crime and what it takes to deal with the problem. Since most crime dramas focus on the investigation of the crime and the conviction of the offender, images of prisoners serve as plot devices. Bill Yousman (2009, 114) examined three popular crime dramas and found images of the incarcerated (e.g., inmates, ex-cons, and parolees) in two-thirds of the episodes, yet no scenes of prison life. Prisoners are depicted in courtrooms and prison visitation rooms being questioned by lawyers or police officers. Viewers can see that the bad guys are being punished, but not much more. Of course, one must consider the purpose of these shows, a popular formula being the investigation of the crime and capture of the criminal. The allure is the mystery and the chase; thus, seeing the bad guy languishing in a crowded cell need only be assumed. The hint of punishment is all that is needed to draw viewers. A recent exception is the third season of AMC's *The Killing* (2013). A central character to the season's story arc is a death row inmate, so scenes of death row are incorporated into each episode. Viewers get an idea of life on death row, but the main purpose of its use is still to serve as a plot device. The inmate gives Detective Sarah Linden motivation to rejoin the police force to clear the man's name before it is too late.

Other than these glimpses of punishment within crime dramas, historically the depiction of prison life on television has been comical. Prison shows briefly appeared on US television from the mid-1970s through the early 1990s, including *On the Rocks* (1975–1976) and Australia's *Prisoner: Cellblock H* (1979–1986). None of these programs offered a serious take on prison life; therefore, one might question whether they had the potential to impact viewers' thoughts about prison. I examine this issue in Chapter 9. More important, these programs aired before the onslaught of modern crime dramas on US television.

The 1990s brought about tremendous change in the development of crime-related television programming. A significant event contributing to the emergence of the first prison drama was the creation of *Law and Order,* which debuted in 1991 and enjoyed a run of more than twenty years. The popularity and impact of this program is undeniable. Not only did *Law and Order* lead to countless other televised crime dramas about the investigation of crime, but it also set the stage for the exploration of other crime-related topics. By the late 1990s the imprisonment binge was in full swing, people were sick of crime despite the fact that the great drop in crime had begun earlier that decade, and many people were willing to support punitive policies. The crime dramas of the 1990s justified and even reinforced these harsh beliefs. This underlying message is one of the reasons why crime dramas became so popular during the get-tough era. According to Arthur A. Raney and Jennings Bryant (2002), crime dramas are about justice. Viewers will enjoy a show only when the idea of justice matches up with their own moral beliefs. In the era of mandatory minimums and three strikes, justice is often equated with imprisonment. The development of crime-related television programming, people's attitudes about crime and punishment, and the increasing use of imprisonment formed the perfect recipe for the development of prison-related programming on US television, including both dramas and documentaries.

We Are Not in the Big House Anymore: HBO's *Oz*

In 1997, the premium cable station HBO became home to the first US television drama about maximum security life. Until this point, Hollywood films served as the primary source of prison tales. Just three years before the debut of *Oz* (Fontana 1997), the highest-grossing prison film of all time was released—*The Shawshank Redemption.* For many, the image of prison presented in this famous film was ingrained in their minds; however, given that it did not take place in the present day, it served more as fantasy than reality. While borrowing a few elements from prison films, *Oz* is set in modern US society, in which crime is thought to be rampant and the government does not want to be seen as soft. What results is a unique take on life behind bars. Viewers are introduced to the worst of the worst, locked up securely where they can only

---

Box 4.1 *Oz:* Fantasy Influenced by Reality

Oz is the brainchild of Tom Fontana, creator of *Homicide: Life on the Streets.* While growing up, he was interested in the infamous Attica prison riot in 1971. Memories of that event made him wonder whether a series could be made about life behind bars. He tried to sell the idea to the major networks. However, most TV executives believed that a show based on the premise of prison life could not possibly include elements critical to successful television programming (Sepinwall 2012). In the early 1990s, HBO aired a couple of prison documentaries that were well received. Therefore, when HBO executives decided to invest in its first scripted drama, a prison show was considered. After seeing a seventeen-minute pilot of *Oz,* they ordered the series (Sepinwall 2012). Fontana was given the green light to do what he wanted with the series since the cable station did not have to rely on advertisers or the same type of censorship as network television. What resulted was a history-making, six-season series containing a total of fifty-six episodes depicting the story of inmates and staff in Emerald City, an experimental unit in the Oswald State Penitentiary, a fictional maximum security prison.

---

hurt one another. Given that this show was the first, and in fact the only, true prison drama, much has been written about the content, messages, and meanings of this pivotal program (e.g., Rapping 2003; Wilson and O'Sullivan 2004; Yousman 2009). What follows is a discussion of the core elements of this program that are influential to the development of prison images (refer to Box 4.1 for background information on *Oz*).

Fantasy Versus Reality

Early prison films contained an underlying promise of offering an authentic prison experience, yet fantasy far outweighed reality. To many critics and viewers, *Oz* fulfilled this promise. But those more familiar with prison life question the ability of this type of programming to truly offer the reality of the incarcerated world. As Brian Jarvis (2006) mentions, much of prison life is about passing time, and to depict the true nature would not attract viewers, yet many viewers believed the nonstop action and violence in *Oz* to be true. Yousman's (2009) discussion of *Oz* includes several quotes from television critics who laud the reality of the program, and many viewers felt the same way. Fans of the show wrote some of the following comments on the Internet Movie Database (IMDb n.d.):

> CHRISTOPHER T. CHANSE: No SHAWSHANK REDEMPTION here, folks, no benevolent GREEN MILE guards or saintly supernatural inmates. OZ tells it like it is, and baby, it ain't pretty.

> CRAZYDOG-2: One thing I really like is this realism: There are no stupid heros [*sic*] that shouldn't be in prison. Everyone there's a criminal and deserves to be there.

> VID STEH: What I like about this show is the fact it has the courage to show the real life in prison without any annoying characters, stereotypes and unrealistic dialogs.

These are just a few examples of how many fans perceived the program. There was a general belief that viewers were finally being shown the truth about life behind bars.

Feeding the belief that this prison show was the real deal was the show's creator, Tom Fontana. In interviews, he discussed how *Oz* was influenced by an Amnesty International report and how he spent time researching prison life before writing the show (Rapping 2003; Smith 1999). While some films and TV shows gain their authenticity from filming at actual prisons, this was not the case with *Oz*, which used a constructed set to present a modern cellblock with glass doors for viewers to see everything (perhaps an ode to Jeremy Bentham's "all seeing eye"; see Throness 2008). Additional realism comes from the filming techniques employed. Many of the scenes were shot with handheld cameras, creating the overall feel of authentic prison images. Despite these elements of realism, *Oz* needed to capture the attention of the audience, and it does just that through negative imagery (Freeman 2000) and predictable melodramatic story lines (Jarvis 2006). Similar to other media representations of prison life, *Oz* relies on violence and the demonization of offenders to entertain.

Demonizing the Inmate Population

Inmate heroes have always been a part of prison tales, providing characters to which the audience can easily relate. In *Oz,* there are no such heroes (Rapping 2003). Viewers may have hope for Tobias Beecher, a new inmate introduced in the first episode. He is a fish out of water; however, by the end of the first episode, his transformation into a hardened criminal has begun. Viewers see the prisonization process firsthand. Beecher's transformation allows the producers to show the effects of imprisonment. In addition, not having an inmate hero allows for the legitimization of the underlying message about the depravity of those behind bars.

Over the entire series, *Oz* offers a complex look at prison life, but that is often overshadowed by violence. The very first scene sets the stage for the level of viciousness contained throughout the entire series. Within seconds of the opening credits, viewers are introduced to the worst of the worst: locked up securely where they can hurt only one another, an incoming inmate is stabbed ("The Routine" 1997). Every day within this maximum security prison is depicted as a battleground. Violence of all types is a common part of the plot. In the fifth season, there was an average of almost fourteen acts of violence per episode (Yousman 2009). Over the course of the series, there were 100 murders and countless nonlethal violent acts (Jarvis 2006). It is not just the sheer amount of violence that may be shocking to viewers, but also the way that the violence is depicted. A review in the *New York Times* begins, "Crucifixion. Cannibalism. Slow death by eating glass. Sexual mutilation. Is there nothing Tom Fontana won't depict on his HBO prison series, *Oz*?" (Smith 1999, par. 1). Most of the violence is committed by the prisoners and only occasionally by smug hacks. For example, in the premiere episode where an incoming inmate is stabbed, another is burned alive (with the help of corrupt guards); Beecher, one of the new inmates, is sodomized and branded; inmates attack one another; and an inmate with acquired immunodeficiency syndrome (AIDS) is smothered to death, albeit per his request ("The Routine" 1997). Violence is a part of prison life but, like many other media images of crime, *Oz* overexaggerates the amount of violence in the prison system. The use of violence in this series serves as a way to thrill viewers while simultaneously distancing viewers and demonizing all people behind bars. It reassures viewers that they belong where they are.

Most analyses of *Oz* highlight the way that it dehumanizes prisoners through its depiction of them, which goes beyond the acts of violence. This story of maximum security life depicts the survival of the fittest (Wilson and O'Sullivan 2004). According to Elayne Rapping (2003, 81), "*Oz* presents a vision of hell on earth in which inmates are so depraved and vicious that no sane person could possibly think they should ever again be let loose upon society." These murderers and rapists are locked away to torture and kill one another in this prison jungle. This depiction of violent criminals matches other media images, including the "Lombrosian undertones" described by Kenneth Dowler, Thomas Fleming, and Stephen Muzzati (2006, 840). It begins to paint these offenders as being different from the viewers, especially in their savageness, thereby drawing a distinct line between us (the viewers) and them (the inmates).

The format of *Oz* allows for a much more comprehensive look at these characters than typical crime dramas that wrap up a case in one episode. The characters are followed throughout the series, or until their demise. The in-depth character development may lead to further demonization or perhaps a better understanding and even humanization of these characters and, therefore, the inmate population. If *Oz* depicted these inmates in a manner similar to prison films then some empathy may be created, but viewers quickly find out that this is not the case.

If one looks past the brutality, there is another interpretation of how the inmates are portrayed on *Oz*. David Wilson and Sean S. O'Sullivan (2004) argue that, in some ways, the show humanizes prisoners. Through the use of flashbacks to their crimes, viewers catch a brief glimpse of who these men were before prison. Each character has his own moral code, even if he has been either directly or indirectly involved in the death of another prisoner (Wilson and O'Sullivan 2004). Viewers see them struggle with questions of life, death, love, and family. For example, in the first episode a prisoner named Dino Ortolani comes to the realization that he will never get out and tells his wife to never visit him again ("The Routine" 1997). However, these morals and struggles are not the main aspects of these characters that are emphasized on the show. Given the fact that viewers are continually inundated with images of vicious inmates, they may be unable to see their humanity. After all, will they really care whether a heartless violent inmate loses his family? Not likely.

Demonization is further enforced by highlighting the impossibility of reforming these awful men. Rehabilitation versus punishment is a common theme in many prison films, and this same debate is at the core of *Oz*. Through the distinction between Emerald City and the rest of Oswald State Penitentiary, viewers capture a glimpse into these different philosophies of punishment. Emerald City is based on liberal ideals pursued by Tim McManus, the head of the unit, and highlights the goal of rehabilitation. McManus can be equated to the reform-minded wardens in the early prison films. He tries to convince the warden and others that, if given a chance, these inmates can be reformed. Yet he must fight against the warden, the governor, and guards who are reinforcing the get-tough stance, not to mention the seemingly out-of-control inmates. In an early episode, a guard mocks McManus's attempts at giving inmates "quiet time" for misdeeds, equating his treatment of them with that of preschoolers ("The Routine" 1997). In contrast, the rest of Oswald State Penitentiary is based on punishment, with linear cell designs and the hole. Even the darkness of the scenes in these parts of the prison reinforces that punishment is the purpose of the institution. In the final episode of the series, the new warden shows the restraint chair to inmates and tells them that it will now be used in solitary confinement, suggesting that even the strictest form of prison punishment is not enough ("Exeunt Omnes" 2003). Of course, like many prison films, punishment wins in the end. According to Brian Jarvis (2006, 167), "Over six years and almost 60 episodes, McManus' experiment to get people to 'learn to live together' was an unequivocal failure." And while *Oz* presents itself as being neutral on prison issues, this neutrality is a facade. It unequivocally "identifies prison as a failing institution" (Wilson and O'Sullivan 2004, 157). In the end, this means that none of these violent human beings can be helped and should remain locked up. The idea that rehabilitation is a failure is once again demonstrated.

Lessons Learned from the Land of Oz

HBO's *Oz* presents viewers with extremely violent images of prison life blanketed in fake realism. At times it repeats common prison-related stereotypes while at others it truly highlights the complexity of prison as a social institution. One might think of *Oz* as the *Law and Order* of prison dramas, a groundbreaking show about this part of the criminal justice system. One that, if done in the right way, could spark countless copycat shows. In the history of crime-related television programming, *Oz* plays an important role. In general, it set the stage for other series such as *The Sopranos* and *The Wire* (Sepinwall 2012). It also marked a change in how the media depicts punishment. According to Rapping (2003, 74),

> It turns away from the model of a publically invisible, relatively benign and "corrective" form of punishment, suited to liberal democracies, to something much more resonant of earlier eras in which punishment for crime was not only physical and brutal, but also publicly

visible. A ritualistic spectacle that served both as a warning and as a moral education for a public socialized to see crime in terms of evil, of unforgivable and unacceptable social transgression.

Despite its impact, to this day *Oz* is one of kind on US television—it is the only true prison drama to air.

Ultimately, *Oz* repeats many of the same messages as other crime dramas, just more so. According to Jarvis (2006, 168), "As public pedagogy the main lesson taught in Emerald City was fear." The show overwhelmingly pushes messages that are supportive of conservative crime control policies while occasionally offering criticism of the system (Yousman 2009). The unbridled reign given to the creators allowed them to show prison as it had never been seen but, just like on network television stations, the aim was to generate viewership. *Oz* did just that through the development of complex characters and story lines that were heavily infused with conflict, violence, and sex.

The Legacy of *Oz*

Oz was an important step in the development of modern prison imagery, but it was not the only attempt to entertain television audiences with the drama and excitement of life behind bars. Ultimately, further attempts have stepped away from the graphic imagery of *Oz* and followed in the footsteps of prison films in two ways. First, there has been a replication of the standard prison film formula, followed by an expansion of the story to outside of the prison walls. A brief look at the programs that have aired since *Oz* uncovers this progression of dramatic portrayals of prison on television.

Back to the Big House

Whereas *Oz* gave viewers a look at prison life like none they had ever seen, the second series to appear on US television is reminiscent of classic prison films. In 2005, Fox added *Prison Break* to its primetime lineup, and it became one of the most popular series in the station's history (Knaggs 2011). According to a media critic, *Prison Break* "has the dark social hierarchies of *Oz* and the clever inventions of *Escape from Alcatraz*" (Flynn 2005, par. 2). Given that it appeared on network television, this program reached far more viewers than its predecessor. Even though *Prison Break* has been off the air since 2009, it currently has more than 11 million Facebook fans (vs. *Oz*'s 453,000 fans), thousands of fan fiction stories, a video game, and mobile episodes. Its impact has reached far beyond the small screen. While there have been extensive discussions of *Oz* in the literature on prison images, to my knowledge *Prison Break* has been absent from the conversation.

While *Oz* had an ensemble cast with no protagonist, *Prison Break* (Scheuring 2005) tells the story of two brothers. The protagonist, Michael Schofield, purposely commits a crime to be sent to prison to help his innocent brother, Lincoln Burrows, escape before his execution. The first season centers on Michael going to prison and putting the plan into motion, and culminates with several inmates on the run after successfully escaping. The seasons that follow diverge from the original formula and, while they contain some prison images, most of the story line has nothing to do with prison life.

As discussed previously, prison films repeatedly use similar characters, scenes, and plot lines, and *Prison Break* borrows heavily from this genre. Michael is the inmate hero to which the audience immediately relates. Viewers witness him before imprisonment, preparing to rescue Lincoln, and are reassured to know that the only reason he committed the crime was to save his brother. He is also handsome, very intelligent, and kind of like the character MacGyver with his ability to solve any issue with ordinary items found in the prison. On the surface, his brother, Lincoln, is not as relatable. After all, he is a death row inmate. Within the first couple of episodes it is established that, while Lincoln is not the innocent that his brother is, he at least did not commit the crime for which he is scheduled to be executed. He is an antihero of sorts; viewers know he is a criminal, but still relate to him and want him reformed.

Michael and Lincoln are contrasted to many of the other inmates. Some of these inmates are sympathetic characters such as Michael's cellmate Fernando Sucre and the old lifer Charles Westmoreland. But many are the stereotypical animalistic inmates often seen in other prison imagery, such as the psychopath (Haywire) and the resident sex offender (T-Bag), as well as a series of gang members and mobsters (Scheuring 2005). The diversity of the inmates is one way in which *Prison Break* is similar to *Oz*. Interracial conflict is also a theme that these two shows share. Yet in *Prison Break* some of these diverse inmates work together, often not by choice, to escape from Fox River Penitentiary.

The story line begins much like many prison films. Michael is convicted, sentenced, and transported to prison (Scheuring 2005). The typical scenes of inmates being processed into the prison are included. As Michael is brought in, he meets Captain Brad Bellick, the epitome of a smug hack (see Box. 4.2), who becomes Michael's nemesis throughout much of the series. Traditional prison films typically contain a reform-minded paternalistic warden. In *Prison Break,* Warden Henry Pope fits this description perfectly. Repeating a scene commonly used in prison films, in the first episode Michael is brought into the warden's office, thereby establishing a connection between the warden and the hero. Warden Pope comes across as somewhat caring and willing to give special privileges to worthy inmates. After a major disturbance in the cell-block, he scolds the inmates like a father would his naughty children. Reminiscent of the wardens in early prison films, he is seeking to rehabilitate offenders. At one point in the series, Warden Pope and Captain

---

Box 4.2 Cruel Guards in TV Dramas

Once something becomes a trope, it is likely to be repeated in all facets of the media. The stereotype of the cruel prison guard that was established in prison films made its way into television dramas. Every TV program contains one or more of these characters. The serial nature of television programming, however, allows viewers to take their time in getting to know the characters. This format provides a more complex look at correctional officers. For example, *Oz* presents viewers with a series of cruel guards, but also tough yet caring prison workers, including the unit manager, chaplain, and prison psychiatrist. Yet can viewers forget the barrage of smug hacks that they have witnessed over the years? Perpetuating this stereotype is problematic because it creates a misunderstanding of the profession of correctional officer. A concerned officer writes, the media portray us "as lazy, crooked, overpaid, system-milking, power-hungry, hardened and desensitized" (Fox 2013, par. 14). They think we "are babysitters who are responsible for making sure the needs of inmates are met. While this is a part of our job, it is society's lack of information of what we really deal with that is also affecting how the media portrays us" (Fox 2013, par. 13). Entertainment media are not alone in sending this message; other media sources, including some documentaries, continue to feed the stereotype of the cruel prison guard.

Bellick express their differing takes on the purpose of the prison system: whereas the warden wants to reform inmates, Bellick is clear that prison is only for punishment. Bellick expresses his views to those above the warden's head. In the midst of a riot, Bellick tells the governor, "These inmates don't mess around . . . sometimes you have to grab the situation by the gonads and take control" (Scheuring 2015). At the end of the season, however, the two become closer in their views. After Warden Pope is betrayed by Michael, his demeanor changes and punishing the escapees becomes a priority: once again, reform is a failure.

Beyond the characters themselves, *Prison Break* incorporates other elements of prison films. There are several disturbances, a riot, and, of course, the big escape in the first season of *Prison Break* (Scheuring 2005). The series also touches on prison rape, inmate-on-inmate violence, and suicide. All of these are also included in *Oz* and, in comparison, their depiction in *Prison Break* is mild. But to viewers of network television, *Prison Break* is fairly violent in contrast to other crime shows that focus mainly on investigation and prosecution. While viewers may be rooting for some of the inmates, the violent savages are still prominent and safely behind prison walls (for the most part).

In order to further the plot of the series, *Prison Break* affords the prisoners an incredible amount of freedom, suggesting that maximum security inmates are allowed to do whatever they want. The inmate work crew that Michael and the others work on is left unattended for hours, allowing them to execute their escape plans. In addition, Lincoln is a death row inmate who is treated similarly to the other prisoners. He is not housed on death row, he is given a work assignment, and he commonly interacts with the general population of inmates even until the night before his scheduled execution. Together, these scenes may feed the belief that inmates are free to do what they want and that serving time in prison is easy.

While on the surface *Prison Break* is much like a traditional prison film, the series is not a pure prison drama. The first season's main story line centers on the conspiracy against Lincoln, who has been framed for the murder of the vice president's brother (Scheuring 2005). About half of the scenes take place outside of the prison, with some characters trying to cover up the conspiracy and others trying to find evidence of the scheme. The intent is obviously not to tell a tale of prison life. Similar to modern prison films, the prison is simply a device to convey an intriguing story.

Like its film counterparts, *Prison Break* ultimately offers viewers escapism, with enough plot twists to keep them glued to their televisions. Perhaps viewers are comfortable watching the familiar images of prison life that have been around for decades, yet it is new enough in its serial format with a conspiracy and the ingenuity of Michael. Within that context are elements of prison life that viewers may take away from *Prison Break,* such as messages about reform versus punishment, with punishment justified by the animalistic behavior of the inmates, and evidence of racial divides in the inmate social system. In the end, however, this program does not add much to the lexicon of popular knowledge of prisons—it is not anything that viewers have not seen before.

Outside the Walls

Oz and *Prison Break* were both hits on their respective channels, each weaving their own tale of prison life. Beyond these two programs, the prison drama has failed to develop any further on US television. Like *Prison Break,* other series that appear to be prison dramas take most of the action outside of the prison walls, yet none have come close to the popularity of this show. This leaves *Oz* as the only true US prison drama. By the time *Prison Break* debuted, there were alternative images of prison available, which were predominately reality based. When people want to look into life behind prison gates, they seem to prefer popular documentary series. Nevertheless, there is room for fantasy and emotional manipulation in the storytelling related to prison life. Some television programs have attempted to draw in viewers with other prison-related tales.

Since *Prison Break* went off the air in 2009, two televised dramas have hinted at being about prison, neither of which was very successful or truly about prison. The first, A&E's *Breakout Kings* (Olmstead and Santora 2011), was created by some of the same producers as *Prison Break.* Its premiere episode was the most-watched original drama on the network (Seidman 2011). The show is based on a formula that has recently become popular in some US crime dramas. In the vein of *Leverage, White Collar,* and even *Dexter,* the story line focuses on offenders getting the truly bad guys. Three inmates, Shea, Erica, and Lloyd, are given a deal—if they help the US marshals find some violent escaped convicts, they can spend their time in a minimum security prison and earn time off their sentences for each capture. While popular with its niche market, *Breakout Kings* lasted only two seasons. A second prison series also highlighted violent inmates. Drawing on what is perhaps the most notorious and for a long time the most mysterious prison in the United States, Fox's *Alcatraz* (Lilien, Sarnoff, and Wynbrandt

2012) is a crime drama infused with science fiction. The premise of the program is that USP Alcatraz did not really close in 1963; rather, every inmate and the staff vanished into thin air. Nearly fifty years later, the inmates and staff begin reappearing one by one in San Francisco, as if no time had passed. This formula was not popular, and the show was cancelled during the first season. In the end, neither *Breakout Kings* nor *Alcatraz* offered anything truly new to viewers. The development of the prison drama appeared to have stalled.

The Failure of the Prison Drama as a Genre

US television is littered with crime dramas. However, those about prison life have not been popular in the United States. People are fascinated with the mysteries behind prison walls and have a general desire to see offenders punished, so why then has this genre enjoyed limited popularity? Raney and Bryant (2002) purport that people enjoy crime dramas when justice is achieved according to their moral beliefs; they call this the "integrated theory of enjoyment." Crime dramas such as *Law and Order* and others typically follow a specific formula for making certain that justice is achieved according to the audience's moral judgments. It seems that prison dramas would fit this equation and, therefore, provide a popular formula for television programming. Each program shows violent offenders locked away, presumably getting the punishment they deserve. Even when prisoners escape, justice is achieved through capture or death, except in *Prison Break* where justice is achieved in another way.

There are other indications that prison dramas have the potential to be popular. Crime dramas are engaging, and they use various techniques to engross viewers with the story lines. One of these ways to engage viewers is to trigger their emotions. In prison dramas, the emotional manipulation comes in part from the types of offenders that are highlighted. Most of the characters in these programs are violent offenders, whose crimes are at times almost unbelievable. It is these serious offenses that trigger the viewers' emotions. Arthur A. Raney (2005) argues that, when viewers see minor offenses, their responses are cognitive; however, when they witness major crimes, they are guided by affective responses. Thus, creators must rely on extreme crimes to keep viewers' attention through emotional manipulation. To maintain viewership, this extreme behavior must continue once the offenders are incarcerated. Since these programs feature violent offenders, the shows must be set in maximum security institutions, the least common type of prison in the United States (Stephan 2008). Regardless of the crime depicted, viewers would expect nothing less than this setting. "In the crime drama world, the punishment cannot fit the crime; it must surpass it" (Raney 2005, 160). If the crime is horrendous enough, it gives viewers "moral amnesty," which allows them to enjoy media offenders receiving excessive punishment (Raney 2005). There is no reason for viewers to feel bad about the system because the offenders are framed as deserving of extreme punishment.

For the most part, US prison dramas use the basic formula popularized by other crime series: violence, drama, mystery, and, ultimately, justice through punishment. While on the surface it might appear that prison dramas should be appealing, perhaps they are limited in their ability to sustain viewers' attention. There are only so many ways to tell stories that happen within the confines of a cellblock. *Oz* was the only program in the United States to engage viewers almost exclusively within the prison, but it relied on shock value to do so. Even *Prison Break* had to rely on stories external to the prison environment to engage viewers for as long as it did. Like prison films, the genre could not sustain itself exclusively within the prison environment. Robert M. Freeman (2000, 51) believes that prison television series were not successful because "they are unable to develop and sustain the intense emotions found in the compressed time frame of the prison movie." But what happens when a show tries to invoke emotions in a new way by presenting modern prison issues? In 2013, two new series debuted— *Rectify* (McKinnon 2013) and *Orange Is the New Black* (Kohan 2013). Each of these series represents a new look at prison life; the latter features a women's prison and will be discussed in Chapter 7.

The Sundance Channel's *Rectify* (McKinnon 2013) tackles the issue of imprisonment, or more specifically punishment, in US society. *Rectify* is a modern commentary on the effects of our system of punishment. The slow thoughtful images of the program seep into viewers' minds. It may lead some viewers to reflect on the purpose of punishment; others may consider the tragedies of an imperfect system. For the purpose of this discussion, however, it is the implications of prison isolation that are important.

The morally ambiguous protagonist, Daniel Holden, is released from prison after new deoxyribonucleic acid (DNA) evidence appears in his case (McKinnon 2013). Daniel has spent two decades on death row. The series begins on the day he is set free. Viewers uncomfortably watch Daniel's transition into a world that has changed considerably over the past twenty years, from tearing apart a down pillow and letting the soft feathers cascade over his naked body and masturbating to a magazine that his stepbrother, Ted Talbot Jr., gave him, to the awkward-ness of every human interaction that he must now have outside the con-fines of his prison cell. These scenes are juxtaposed with flashbacks to his years in prison. Viewers see his hours in the solitary cell, during which Daniel reads, meditates, and talks to the inmate in the next cell through the vent (McKinnon 2013). Standard elements are incorporated, including a cruel guard and a bloodthirsty death row inmate, thus rein-forcing popular ideas about prison life even if Daniel appears to be a contradiction. If Daniel is not the bloodthirsty killer that everyone thinks he is, then moral amnesty no longer applies, potentially leaving viewers to question justice in this series.

Doubts are raised about whether Daniel could have killed his girl-friend (McKinnon 2013). A scene near the end of the first season leaves viewers wondering—was he capable of the crime or did twenty years of isolation affect his psyche? After Ted pushes his buttons too many times, Daniel strangles his stepbrother. Viewers next see Ted face down in the family's tire shop. He is alive, but his pants are pulled down and coffee grounds cover his butt (McKinnon 2013). The entire scene is dis-turbing, leaving one questioning everything else that had been seen about Daniel. *Rectify* is an interesting take on the modern justice sys-tem. While a critically acclaimed program because it is not on network television or even the most popular premium channels, *Rectify* reaches a limited audience in comparison to other prison dramas (e.g., *Prison Break*). And for some, the morally ambiguous images may be just too uncomfortable to watch.

Conclusion

People draw from various sources in their social construction of prison; for some, prison dramas are a part of the formula. This imagery is based on either the shock of reality or the entertainment provided by tales of injustice similar to prison films. From *Oz* to *Alcatraz*, viewers are con-fronted with tales of violent prisoners in maximum security prisons or, as in the case of *Breakout Kings*, their escape from these institutions. The majority of the inmates are bloodthirsty and cruel. Occasionally, there are prisoners to whom viewers can relate, such as Michael in *Prison Break*, but his innocence is immediately established. Each of these dramas shows an exciting version of the prison routine. There is not much idle time or monotony; nearly every inmate is in the mix, hustling and fighting their way through the prison jungle. After all, it is entertainment television and, as previously discussed, negative imagery and emotional manipulation attract viewers (Freeman 2000; Jarvis 2006). Violence and hustling provide a powerful source of both, and this is particularly true of *Oz*. However, the other programs use prison as a backdrop for another type of story. So, while there is some negative imagery of prison life and prisoners, the main entertainment factor comes from the conspiracy, the mystery, or the chase. The rest becomes background noise.

The takeaway from watching these programs is simple. For the most part, the messages contained within these prison dramas are a continuation of those found in crime dramas featuring the front part of the justice system. The message remains that prison is a necessary social institution and, perhaps, is not harsh enough for some. These dramas about prison do not add much to the social construction of imprisonment beyond what prison films have already contributed. Whether watching the movies *Cool Hand Luke* and *Felon* or the TV series *Prison Break* and *Oz*, the results are much the same. Viewers walk away with a sense of knowledge about prison life, without ever truly understanding the complexities of the social institution.

Entertainment of all kinds is shaped by many factors. The prison drama emerged in a time of declining prison movies and increasing interest in reality-based programming. *Oz* filled a niche that is now filled by infotainment television programming, but there is room for additional storytelling. At no other time in US history would it have been particularly relevant to challenge viewers' beliefs about punishment as *Rectify* does so eloquently. While a critically acclaimed series, it remains to be seen how this morally ambiguous drama will sit with viewers. One must remember that these prison dramas do not exist in a vacuum. It is unlikely that their imagery is all that people have seen during the imprisonment binge. More influential images were brewing in the form of the televised prison documentary, which I discuss in the next two chapters.

5

Early
Prison Documentaries

PRISON FILMS AND TELEVISED DRAMAS HAVE PROVIDED PEOPLE
with decades of entertainment. While these undoubtedly unlock secrets
of prison life, viewers are aware that these accounts are fictionalized.
Real images of prisons and inmates are more influential but, given that
news media coverage of prisons is limited, people must turn elsewhere
to find these images. Today, documentaries fulfill this role. Although
prison documentaries were slow to develop, they now play a pivotal
role in many people's understanding of this social institution.

Documentary is one of the main creative modes in filmmaking.
While Hollywood films are meant to entertain, documentaries are "part
record of what exists, part argument why and in what ways it should be
changed" (Ellis and McLane 2005, ix). While the term *documentary*
was not used until the 1920s, documentaries have existed in one form or
another since films were first created (Ellis and McLane 2005). Over
the course of the twentieth century, documentaries underwent major
transformations, appearing not only in theaters but also on television
and the Internet (see Table 5.1). History, culture, and technology shape
the format and content of documentaries. These factors explain the
development of prison documentaries and why they are more popular
today than ever before. Examining the evolution of early prison documentaries uncovers the factors that shaped these films and provides an
understanding of modern prison imagery.

The Development of Prison Documentaries

Within the ever changing world of documentary filmmaking, a slow
progression toward prison documentaries as a genre can be seen. Early

Table 5.1 Development of Documentary Films

■ Theatrical and Government Documentaries, 1930s–1940s

Movie theaters were used for more than just entertainment. The public remained informed through newsreels and documentaries. Series such as *March of Time* allowed people to learn more about social issues (Ellis and McLane 2005). The US government also produced documentaries during this time, making some available to the public at large (Ellis and McLane 2005). Poverty, unionism, war, and international relations were some of the major social issues that were covered by documentarians.

Prison Documentaries

Prison documentaries were not common.

■ TV Documentaries and Cinema Vérité, 1950s–1970s

Technological advances led to significant changes to documentary filmmaking. Documentaries moved from the theater to classrooms and living rooms. Most accessible were the network documentary series that emerged in the 1950s. Shows such as *See it Now* on CBS and *Project XX* on NBC became a popular source of information (Ellis and McLane 2005). In the 1960s, these programs developed into televised news magazines, which attracted viewers with their soft news format, the content covered, and the on-air personalities. However, unlike documentaries, these programs leaned more toward entertaining viewers than offering a critical look at society (Spragens 1995). Filmmaking also changed considerably. New technology allowed filmmakers to capture sight and sound simultaneously and to film subjects from a distance. Documentarians could now capture more images than ever before. As a result, a new form of documentary film known as cinema vérité was created. These documentaries feature voyeuristic recordings, with no narration or interviews; the audience simply observes (Ellis and McLane 2005).

Prison Documentaries

Prison documentaries began to emerge in the 1960s. While still not common, technological advances allowed filmmakers to capture life behind prison walls.

■ Public Television and Cable Documentaries, 1980s–1990s

By the end of the 1970s, documentary programming on network television had almost disappeared, having been replaced by soft news programs (Moore, Bensman, and Van Dyke 2006; Spragens 1995). At the same time, documentaries were becoming even more prevalent due to the development of video recordings, which made it easy for small film crews to tape hundreds of hours of footage (Ellis and McLane 2005). Public television and the development of cable television kept documentaries alive, although the genre was substantially altered in the transition from network television to cable. These popular documentaries were designed to entertain as well as educate viewers and became known as infotainment (Moore, Bensman, and Van Dyke 2006).

Prison Documentaries

Prison documentaries became more prevalent and the modern prison documentary was born.

on, there were technological challenges to making these films as well as a general lack of interest in the topic. Things began to change in the 1960s when the technology became available to facilitate filming in a prison and the public began to show interest in what was happening behind prison gates. In 1965, President Lyndon Johnson officially declared a War on Crime (Flamm 2005). That was the beginning of a shift toward conservatism and, eventually, get tough crime policies. Prison documentaries emerged at this time and slowly developed into a genre of filmmaking. By the end of the twentieth century a variety of prison documentaries existed, although not all were easily accessible to the public. Regardless of accessibility, these films were some of the few sources of real prison imagery available. Viewers were able to catch a glimpse of life behind prison walls.

Types of Prison Documentaries

When a genre is first established, variety exists. Frames and other standard storytelling techniques have yet to be developed. Each of those early films weaves a unique tale of prison life, using distinctive frames. There are, however, some similarities in the underlying messages or purpose of the films. In general, prison documentaries made during the twentieth century can be divided into three different types: historical prison documentaries, deterrence-based prison documentaries, and investigative prison documentaries (see Table 5.2). These are not steadfast classifications, but they are a helpful way of looking at how these films have developed over time.

Historical Prison Documentaries

Documentarians love history. Historical information is commonly used in films to establish context since viewers would not understand the uniqueness of an institution unless they were made aware of its past. The historical references commonplace in many prison documentaries provide valuable insight into imprisonment in the United States. Many early prison documentaries focus exclusively on providing a history lesson in penology. These films allow us to witness institutions, customs, and penal practices of the past. Through films such as *Let the Doors Be of Iron* (1987) and *Eastern State Penitentiary* (1998), viewers can step back in time and enter the first prison in the United States through reenactments, photos, and new footage shot at the crumbling institution.

Table 5.2 Types of Early Prison Documentaries

Historical	Deterrence	Investigative
Afro-American Work Songs in a Texas Prison (1966)	*Life at Stateville: The Wasted Years* (1960)	*Titicut Follies* (1967)
Alcatraz Island of Hate (1971)	*Scared Straight* (1978)	*Three Thousand Years and Life* (1973)
Alcatraz: America's Toughest Prison (1977)	*Squires of San Quentin* (1978)	*Attica* (1974)
Let the Doors Be of Iron (1987)	*Scared Straight! 10 Years Later* (1987)	*Shakedown in Santa Fe* (1988)
The Big House series (Miranda 1998)	*Scared Straight! 20 Years Later* (1999)	*Investigative Reports* series (Kurtis 1991)
Eastern State Penitentiary (1998)	*Beyond Scared Straight* series (Shapiro & Coyne 2011)	*The Farm: Life Inside Angola Prison* (1998)
Escape! Breakout from Alcatraz (2000)		*Doing Time: Life in the Big House* (1991)
Lonely Island: Hidden Alcatraz (2003)		*Prisoners of the War on Drugs* (1992)
The Children of Alcatraz (2003)		*Ghosts of Attica* (2001)
Alcatraz: Living Hell (2007)		*The Farm: 10 Down* (2009)
Alcatraz Reunion (2008)		*Criminal Injustice: Death and Politics at Attica* (2012)
Eastern State: Living Behind the Walls (2008)		

They can witness African American prisoners singing while working in the fields in *Afro-American Work Songs in a Texas Prison* (1966). Even the first televised prison documentary series, *The Big House* (Miranda 1998), adopted this perspective with each episode providing a history lesson on a specific institution.

While there are more than enough prisons in the United States to produce a variety of historical documentaries, one institution in particular has been the subject of many of these films. USP Alcatraz is perhaps the most famous prison in the world. Located on an island and known for housing infamous criminals such as the Birdman of Alcatraz (Robert Stroud), Al Capone, and "Machine Gun" Kelly, it is no wonder that people are curious about this institution. For much of its history administrators kept the media at bay, thereby limiting people's knowledge of what was taking place there. Filmmakers of all types have taken advantage of the lore surrounding Alcatraz, creating both fictional and nonfictional accounts of life on the Rock. One of the first of these films was *Alcatraz: Island of Hate* (1971). Narrated by Howard Duff, this film traces the history of Alcatraz Island, the daily routine in the prison, and the 1946 siege through the use of still photos, newsreels, and interviews. Duff weaves most of this tale from a boat off the shore of the island. This film was made before Alcatraz became a part of the National Park Service and was opened to the public; therefore, the filmmakers were constrained by their inability to film in the institution. Despite this challenge, they created a visual history of a US landmark. Since then, many other documentaries have been produced as well as episodes of various paranormal television programs. Each film attempts to craft a unique take on the history of the institution. One example is *The Children of Alcatraz* (2003), which depicts the story of children growing up on the island because their parents worked in the prison. The filmmaker infuses interviews of several people reflecting on their childhood on the island with still photographs and footage of their time there. Their stories present a unique look at events that unfolded at the prison. Media images of all types have contributed to people's understanding of Alcatraz, but these historical documentaries provide the best knowledge of life on the rock.

Most prisons are not as well known as Alcatraz, but historical documentaries unlock the mysteries of the past and introduce viewers to other kinds of prisons too. This type of prison documentary serves as an educational tool. Viewers can witness the complex history of incarceration in the United States, which is an important consideration when critiquing current policies. It makes sense that this type of film was popular in the early development of prison documentaries. Filmmakers did not need direct access to the institutions when they could incorporate archived materials and interview living witnesses to recreate the events that unfolded in these prisons. Today, historical documentaries are less common. History is not ignored; instead, it is a smaller part of the story in the quick-paced sensationalistic imagery that is now popular.

Deterrence-Based Prison Documentaries

There is a long-held belief that the threat of punishment can be used to dissuade people from committing crime but, for this to work, people must be aware of the consequences of their behavior and at times the media are used as the messengers. The most well-known attempts are the public service announcements that were popularized early in the war on drugs. The second type of prison documentary is rooted in this philosophy, its primary purpose being to deter youth from crime. These deterrence-based prison documentaries use the penal system as an example of what can happen if a young person makes the wrong choices. With today's get-tough polices, it is not surprising to find prison documentaries crafted in such a way.

One of the earliest prison documentaries is deterrence based. Before people became overly worried with crime, they had other social concerns, including out-of-control youth. *Life at Stateville: The Wasted Years* (1960) was crafted with this in mind. Locally produced and shown on Chicago's CBS affiliate, WBBM-TV, it is an example of the use of prison images as a deterrent. The narrator, Hugh Hill, quickly establishes the purpose of this special—to present an accurate picture of what life is like in a maximum security prison, with the purpose of deterring young viewers. This documentary uses footage of the daily routine at Stateville Penitentiary as well as interviews with inmates and the warden.

The scenes in this documentary highlight two points. First, time in prison is mundane and a waste of one's life. In his concluding remarks Hill says, "To this reporter it seemed that the real punishment here is left up to one thing and one thing only, the finality and completeness of the regimentation, the separation from the insignificant pleasures and freedoms of the outside world. That punishment is what turns day into night and the months to the wasted years" (*Life at Stateville* 1960). Second, these inmates are wasting their lives behind prison walls because they dropped out of school. This point is demonstrated in the life stories that the inmates share, but is really hit home in the ten-minute editorial following the documentary. Clark B. George, the manager of WBBM-TV, expresses his belief that many of Chicago's youth are on the inevitable pathway to a prison cell, commenting that, "One of these paths leading to tragedy begins when a man or woman drops out of school" (*Life at Stateville* 1960). The impact of this documentary is not known, but it is a reflection of people's concerns at the time. As people shifted their attention to crime, deterrence-based prison documentaries changed their focus specifically to crime prevention rather than to prematurely leaving the educational system.

One of the most well-known prison documentaries of all time is deterrence based. Even if they have never seen the film, it is likely that almost everyone knows about *Scared Straight* (1978), an Emmy- and Academy Award–winning documentary directed by Arnold Shapiro. Its viewers are introduced to a deterrence-based program in which juvenile delinquents are confronted by a group of maximum security inmates. Images of the program are interspersed with scenes of the juveniles talking about their behavior and attitudes. Some scenes of Rahway Prison in New Jersey are included; however, the main focus is on the interactions between the inmates and the juveniles. The program depicted is run by inmates serving life who attempt to scare the delinquents so that they will not be involved in any more criminal behavior. During this time, some harsh lessons about prison life are revealed. The inmates threaten the juveniles. They tell them what will happen when they are raped by a group of inmates and how they will not be able to escape victimization. Interviews with the juveniles following the intervention send a message to viewers that the program was an effective tactic to change their attitudes. Gone are the cocky and tough delinquents who did not see anything wrong with their actions; in their place were shell-shocked kids who began to regret their actions and question their futures.

Unlike most prison documentaries at this time, *Scared Straight* was shown all over the country, first airing in November 1978 on a local Los Angeles television station. On March 5, 1979, the film was shown in over 200 markets nationally (Cavender 1981). Some stations also aired specials on similar programs in their area. For example, *Squires of San Quentin* (1978) depicts the same type of program contained in San Quentin Prison in California. WTCN-TV, a Minneapolis–Saint Paul station, aired the documentary along with commentary and a town hall meeting discussing the effectiveness of the program. The popularity of this documentary is undeniable. Not only is it commonly referenced in popular culture, but there have been subsequent documentaries that followed up on the participants and, most recently, a television series based on the same premise.

Whereas historical prison documentaries educate viewers about many aspects of the institutions themselves, deterrence-based documentaries give viewers a glance at prison life. Frightening inmates unveil the horrors of time inside. The negative aspects, especially violence and rape, are highlighted with the intended purpose of deterring viewers from a life of crime. The imagery supports the belief that deterrence is an effective crime control method. Out-of-control youth were a social concern for much of the twentieth century. Deterrence was offered as the answer to the problem, and adult viewers wholeheartedly embraced the idea. But this solution was a false promise. In the nearly four decades since the original *Scared Straight* documentary was released, research has consistently indicated that these types of programs are not effective in reducing criminal behavior (OJJDP 2011). Despite this, support for deterrence continues to be perpetuated by crime-related media imagery and viewers continue to be enthralled by it. In 2011, the television series *Beyond Scared Straight* (Shapiro and Coyne 2011) debuted on A&E and aired its seventh season in 2014, continuing the tradition of deterrence-based documentaries.

Investigative Prison Documentaries

Many mysteries existed behind prison walls. Without media attention on these institutions, people were simply unaware of what was happening. Early documentarians uncovered some of the issues plaguing the prison system. In the third type of prison documentary, viewers receive the most in-depth look at life in prison. These investigative documentarians follow in the footsteps of investigative journalists who spend extended time researching their subject in order to produce comprehensive stories. While there are many different definitions of *investigative journalism,* in general it uncovers scandals, examines the inner workings and policies of organizations, and brings awareness to societal trends, including political, economic, and cultural issues (Journalism Fund n.d.). Documentary filmmaking has many similarities to journalism. The documentarians who use investigative techniques have uncovered scandals and abuses in the system, exposed problematic policies, and highlighted trends of which the public should be aware. These types of films were particularly prominent in the early stages of prison documentaries. Once prison imagery became more common, investigative qualities diminished.

When filmmakers begin to document their subject, there is no telling what might actually be captured on film or what stories might be unearthed. In the 1960s, Frederick Wiseman was given permission to film at the Massachusetts Correctional Institution at Bridgewater, an institution known for housing the criminally insane. What resulted was one of the most controversial prison documentaries to date, *Titicut Follies* (1967). While Wiseman perhaps did not set out with the intention of uncovering abuse in the system, in the end his film did just that. It became the only US film to receive court-imposed restrictions not based on obscenity or national security, but for breaking an oral contract and violaction of privacy (Anderson and Benson 1991). Thus, it would be more than twenty years before most of the public would have access to this film.

Titicut Follies (1967) is a cinema vérité film that makes the audience voyeurs. The scenes that unfold before their eyes may be confusing at first, but soon the imagery becomes rather disturbing. The film opens with the annual talent show. Various men are on stage singing and waving pompoms. The scene itself is an odd one to behold. Using the standard style of cinema vérité filmmaking, the film provides no narration or explanation of what viewers are witnessing; they must figure it out on their own. Viewers are then confronted with images of the day-to-day lives of these inmates. The men are nude in many of the scenes—from shots taken of the men in their cells to inmates being paraded up and down the corridors. The camera captures several inmates breaking down. One inmate is taken by the guards to be shaved. The guards seem to be agitating this inmate by constantly telling him to clean his cell. When he is brought back to his cell, still naked, he begins to stomp his feet rhythmically. He stops in a corner with his hand over his mouth and, as the camera gets a close-up of his haunted eyes, viewers hear the guards ask him once again if he is going to clean his cell. He is stirred up again by officers who are the epitome of the cruel guards seen in Hollywood films (see Box 5.1).

Perhaps the most disturbing part of the film involves the force-feeding of an inmate. In the approximately eight minutes of the film that this scene encompasses, viewers watch a nude inmate being strapped down, a feeding tube being inserted, and a doctor feeding him while his cigarette dangles over the funnel. Interwoven in these scenes are clips of an inmate, who appears to be catatonic, being shaved. But the truth is revealed when cotton is shoved into the man's eye socket; the inmate is dead and they are prepping the body for burial. This section of the film ends with the inmate's body being pushed into a drawer in a morgue.

Box 5.1 Correctional Officers in Documentaries

Hollywood films firmly established the stereotype of the cruel guard. And as they say, there is some truth in fiction. Like in any other profession, there are a few rotten apples; thus, a version of the smug hack can be found in some prison documentaries. Investigative prison documentaries that have uncovered scandal or abuse highlight these types of correctional officers. Their cruelty is the root of the problem. Despite their inclusion in this imagery, smug hacks are not the primary representation of correctional officers in documentaries. More often than not, prison documentaries use the experiences of the people who work behind prison walls to enhance the story. The correctional officers become tour guides and educators. In *Life at Stateville: The Wasted Years* (1960), the correctional officer literally guides the cameras through the prison on a tour of life in the maximum security prison. In many others, correctional officers provide information via on-camera interviews. They describe their jobs, voice their views of the inmates, and explain inmates' behaviors. The stories would be incomplete without their input. Overall, a much more positive representation of the men and women working behind bars is found in these films. This trend has continued in the documentaries that have become popular in the twenty-first century.

The film quickly shifts to a birthday party held in the prison, with inmates singing and playing games. The film closes the way it started—with the annual talent show as if this is a perfectly normal place and one can forget the disturbing images contained within.

Titicut Follies made its debut at the New York Film Festival in September 1968 and, shortly thereafter, it was released commercially in New York City but not for long. The distribution of this film was halted by *Commonwealth v. Wiseman,* the proceedings of which began on November 17, 1968. This case alleged that Wiseman violated privacy rights of an inmate and broke an oral contract that gave the state editorial control over the films (Anderson and Benson 1991). The legal battle continued for more than two decades until 1991, after which the film was shown on PBS (Goodman 1993). The atrocities uncovered by Wiseman were not uncommon at the time. Prisoners did not have legal rights. Due to the legal restrictions, the potential impact of this investigative documentary will never be known. By the time *Titicut Follies* aired on PBS, inmates had earned the right to adequate medical care and other things. Viewers could watch it in disbelief that this type of treatment had occurred within the system, but it already was a part of history.

Abuses were also uncovered in documentaries on the infamous Attica prison riot of 1971, one of the bloodiest uprisings in US history. Journalists were allowed to film in the prison yard during the four-day siege, giving an unprecedented look at the events as they unfolded. The disturbance ended when the National Guard stormed the prison, which resulted in thirty-nine deaths. The many unanswered questions following this tragic event made it the perfect subject for an investigative documentary such as *Attica* (1974) by Cinda Finestone. Footage from the riot and the subsequent investigations, as well as interviews with prisoners released after the uprising, are combined to tell the story. The film presents "a sobering and revealing look into the heart of American justice, weighing the costs of institutional dishonesty and abuses of power against the price some will pay to retain human dignity" (Shell Castle Film Corporation 2007). Despite the importance of the story, *Attica* remains relatively unknown. It never aired on television and only recently became available for screenings (Castle Film Corporation 2007). But the riot is far from forgotten; legal cases related to the event were settled as recently as 2004. In 2012, *Criminal Injustice: Death and Politics at Attica* revisited the subject. The film's description says it all:

> Forty years after the bloodiest one-day encounter between Americans since the Civil War, the dead remain buried along with the truth. Until now. Based on interviews with eyewitnesses who just now are telling their stories, as well as access to newly discovered documents, the film sheds new light on exactly what happened at Attica between September 9–13, 1971. *Criminal Injustice* raises compelling new questions about the 39 deaths at Attica, White House involvement, and the corrupting influence of Nelson Rockefeller's political aspirations before, during, and long after the deadly retaking of the prison. Former hostage Michael Smith said that "the cover up started as soon as the shooting stopped." This film reveals that the truth actually may have been concealed long before that. (Blue Sky Project n.d.)

Criminal Injustice: Death and Politics at Attica is the epitome of an investigative documentary.

Not all investigative prison documentaries uncover such blatant abuses. Many other early prison documentaries focused on policies and trends. Not everyone may agree that these are investigative in nature but, given their placement in the initial development of this genre, they do uncover issues that not many were aware of at the time. *The Farm: Life Inside Angola Prison* (1998), which originally aired on *Investigative Reports,*[1] is an example of this type of investigative documentary.

The Farm: Life Inside Angola Prison (1998) is an award-winning and Academy Award–nominated documentary produced by Jonathan Stack and Liz Garber (it won eleven different awards from various film festivals, as well as two Primetime Emmy awards). It presents a haunting look at life in what was once one of the most brutal prisons in the United States: the Louisiana State Penitentiary, also known as Angola. Under the leadership of Warden Burl Cain, this institution has developed into one of the most interesting prisons in the country, as is evident by the amount of media coverage it receives. The film examines the effects of sentencing people to life without the possibility of parole. The prison population at Angola is made up mainly of lifers. Viewers learn in the introduction that 85 percent of the prisoners in Angola will die there. To put the issue on a personal level, the film follows six men, including a twenty-two-year-old who is just beginning his life sentence, an inmate who has been in Angola for thirty-eight years, and a lifer who is dying from cancer. Using the stories of these men, discussions with the warden, and images of the prison, the filmmakers tell an incredible story of transformation, freedom, and death. Rather than demonizing lifers, as many media images do, it puts a face on the thousands of inmates who will die in Angola. While depicting these inmates' stories, the film also introduces viewers to some of the unique aspects of this particular prison, such as prisoners working the fields of what was once a plantation, the prison radio station and newspaper, and the cemetery where many of these prisoners will be buried. By presenting this story, the filmmakers demonstrate the effects of life sentences and how institutions deal with issues such as elderly inmates. It questions the usefulness of incarcerating so many prisoners for life. *The Farm: Life Inside Angola Prison* is the first of many documentaries to examine the unique culture of Angola, including a follow-up on the inmates featured in the original documentary in *The Farm: 10 Down* (2009).

Investigative documentaries play an important role in the development of prison imagery. Prisons are closed institutions; therefore, what happens behind the walls is not always transparent. These types of films bring to light prison issues. Changes to the genre at the end of the twentieth century decreased the number of investigative films and issue-based documentaries began to take their place.

Moving Toward Serialization and Sensationalism

Changes in television programming influenced the development of prison documentaries in the 1990s. Crime-related programming was always popular on television but, as discussed in Chapter 4, prison programs were not common. The development of reality-based programs and new crime drama formats influenced documentary filmmaking during that decade and paved the way for the prison documentary to flourish on US television after the turn of the century.

In 1989 *Cops* burst onto the screen as the first reality-based crime show to rely on real footage instead of reenactments. Its popularity demonstrated that viewers were enthralled by real images of the justice system. Shortly thereafter, in 1991, *Law and Order* emerged to change the face of the televised crime drama. That same year, Court TV began its gavel-to-gavel coverage of court cases. This station is probably best known for its coverage of the O.J. Simpson trial but, over its twenty-year run, the channel covered many other sensationalistic trials. Simultaneously, people were being exposed to more crime-related programming and being entertained by more sensationalistic coverage of real events. Both of these changes were reflected in prison documentaries of that decade.

Ratings demonstrated that the more exciting and entertaining the information was, the more viewers tuned in. Whether on purpose or not, some documentarians began to adopt that belief. Sensationalistic imagery became a tool of storytelling even in prison documentaries. Two of these films are *Doing Time: Life in the Big House* (1991) and *Prisoners of the War on Drugs* (1992). The images presented in both are more shocking and violent than previous imagery, which provides a glimpse into the future of prison documentaries.

Doing Time: Life in the Big House (1991), produced by Alan and Susan Raymond, comprises footage shot over five weeks inside the federal penitentiary in Lewisburg, Pennsylvania. What resulted was an Academy Award–nominated film exposing life in a maximum security federal prison. The opening sounds set the stage for the journey that viewers are about to take: the loud echoing voices of many inmates talking at once in a cellblock indicate the chaos and anger within the walls of this prison. The first inmates that viewers see are being processed into the prison and, from photos to strip searches, viewers see it all. The film incorporates many images of prisoners yelling at the camera, demonstrating an out-of-control prison population. It examines SHU, yard time, prison industries and other work duties, a disciplinary hearing, the Special Operations Response Team training and removing inmates from cells, and the warden walking the cellblock talking to inmates. These were somewhat new scenes to many viewers; however, they soon became commonplace in prison documentaries, especially those on cable television. Viewers get an overall view of the inner workings of this institution. The types of inmates highlighted and the way they are depicted became a standard in many televised prison documentaries. Instead of creating a portrait of typical inmates serving time, the focus is on some of the most unique and dangerous inmates, including a former mob boss, a triple murderer, and a man who threatened President Ronald Reagan's life. Whereas *The Farm: Life in Angola Prison* humanizes lifers, this film contains footage of angry, violent, and mentally ill inmates. What is clear when watching this documentary is that USP Lewisburg is not a pleasant place, but this treatment is acceptable because of the crimes that these inmates have committed. The sensationalistic imagery supports this idea. Despite the way that the inmates and day-to-day life are presented in this documentary, it is at the same time an educational journey through a federal prison. The narrator provides a history of the institution and of prisons in the United States as well as statistics on the inmates held in this penitentiary. The information that is presented is clear and it provides context for the story, something with which future documentaries would struggle.

Taking sensationalism even a step further is HBO's *Prisoners of the War on Drugs* (1992), which presented a view of prison few HBO subscribers had seen before. On the surface, this film is an investigative documentary to examine drugs in the prison system; however, the tactics employed to depict the stories may not have had the intended results. Comedian Chris Rock uses a scene from this film in one of his stand-up routines. The opening scenes depict several inmates using drugs or talking about drug use while incarcerated, shocking viewers by showing extreme behavior within the prison system. The film is broken into three segments. The first segment features the same prison in Rahway, New Jersey, in which *Scared Straight* (1978) was filmed. This is followed by a segment on women incarcerated at Bedford Hills Correctional Facility in New York, and the film is wrapped up with a segment on the Oklahoma State Reformatory.

The inmates in the film are brutally honest about drugs, sex, and violence in prison. Viewers are given graphic descriptions of sexual acts that are sometimes traded for drugs and hear about inmates smuggling drugs in various orifices. Prison staff speak candidly about the war on drugs that is being waged behind prison walls, one that appears to be a losing battle. To reiterate this, there are many scenes of inmates shooting up and smoking. In addition, the segment on Oklahoma State Reformatory shows an inmate known as the "Grand Marshall of Meth" using a chemistry textbook to teach his cellmate how to make meth so that he can have a career on the outside. A slightly gentler view is taken of the women, presenting a deeper understanding of their drug issues and highlighting the harsh sentences they received for drug crimes. For the most part though, throughout this documentary, the story does not lend itself to sympathizing with the inmates or the issue of addiction. The film fits well with the mainstream views of a time in which people were becoming more intolerant of drug offenders (see Tonry 2004). *Doing Time: Life in the Big House* and *Prisoners of the War on Drugs* displayed sensationalistic qualities that were becoming more commonplace on crime-related television programming and eventually would become a standard characteristic of televised prison documentaries in the new millennium.

The second transformation to take place in the 1990s was the development of the prison documentary series. *The Big House* (Miranda 1998) premiered on the History Channel. The thirty episodes over its five-year run trace the history of some of the most infamous institutions in the country, including Eastern State Penitentiary, San Quentin, Folsom, Sing Sing, and Leavenworth. Similar to other historical prison documentaries, this series uses archived photographs and footage, along with interviews with administrators, correctional officers, and inmates of the past and present. From inmate laborers building institutions to major disturbances within the prison system, this series exposes viewers to the complicated history of imprisonment in the United States. It did not employ the sensationalistic storytelling techniques that were becoming popular at the time; instead, *The Big House* provided an educational journey through some of the most infamous prisons in the United States. This insightful series was to be one of a kind. The US public's viewing preferences were rapidly changing and television executives took notice. The format used by the producers of *The Big House* would not be repeated. It is the sensationalistic imagery that wins in the end.

Conclusion

By the end of the twentieth century, viewers had more access to realistic images of prison life. Historical documentaries uncovered the development of prisons in the United States to provide context. Deterrence-based documentaries highlighted the scary parts of imprisonment so that the youth of the nation would not go down that same pathway. And investigative documentaries uncovered abuse, scandals, and potentially problematic prison policies. Regardless of any shortcomings, at the time each type of documentary played a role in the social construction of prison. Viewers walked away with more real knowledge of prisons so they would not need to rely on Hollywood-generated fantasies.

Regardless of the type of documentary, viewers expect these films to tell them "something about the workings of the socio-historical world" (Kilborn and Izod 1997, 4). These early prison documentaries do just that. Viewers are presented with imagery of the inner workings of the prison system. They learn about inmates wasting big chunks of their lives behind bars and some inevitably dying in prison because of their incredibly long sentences. They are able to see stories of African American inmates carrying on traditions of their enslaved ancestors, and the treatment of mentally ill inmates before prisoners were ensured certain rights. Finally, they revisit historical turning points, including the Battle of Alcatraz, an event that ultimately led to the closing of the infamous prison, and the uprising at Attica, which pushed along the prisoners' rights movement. To revisit the description of documentary presented by Jack C. Ellis and Betsy A. McLane (2005, ix), documentary is "part record of what exists, part argument why and in what ways it should be changed." Most of these documentaries accomplish two of these three things: they record what exists behind prison walls and they explore why. Few go on to examine the ways that the system should be changed. Those that perhaps could have sparked concern on the part of viewers and incite change, such as *Titicut Follies* and *Attica,* were not readily available to the public. Viewership was limited; thus, the potential impact is dampened. This pattern is one that would be repeated after the turn of the century; the most impactful and critical documentaries have not been as readily available as those designed to entertain and shock viewers.

Despite the development of prison documentaries, there were challenges to their creation. Interest in telling these stories existed; however, film crews were often stopped at the gates. Prison administrators were restrictive in allowing the media to enter their institutions. In the 1990s, requests to film at US prisons were often denied (Sussman 2002). For many years, these decisions limited the development of the prison documentary. This restriction is likely one reason why the first series relied on historical storytelling.

By the 1990s, televised documentaries had substantially changed. According to Ellis and McLane (2005, 294), there "was a marked decline in the overall quality of most televised documentary, even as the number of television hours devoted to nonfiction increased exponentially." With all of the competition, television executives needed to catch viewers' attention; thus, entertainment became a part of the equation. Executives found that they could provide information in such a way as to entertain and educate their viewers simultaneously. Televised news magazines and pseudodocumentary programs, such as *Investigative Reports,* were growing. While the value of this technique is a topic of much debate, it is within this format that prison documentaries began to reach the masses, as I discuss in the next chapter.

Note

1. *Investigative Reports* (Kurtis 1991) aired more than 400 episodes on A&E between 1991 and 2008. This program is an example of the type of television programming that became popular in the 1990s. Televised news magazines grew in popularity and some documentary programming adopted various qualities of these shows. The emphasis was on the sensationalistic side of crime and justice, from rare types of criminal behavior to several episodes on the dark side of parole. The series also included seventeen prison episodes. Instead of using common documentary film techniques, such as letting the story unfold or using a narrator, *Investigative Reports* relied on a host, a technique borrowed from TV news magazines. Bill Kurtis guided viewers through the story adding drama and excitement with the intonation of his voice. This style became the template for many televised prison documentaries.

6

Modern
Prison Documentaries

MODERN IMAGES OF PRISON FALL PREDOMINATELY WITHIN THE
realm of documentary filmmaking, although whether some of these are
actual documentaries or just another form of entertainment television
is debatable. Continued technological advances, combined with an
appetite for reality television and the use of imprisonment, have created
a climate in which prison documentaries flourish and are more common
than ever before. The potential reach of these images is indeterminable.
Today, viewers can catch countless of these documentaries on television
as well as on DVDs and the Internet. Ultimately, people are able to see
more real-life images of prison than ever before; however, more does
not always mean better. Just because viewers have seemingly endless
opportunities to access these images does not ensure that they are more
knowledgeable about the prison system. Once the prison documentary
genre found its footing, commodification became inevitable. Early on, a
winning formula was found and repeated time and again. Basic scenes,
frames, and messages can be found in many televised prison documentaries. The message becomes loud and clear—prisons are a social necessity. It is only when one examines independently produced documentaries that the tone changes and the complexities of incarceration are
uncovered.

The Birth of a Genre: MSNBC's *Lockup*

Although *The Big House* was the first televised prison documentary
series, its formula was not popular. Historical prison documentaries still

85

exist, but they are not the main type of prison imagery presented today. It was not until the emergence of *Lockup* on MSNBC that the modern prison documentary series was born. As seen in the development of documentary filmmaking, there are several factors that shape the end product. In the age of cable television, one of these factors is the station on which the program appears. Television programming used to rely on *broadcasting,* where stations attempted to reach a wide segment of society. However, today's market relies on *narrowcasting:* with all of the competition, a station cannot expect to attract all viewers; thus, many now cater to more specific audiences. There are channels for all walks of life and interests. Viewers can find prison documentary series on a variety of stations, each presenting a slightly different take on the issue. This trend began on a twenty-four-hour news station.

Lockup is the quintessential prison documentary series. It has been airing on MSNBC in one form or another since the turn of the twenty-first century. MSNBC describes itself as "the premier cable destination for in-depth analysis of daily headlines, insightful political commentary and informed perspectives—24/7. MSNBC defines news for the next generation with world-class reporting and a full schedule of live news coverage, political analysis and award-winning documentary programming—24 hours a day, seven days a week" (MSNBC n.d.). The channel reaches 95 million households in the United States (MSNBC n.d.). MSNBC has become known as a liberally slanted news organization and it is viewed as an influential source of US news. Like many other cable news stations, it responded to the competition by expanding its programming beyond typical news broadcasts. One change was the addition of documentaries to the lineup. In 2000, the channel's original documentary series titled *MSNBC Investigates* debuted, covering a wide range of newsworthy topics. Between 2000 and 2005, prisons and jails were the focus of twenty episodes of *MSNBC Investigates* (2000). In 2005 *Lockup* (Drachkovitch 2005a) became its own series, adding an additional twenty episodes to the collection. Today, *Lockup* is the longest-running prison documentary series on cable television and it has developed into a media franchise (see Box 6.1). This series set the stage for others to come by creating the template used in many other televised prison documentaries. While exposing more people to life behind prison walls, *Lockup* was the first step toward the commodification of prison documentaries; therefore, it warrants an extensive discussion.

In all, twenty-four prisons were featured on *Lockup* (Drachkovitch 2005a), including Utah State Prison, Kentucky State Prison, Anamosa, Pelican Bay, Brushy Mountain, Folsom, and San Quentin. The stories

---

Box 6.1 The *Lockup* Franchise

MSNBC Investigates Lockup (2000): This series featured a variety of documentaries on newsworthy topics, including twenty prison- and jail-related episodes from 2000 to 2005.

Lockup (Drachkovitch 2005a): The original series developed from episodes featured on *MSNBC Investigates*. Beginning in 2005, twenty episodes were produced that featured prisons and a few county jails.

Lockup Extended Stay (2007): In 2007, the producers of *Lockup* expanded their series by focusing on a single institution for an entire season. This ongoing series has grown to include jails.

Lockup Raw (2008): Debuting in 2008, this ongoing series features never-before-aired footage as well as producers and film crew talking about their experiences and why they chose specific stories.

Lockup Special Investigation: Lake County Juvenile (2009): This was a six-episode series featuring the stories of juveniles incarcerated in an Indiana detention center.

Lockup World Tour (2009): This was a three-episode series highlighting prisons in Eastern and Western Europe as well as Israel.

Life After Lockup (2011): This was a two-episode look at some of the most infamous inmates featured in other episodes of the program. It followed some of these inmates on release to uncover the challenges of reentry.

---

presented in each episode are shaped by the unique characteristics of that particular institution. However, all the episodes use a standard format and employ the same frames to send the message that prisons are needed in society.

The purpose and style of *Lockup* is quickly established in the opening credits. Through the advisory given at the opening, viewers know that they are about to witness some potentially violent and shocking material. They are then led to believe that they will learn secrets of prison life when the voice-over says, "There are two million people behind bars in America. We open the gates" (Drachkovitch 2005a). If *Cops* is considered a televised ride-along, one can consider *Lockup* to be a televised prison tour. What follows is a titillating story of the people who work and live behind bars in the United States.

Each episode follows a standard structure. Before documentary footage is shown, the host, John Seigenthaler, sets up the story while introducing the prison. Midway through the episode, he segues into another major story and finally wraps up the episode with concluding remarks. All of Seigenthaler's statements tie the segments together to create a story about that institution. For example, in an episode about the notorious Corcoran Prison in California, Seigenthaler weaves a tale of violence and control ("Return to Corcoran" 2005). The introduction highlights the sordid past of this maximum security prison, which involved gladiator fights between inmates orchestrated by staff. The opening statement suggests that the purpose of this episode is to follow up on how the institution has changed since the guards were caught staging prisoner fights. New inmate programs and prison procedures are featured. Midway through the episode, Seigenthaler reminds viewers of the point of the story by calling the prison a "war zone," which is due to the prevalence of prison gangs and a lucrative drug trade. He wraps up the episode by acknowledging the effectiveness of the new programs, but reminds viewers that "with new defiant inmates coming into Corcoran every day there are plenty of challenges ahead" ("Return to Corcoran" 2005). This final statement reinforces the main message of the tale; even though there may have been some changes, the violence and chaos will always be an issue. Whether focusing on the issue of the death penalty and violence ("Inside Riverbend" 2005); overcrowded institutions, long sentences, and elderly inmates ("Inside Anamosa" 2005); or prison gangs, violence, and Security Housing Units ("Return to Pelican Bay" 2005), the host guides viewers through the story.

The episode structure is not the only commonality found throughout the series. In a comprehensive study of *Lockup,* Dawn K. Cecil and Jennifer L. Leitner (2009) conclude that the series uses specific frames to show viewers a day in prison, thereby not truly presenting the unbiased view that was intended. Filming in large maximum security prisons, producers present life in a type of institution that constitutes only one-fourth of those in the United States. The stories highlight unusual inmates, gangs, and prison violence. Viewers are left with the impression that almost all inmates are monsters and that prisons are a constant battleground, thereby supporting current crime control policies while ignoring many of the pressing issues related to mass imprisonment (Cecil and Leitner 2009). In the end, *Lockup* does fulfill its promise of unlocking the gates, but viewers are not truly given open access. The images are crafted together to tell specific stories that are repeated time and again.

Lockup proved to be a winning formula for MSNBC. Nielsen ratings for this channel make one thing clear—MSNBC may not be the top cable news station but, when *Lockup* is airing, it often has the highest viewership (Knox 2012). Even when major world events have occurred, *Lockup* has been the preferred programming. For example, in February 2011 when the major unrest in Egypt was being covered by other cable new stations, MSNBC drew in the highest number of viewers with reruns of *Lockup* (Joyella 2011). Viewers seemingly cannot get enough of life behind prison walls.

Extending the Lockup Story

When *Lockup* emerged, it was one of a kind; however, there soon were copycat versions. Perhaps in response to that competition, the format of the show changed. Providing a complete picture of life in prison within an hour-long television format is nearly impossible. So, instead of filming for nine days and presenting a single day behind bars, the show was filmed for several months to create *Lockup Extended Stay*. Debuting in 2007, each season of *Lockup Extended Stay* provides a multiple episode–look at one institution. Seven maximum security prisons have been featured in this series, most of which had been visited in the original series. The new format allows for a more comprehensive examination of these institutions than was possible in a single episode. However, it is undeniable that the original formula was a hit, so elements of the original format are infused into the new series.

California's San Quentin Prison was featured in the premiere season of *Lockup Extended Stay*. The producers originally visited this infamous prison in *Lockup*'s "Inside San Quentin" (2003) episode. Comparing the original episode to the extended version illuminates both similarities and differences in how prison life is presented. "Inside San Quentin" depicts the story of an old institution that is ill-equipped to handle its current population. The stressful and violence-filled environment is a battlefield, with officers fighting to control the inmates. The outdated design of the prison, combined with the number of inmates, creates an environment in which the staff is in constant danger of being attacked. Shakedowns, investigations, and administrative segregation are used to combat this problem. This formula is typical of the episodes in the original series, which concentrate on violence and the ways to control this

behavior, especially cell searches and the use of administrative segregation or SHU (Cecil and Leitner 2009). The intense and unbearable environment is highlighted until the last segment, which examines how staff
and inmates deal with prison life. Escape for the staff is home, even
when they live on prison grounds. For some inmates, escape is found
through worship, which offers them a release from the prison game
played on a day-to-day basis. Although in the end, the choice to escape
the mix is framed as an unusual one, because most featured inmates are
ingrained in the inmate subculture. Although San Quentin is an old,
infamous maximum security prison, filled with inmates who have been
convicted of violent crimes and even of inmate violence within prison,
the true stories of many of those incarcerated there are barely touched
on in this single episode. Some of the men have gone through major
transformations while incarcerated. Some devote their time and energy
to the many different and unique programs offered in this prison—
including sports teams, a newspaper, and a scared straight program.
These stories of hope and redemption are excluded from the original
documentary; with more episodes devoted to San Quentin, viewers may
get to hear these stories.

In 2007, *Lockup Extended Stay: San Quentin* aired (Drachkovitch
2007a). Each episode opens with: "America's prisons, dangerous; often
deadly. There are two million people doing time. Every day is a battle to
survive and to maintain order. Among the nation's most notorious institutions is San Quentin State Prison. Our cameras spent months documenting life on the inside, where gangs, drugs, and sheer boredom make
up a violent mix" ("The Gang's All Here" 2007). The introduction suggests that there is not much different about this extended look, yet it is
in fact better able to capture the overall environment of the institution
and the stories of the inmates involved.

A similarity between the two series is the use of violence as the
main frame through which the stories are told. The series reiterates that
San Quentin Prison is an old institution with an extensive history of violence. The first episode of the series opens with officers responding to a
stabbing, with the siren blaring, inmates crouched on the ground, and
officers rushing to the cellblock. Images of blood and the victim on a
stretcher with a bandage around his head are also included; the inmate
has been severely slashed in a suspected gang attack ("The Gang's All
Here" 2007). This incident allows the producers to follow the way that
the prison administration deals with specific cases of violence, from the
investigation by the Institutional Security Unit to the arrest of four
inmates involved in the stabbing. The root cause of this type of violence

is traced to gangs. A featured sergeant states, "All violence in prison is gang related" ("The Gang's All Here" 2007). Later in the series, the narrator comments that "gang violence is endemic at San Quentin" ("Bad Boys, Bad Boys" 2007). This theme is one that is repeated from the original series. One might conclude that the extended series simply retells the same stories of animalistic inmates, violence, gangs, and segregation, but this is only partially true.

A difference between the two series is the depiction of inmates; the original series offers a one-dimensional look while the extended series provides a multidimensional picture of the prisoners behind bars. As noted by Cecil and Leitner (2009), *Lockup* typically frames inmates as others, thereby allowing viewers to distance themselves. In *Lockup Extended Stay* some of the representations of inmates diverge from this characterization. The extended series is better able to humanize the inmates by delving deeper into their stories. While not excusing their behavior in or out of prison, the depth of the stories allows viewers to better understand the lives these men lead—the good, the bad, and the ugly. While several inmates are introduced to viewers, there are three main prisoners whose stories are told extensively throughout the series. One of these is Angel Rodriguez, who is introduced in the first episode. The representation of Angel's story is an example of the complexity uncovered in this series. Angel is serving a ten-year sentence for attempted domestic violence and, as a validated gang member, is serving his time in solitary confinement. The only way to get out of segregation is to debrief or give up the names of other gang members, but he tells the producer that he does not know anything. Angel opens up, allowing viewers to see a softer side of inmates: "What the cameras don't see is when it's quiet, people are sitting here doing their time. . . . We cry too . . . I cry. I don't let my neighbors hear it . . . I miss my girl" ("The Gang's All Here" 2007). He spends time in his cell painting a mural that depicts his story—one of violence, drugs, and love ("Killing Time" 2007). Angel was a violent man with an addiction. For a while he was clean, fell in love, and had a child; then, addiction reared its ugly head. While on drugs he had an altercation with his girlfriend, which they both describe in detail on camera, resulting in his current prison term. His girlfriend decided to stand by him ("The Conjugal Visit" 2007). By telling his story throughout the series, viewers get a glimpse of the issue of addiction and the complexity of the relationships that exist when one is in prison. It does not excuse Angel's behavior; rather, it provides the context needed to have a better understanding of the men in San Quentin.

The officers also add to this more humanistic view of prisoners. According to Officer Maddox, "You expect monsters when you come to prison and they're not. They look like your neighbors and a lot of them are very young. All these guys have parents and nobody thinks 'Oh, someday you're going to prison'" ("Bad Boys, Bad Boys" 2007). And while a specific image of inmates is utilized in the original series, Officer Alejos demonstrates that there are many different types of people in prison: "Every inmate is like a snowflake; they are unique and different" ("Bad Boys, Bad Boys" 2007). Stereotypes of some types of prisoners are dispelled through the featured stories. For example, a typical misconception of lifers is that they are the most dangerous and problematic inmates in an institution. In reality, most lifers go through a major transformation while in prison and become some of the most well-adjusted and productive inmates (Irwin 2010). In *Lockup Extended Stay: San Quentin* viewers learn about the San Quentin Squires, a scared straight–type program run by the lifers. They are also introduced to David Silva, who is serving eleven life sentences and is excited to tell the cameras all of the crimes he has committed ("Slammin' in the Slammer" 2007). Featuring differing types of lifers sheds light on the lives of typical lifers while also reminding viewers that there are inmates who definitely deserve to spend their remaining days behind bars. Given that the most common representation of lifers is a negative one, the chances are that many will remember David's story before remembering the contributions of the other lifers.

Overall, *Lockup Extended Stay* reuses the same frames as the original series while providing deeper understanding into the prison environment and the people incarcerated in these institutions. The season featuring San Quentin still tells many tales of gangs and violence, yet viewers learn more of the culture that creates these problems. While inmates are commonly demonized, viewers are privy to the lives of those serving time, which allows for a deeper understanding of the men behind bars. Nonetheless, the audience is entertained by bad guys behind bars. Similar to the original series, careful attention is paid to administrative segregation units; however, context is provided, thereby capturing the complexities of this type of housing unit with the extended images. Finally, viewers learn more about programs that are available to the inmates and about the inmates who choose to participate in them. This mix of shocking and humanizing images and stories becomes the template for seasons to come.

Similar to other media representations of prisons, *Lockup Extended Stay* has limitations. Perhaps because the producers had already established relationships with specific institutions and demonstrated their filming and storytelling techniques to the prison administration, they revisit many of the same prisons featured in the original series. These are some of the largest maximum security prisons in the country. Maximum security institutions are not as common as medium and minimum security prisons. However, since maximum security prisons are the institutions where the most troublesome inmates are housed, it makes sense for this particular program to film at them. Once all of the duplicate TV shows began to emerge, however, the producers of *Lockup Extended Stay* shifted their focus to county jails, another institution in which anything can happen at any moment when processing in mentally ill, drunk or high, and sometimes combative inmates, thereby allowing them to use a similar formula (see Cecil 2010).

The programs in the *Lockup* franchise have transmitted prison life straight into US homes like never before. These televised prison tours set out to be educational, but many times any true pedagogy is undermined by the entertainment value. The programs flourished in the midst of the ever increasing popularity of infotainment-type programming and stiff competition among cable news channels. Shooting behind prison gates allowed MSNBC to entertain the masses, and the gamble paid off. Jack Curry of the *Washington Post* wrote, "*Lockup* is the crazy rich uncle of MSNBC, the relative whose gifts you accept, but whom you keep stowed away in the attic" (Curry 2011, para. 1). Since their ratings are lower than other news stations when regular programming is airing, they must rely on these programs to draw in viewers (*Breitbart News* 2014; Kirell 2014). No other prison documentary series is as well known and popular as this one. Their stories of maximum security life here and abroad are perhaps some of the most influential images of prison in the new millennium. Of course, a format this popular does not remain unique for long.

The Expansion of Televised Prison Documentaries

Due to an increased interest in terrorism following the September 11 terrorist attacks, there was a lull in prison documentary programming in 2001 and 2002. Eventually, other cable stations began to jump on the bandwagon, following in the footsteps of MSNBC. Court TV, Discovery Channel, National Geographic Channel, and even Animal Planet each contributed their own prison stories to the lineup, although some struggled to find an original take on the subject (see Table 6.1).

Table 6.1 Prison Documentaries on Cable Television

Cable Station	Documentaries	Documentary Series
Discovery Channel	*San Quentin: Inside the Big House* (2001), *Dungeons of Alcatraz* (2003), *Convict Air* (2003), *Prison Boot Camp* (2003), *Prison Medical* (2003), *Engineering Supermax* (2004)	*Supermax* (2001)
Court TV	*Inside:* "Prison Gangs" (2006), "Supermax" (2006), "Prison Code" (2007), "Prison Tactical" (2007), "Alaska's Toughest Prison" (2007), "Gangs Behind Bars" (2007), "Surviving Prison" (2008)	
National Geographic Channel	*Prison Nation* (2007), *Explorer:* "Surviving Maximum Security (2005), "Solitary Confinement" (2010)	*Lockdown* (Mitchell 2007), *Hard Time* (2009)
Animal Planet		*Cell Dogs* (Drachkovitch 2004), *Louisiana Lockdown* (Dugger 2012)

Similar to *Lockup,* many of these programs rely heavily on negative imagery, violence, and gangs to convey the reality of life behind bars. One example is the prison programming on Court TV. Originally known for its gavel-to-gavel coverage of court cases, especially some of the more sensationalistic trials, station executives eventually responded to the ever changing landscape of television programming by delving into the world of crime-related reality programming. In 2005, Court TV began airing a variety of reality-based shows during primetime to draw in younger viewers; its motto became, "Seriously Entertaining" (Associated Press 2005). This tagline establishes the main purpose of the new programs. One such series was *Inside,* which debuted in 2006. This program explored many crime-related topics, including prison life. The nonstop action and suspense used in the prison episodes had one purpose—to entertain. Episodes such as "Prison Gangs," "Supermax," and "Prison Tactical" did just that by examining the most exciting and dangerous parts of prison life. Even though *Lockup* told many of these stories with a flair for sensationalism, its techniques paled in comparison to *Inside.* Prison programming on this station was short-lived. In 2008 Court TV became truTV, replacing this type of crime-related programming with shows such as *Hardcore Pawn.* In the end, other than potentially reaching a different audience base, Court TV's offerings did not add anything new to existing prison imagery.

Many other prison documentaries on cable television followed in the footsteps of those seen on Court TV. Even in an effort to present unique stories about prison life, the focus of many of these documentaries remains on maximum security prisons, violence, gangs, and SHU. Sensationalism commonly trumps pedagogy, and some series were at least successful in presenting a slightly different take on prison life.

Explorations into the Prison World

National Geographic Channel followed in the footsteps of MSNBC by airing a variety of prison programming. At first glance, one might not expect National Geographic to air prison documentaries. After all, it is known for exploring exotic cultures and places unknown to most. Yet to many viewers, prison might as well be a faraway land and it does in fact have a unique culture. While offering a variety of prison programs, National Geographic is most well known for entertaining viewers with tales of people locked up in correctional institutions around the world in *Locked Up Abroad.* There are, however, other series on this channel that have explored prison life in the United States.

National Geographic Channel began its prison programming on *Explorer,* a documentary series opening "a window on hidden parts of the world" (National Geographic 2012). This series covered a variety of topics, including prison life. The station expanded its look at prison life in another series titled *Lockdown* (Mitchell 2007), which debuted in 2006. There really is nothing unique about this particular series. With episodes such as "Gang War" and "Predators Behind Bars," it continued to entertain viewers with the same prison tales. *Lockdown* is a carbon copy of many other documentaries, adding to the already existing chatter. It was not until this channel took a page from *Lockup Extended Stay* that differences began to appear.

National Geographic's *Hard Time* is a natural extension of its other prison documentaries. It explores the world and culture that develop behind prison walls, and delves into the environment, practices, values, and customs of prison life. Debuting in 2009, the first three seasons featured US prisons, before switching to jails. This series is unique in that each season focuses on the prison system within one state, allowing for an in-depth look at the system instead of just one institution.

The second season of *Hard Time* (2011) explores the Ohio Department of Rehabilitation and Correction. Most of the scenes were shot at Ross Correctional Institution, but images from the Correctional Reception Center, the Ohio Reformatory for Women, and the Southern Ohio Correctional Facility are also included. The filmmakers essentially followed the system from intake to release, from the reception center to maximum security prisons and supermax units. These elements are seen in many prison documentaries, but the difference is in the detail allotted by the format of the series.

The second season of *Hard Time* (2011) consists of eight episodes. The first episode, "The Hustle" (2011), sets the stage for the main themes seen throughout. Suggesting that there is more than one way to do time, the episode opens with: "*Hard Time* begins at Ross Correctional Institution, a place of tough choices and easy mistakes. Find your place and you might serve your sentence in peace, but just one wrong move can change everything" ("The Hustle" 2011). Most of the featured stories focus on these wrong moves. The emphasis is on inmates playing the system to lead more comfortable lives behind bars, rather than on those making the decision to better themselves in preparation for release. The choice presented is to either hustle behind bars or to partake in the myriad treatment programs available to inmates in the Ohio Department of Rehabilitation and Correction. In this episode viewers are introduced to Chaz, a new inmate who is serving a twenty-seven-year sentence for armed robbery and attempted murder. He spends his early days at Ross Correctional Institution in close security. He confesses to the camera that he wants to look at his sentence as a way to make changes in his life. The narrator foreshadows what is to come in Chaz's story: "Prisons are full of traps and temptations that can make hard animals even worse" ("The Hustle" 2011). Despite what Chaz says, he is already a part of the hustle and is ready to fight. While still at the reception center, he begins to trade commissary items and is busted. At Ross, he immediately surveys the situation and decides to deal instant coffee. What may appear on the surface to be fairly benign behavior is described as dangerous to the security of the prison since things like unpaid debts contribute to inmate violence.

Avid viewers of prison documentaries are already familiar with hustles and the inmate economy, but the producers of *Hard Time* explore these elements like no other program. Inmates featured throughout the series confess to many different types of hustles on camera. Juice Reynolds robs people after they leave commissary. He is suspected of attacking another inmate for his shoes. While the disciplinary board finds him not guilty, he confesses to the camera that he did it ("The Hustle" 2011). In the maximum security prison in Lucasville, John Sheer and John McAllister run a sports betting operation; one researches the games and sets the odds while the other takes the bets ("The Worst of the Worst" 2011). Other inmates are jailhouse lawyers or tattoo artists. The ways to hustle are endless. The main theme is that many, if not most, inmates continue the game behind bars; therefore, there is no actual rehabilitation in the Ohio Department of Rehabilitation and Correction.

The message in season two of *Hard Time* is clear—most inmates are in the mix, hustling in any way that they can. In reality, many inmates are not playing the prison game. While not the main focus, their stories are not completely neglected. David Applegate is one of these inmates. Despite facing a twenty-year term, he has decided to not waste a moment of time in prison. He works in the furniture factory and, when it closes, chooses to settle for a maintenance job instead of joining the hustle. As his story unfolds in the series, it is almost as if the cameras are just waiting to capture the moment that he strays from this path.

Institutionalization is another aspect of the prison culture examined in *Hard Time*. Many of the inmates featured begin to rely on the prison routine and the prison game—this world is what they know best. When these men face the prospect of release, many do not know how to feel or how they will adapt. This theme is seen in the stories of Dwayne Rosier (aka Squirrel) and Stacy Ayers. At twenty-seven years old, Dwayne is being released after spending more than ten years in prison. He says that he is really just a sixteen-year-old, the age at which he was imprisoned. His institutionalization is clear in his on-camera confessionals as well as his appearance. Dwayne's prison history is depicted over his body in the many prison tattoos he has acquired, including the word "freak" across his neck. This tough-looking inmate has no idea what to do once he is released. In the last shot viewers see of Dwayne outside the prison gates on release day, he appears to be on the verge of tears waiting for his ride ("Prison City" 2011). Stacy contemplates life on the streets as his release hearing approaches. He says that he is not ready and feels that he has not earned his freedom. He finds himself in the hole for fighting and, thus, his release is denied. Stacy is an example of the ends that institutionalized inmates will go to in order to remain where they feel most comfortable ("Back on the Streets" 2011).

The challenges of reentry are also depicted in this series. In the episode titled "Back on the Streets" (2011), the cameras follow Maurice Adderson's release and compare his story to that of David Mahoney, who has been out for eight months. While David confesses to the challenges of being released after serving twenty years, the camera cuts to Maurice as he navigates his first days of freedom. Maurice's father has taken him in, yet within a matter of hours he is hanging out with his old gang buddies. One can only assume that Maurice will soon find himself back in the prison hustle. The way that David sees it, he will never be free, especially not knowing the boundaries of the free world. David weeps slightly as he confesses to the camera that he might be better off back in prison. Similar types of struggles are incorporated throughout this series and others, but this episode in particular truly highlights the difficulties of transitioning back into the free world.

The institutions featured in any documentary shape the stories that unfold before the cameras. *Hard Time* is an example of this variance. The first and third seasons feature the Georgia Department of Corrections. The paramilitary structure used in its system is in sharp contrast to that of Ohio, one of the few states with rehabilitation in its department name. The *Hard Time* series in general focuses on the conflict between prison and inmate rules. The first season begins with the discussion of prison protocol versus the inmate code, and serving hard time versus easy time (*Hard Time* 2009). Viewers meet hustlers and violent inmates, but there is also a discussion of transformations—some good, some bad. As the narrator declares, "Doing time in a world this extreme can change anyone" (*Hard Time* 2009). Some inmates' transformations are physical, such as covering their bodies in prison tattoos or taking on a female identity behind bars. Other transformations are internal. Some inmates become convicts while some killers become converts, according to the narration. The first season also offers insight into aspects of the correctional system that are not seen in the second season: cadet training and boot camp, the hours before an inmate's scheduled execution (which is commuted to life just a few hours before his scheduled death), and a manhunt for two escapees (*Hard Time* 2009). While there are several overlapping themes between the seasons, the first season presents a more stringent prison system.

Next to MSNBC, National Geographic Channel offers the most comprehensive images of prison life. Its representation of prison is a diverse one. From people imprisoned in faraway lands to the nuances of the various institutions in the United States, it is a true exploration into territory that is foreign to many viewers. Yet like MSNBC, it relies on similar frames, themes, and messages in crafting stories of prison life. Viewers are still left with an incomplete view of the prison system, and this affects their social construction of the institutions.

Animals Behind Bars

MSNBC and National Geographic Channel have fairly strong prison lineups, each offering their own spin. Animal Planet is another, albeit surprising, channel to tackle prison life. This channel is known for tales of cute puppies and kittens as well as stories about rescuing animals. The station's motto is "Surprisingly Human" and, over the years, this motto has been exemplified in the new programming developed in response to changing appetites of the viewing audience. An example of this change is the reality-based program *Pit Bulls and Parolees,* which features a center that hires ex-convicts to rehabilitate rescued pit bulls. In the end, the program "humanizes" both societal outcasts and one of the most feared dog breeds in the nation. Given the purpose of the channel and the interests of its viewing audience, the prison documentary series on this station are like no other.

In 2012, Animal Planet aired one of the most recent prison documentary series, *Louisiana Lockdown* (Dugger 2012). This eight-episode series features one prison—Louisiana State Prison at Angola. The uniqueness of this institution allows producers to depict several stories related to Animal Planet's programming. A blog on the channel's website explains how this program ended up in its lineup. Angola's warden Burl Cain is a well-known fixture not only in the field of corrections, but also in the media representations of his prison. Several documentaries have been made about this infamous institution since he took charge. In dealing with a population of men who will most likely die behind bars and who live in a prison housed on 18,000 acres that are surrounded on three sides by the Mississippi River, the warden has instituted policies aimed at promoting good choices. His philosophy is simple—make the right choices and get rewarded, make the wrong ones and do hard time. Many of the privileges afforded to the inmates include opportunities to work with animals, but the most well-known is the chance to participate in the prison's annual rodeo. While the original intention was to tell the stories of the rodeo participants, many other stories emerged (Chu 2012). From horses and bulls to dogs and alligators, the animal-related stories from Angola are abundant.

Taking a slightly different approach, the opening credits of *Louisiana Lockdown* are reminiscent of popular crime dramas, with some of the staff highlighted as stars of the show (Dugger 2012). Warden Cain, Assistant Warden Cathy Fontenot, Major Ronnie Frugé, and Lieutenant Colonel Harvey Slater are featured in each episode. The realities of life in what was once one of the toughest prisons in the United States are highlighted. The type of prisoner sent to Angola becomes clear early in the series. These inmates have been convicted largely of violent offenses and have extensive histories of criminal behavior, yet violence is not a frame employed by the producers of this series. Upon entering the "land of new beginnings," as Warden Cain refers to Angola, the men face the inevitable choice of hard time or a new life—even if it is behind prison walls. For most, the realities of this choice take time to settle in, and several of the inmates who had been in Angola for many years describe the process that they went through.

Tiger, a featured inmate, is a good example of new beginnings. He has been in prison for more than ten years, serving a life sentence for second-degree murder. The inmate that viewers see seems to have some of the same worries as many free men. Tiger has been waiting to hear from his son for over ten years. Early in his sentence he was ingrained in the inmate subculture, but has since worked his way up to be a trustee on the cattle ranch and has competed in the rodeo for several years. According to the narrator, Tiger is on "a path of self-improvement." Tiger's story ends with a reunion with his son at the annual prison rodeo, after he has just won his event ("Drug Bust" 2012). The way that he is emotionally touched by this meeting might be an unexpected surprise to viewers, given the way that many prisoners are portrayed on similar series.

From picking vegetables in the hot sun to breaking horses to sell and even raising and training dogs, the scenes that unfold depict the men hard at work, each navigating prison life the best that they can. Viewers even see a wedding and a funeral, natural parts of many people's lives. They learn what these men will do to feel normal, even for a few seconds. Cracker is about to participate in his nineteenth rodeo, loving the feeling of freedom so much that he swears to ride until he dies. But his freedom rides come to an end when the medical staff prohibit him from participating because he lost a kidney due to an injury in another rodeo and might die if he participates again ("Death Ride" 2012). When evacuated from the prison due to the rising Mississippi River, one inmate is thrilled to see the road and trees outside of the prison walls, despite being shackled on a bus ("Killer Road Trip" 2012). These men are incarcerated for so long that even the slightest hint of freedom brings them joy.

Another theme of *Louisiana Lockdown* is that people who work in prison are in some ways similar to those incarcerated. Almost 200 of the staff have chosen to live on the B-line, which is a residential community on prison property. Not only are the inmates serving life sentences on prison grounds, but so too are many staff. Lieutenant Colonel Slater was born and raised on the B-line. After a series of choices that could have landed him on the inside of a cell, he came to work at Angola. He is now raising his own children there. Major Frugé has been living on the B-line for forty years. Inmates and staff alike have difficult relationships with others. Kathy Fontenot struggles to fulfill her dual roles as assistant warden and a single mother. Lieutenant Colonel Slater's first wife committed suicide and, while the series was being filmed, his second wife left him. He now struggles to raise his children on his own. In other prison documentary series, viewers do not learn much about the lives of the correctional officers and administrators; therefore, they may be surprised to see that people on both sides of the cell doors are remarkably similar to one another. Whereas other series paint inmates as others, this series closes the distance between us and them.

While *Hard Time* highlights the many bad choices made by inmates, *Louisiana Lockdown* focuses on those who have made the choice to live a full life behind bars even though they may never see the free world again. Oliver Howard is serving a fifty-year sentence for armed robbery. He has a job in the prison and makes alligator bags in his spare time to sell at the rodeo. He says, "I chose to be a man not a predator" ("Escape!" 2012). He even gets married while an inmate in Angola. There is no doubt that hustles and other aspects of the prison culture exist at Angola and that many of the inmates are a part of the mix, yet the producers of this series have chosen to highlight stories of redemption in the "land of new beginnings." Angola, however, is a unique institution in its location, structure, programs, and the warden and other staff—there simply is no other institution like it. It is no wonder that Angola has been the topic of many documentaries. The stories that can be told from this institution are vastly different from those from other institutions.

It is undeniable that Animal Planet presents a unique look into prison life in the United States; however, these series have failed to reach the extreme popularity of *Lockup*. Its first series, *Cell Dogs,* is not currently available. *Louisiana Lockdown* is available digitally, but remains a relatively unknown documentary series. When it was on the air, it was near the bottom of television cable ratings (The Futon Critic 2012) and was not renewed.

Whether on MSNBC, National Geographic Channel, or even Animal Planet, prison documentary series have become prevalent in the United States. As I have demonstrated, the channel itself shapes the slant of the program, but there is a general tendency to place an emphasis on violent offenders in maximum security institutions. Surprisingly, the storytelling varies slightly. Some programs further demonize inmates while others attempt to show that they are also humans. The most empathetic depiction is found on Animal Planet, but this humanistic view is the least popular of the main series I have discussed. Looking beyond these serialized prison documentaries, there are additional opportunities for viewers to learn about the complexities of imprisonment in our society through nonserial documentaries on cable television and other venues.

An Independent Look at Prison Life

Modern prison imagery has been dominated by the infotainment-type programming popularized during the twenty-first century. The tradition of early prison documentaries, however, has been carried over in the form of independent documentaries. While not all of these are as readily available as the previously discussed cable documentaries, they are easier to access than those of the past. PBS continues to be a popular avenue for the work of independent documentarians with shows such as *P.O.V., Frontline,* and *Independent Lens* featuring their films. Prison documentaries have been shown on each of these programs, including *The New*

Asylums (2005), *Prison Town, USA* (2007), *Herman's House* (2013), and most recently "Prison State" (2014) and "Solitary Nation" (2014). In addition, this type of documentary is aired occasionally on cable television, and it is readily available on DVDs, streaming videos, and the Internet. This availability allows a wider range of viewers to have access to documentaries that are more critical than entertaining. These films add context to the issues. Yet by informing more than entertaining, the number of viewers who choose to watch is small in comparison to the highly stylized, sensationalistic versions with the highest viewership.

Early in the development of documentaries on prison life, the main types of films produced were historical, deterrence based, and investigative. Although they are made today, other types are more common. Modern independently produced documentaries continue to cover innumerable issues and can be divided into two general categories: treatment-based and issue-based documentaries. However, some documentaries do not fit neatly into these two classifications. For example, some explore cultural aspects of prison life such as *In a Day's Time: Songs of the California Men's Colony* (2007) and *Follow Me Down: Portraits of Louisiana Prison Musicians* (2012). Both of these films capture the role of music in the lives of prisoners. This type of documentary is not prevalent, but it does uncover relatively unknown aspects of the prison system. Treatment-based and issue-based prison documentaries are much more common, each providing insight into parts of the prison system not often seen (see Table 6.2). The underlying messages are in contrast to those found in commodified documentaries.

Treatment-Based Documentaries

The prison system has different goals. Most often people talk about the deterrent effect of prison, which is reflected in early deterrence-based prison documentaries. While this type of documentary continues to be popular, especially as a form of infotainment on the series *Beyond Scared Straight* (Shapiro and Cohen 2011), since the turn of the century viewers have seen a different view of prison life through treatment-based documentaries. One goal of the prison system is to return inmates to a law-abiding way of life. In the past, rehabilitation was one of the main goals of the system; however, it has long since been overshadowed by the get-tough movement. Yet programs aimed at helping inmates with the intent of rehabilitation continue to exist. Though not all rehabilitation programs are directly related to skills needed for successful reentry, all are meant to improve the people who participate. The types

Table 6.2 Independent Prison Documentaries by Type

■ **Treatment-Based**
Shakespeare Behind Bars (2006)
Bad Boys of Summer (2007)
Six Seconds of Freedom (2008)
Concrete, Steel and Paint (2009)
San Quentin Film School (2009)
The Redemption Project: Inmates Got Talent (2010)
At Night I Fly: Images from New Folsom Prison (2011)
University of Sing Sing (2011)
Conducting Hope (2013)

■ **Issue-Based**

   Economic Impact
Corrections (2001)
Profits of Punishment (2001)
Prison Town, USA (2007)
Prison Valley (2010)

   Imprisonment Binge
Ted Koppel's Breaking Point (2007)
"Prison State" (2014)

   Solitary Confinement
Concrete and Sunshine (2002)
Herman's House (2013)
"Solitary Nation" (2014)

   Special Populations
The New Asylums (2005)
Cruel and Unusual: Transgender Women in Prison (2006)
Serving Life (2011)
Prison Terminal: The Last Days of Private Jack Hall (2013)

   Other
Torture: America's Brutal Prisons (2005)
Attica: The Bars that Bind Us (forthcoming)

■ **Miscellaneous**
In a Day's Time: Songs of the California Men's Colony (2007)
Follow Me Down: Portraits of Louisiana Prison Musicians (2012)

of programming available to inmates are dependent on many factors, including security level, departmental philosophy, and resources. Several modern prison documentaries focus on specific prison programs and the transformation of the participants.

Prison programs run the gamut from art therapy to therapeutic communities, some of the most common of which are education programs, counseling, and drug treatment. For the most part, however, the programs featured in these treatment-based documentaries are some of the least common and unusual programs in the country. By featuring unique programs, the documentarians are able to highlight some of the most interesting stories about inmates and prison life. Two examples of this type of documentary are *Bad Boys of Summer* (2007) and *University of Sing Sing* (2011). The first explores San Quentin Prison through the tale of the San Quentin Giants, a baseball team comprised solely of prisoners, while the other highlights a college program in Sing Sing. The stories presented in each of these films highlight an aspect of prison life not typically seen.

Education has long been a part of the prison system. Prisoners are twice as likely as the general public to have not graduated from high school. If given an education behind bars, they are half as likely to recidivate (Davis et al. 2013). Despite the benefits, in-prison educational programs have dwindled significantly during the imprisonment binge, especially college-level courses. In some states, there is renewed interest in providing inmates with an education to decrease the likelihood that they will return to prison after their release. New York is one of these states. Governor Andrew Cuomo has instituted funding for college classes in ten of the state's prisons (Editorial Board 2014). *University of Sing Sing* takes viewers into one such a program. Two things are achieved through the stories of the inmates involved and interviews with the professors who teach the classes. First, the film informs viewers about this type of program, thereby highlighting the benefit of investing in such programming. Second, it shows viewers that even inmates incarcerated in this infamous maximum security prison want a second chance and are willing to work toward their goals. Viewers may be surprised to hear that these students are more dedicated than some of those who the professors teach in the free world.

At the core of most treatment-based documentaries are stories of redemption and inspiration. The men highlighted in *University of Sing Sing* are very different from when they were sentenced to prison. The inmates and their families are candid about the transformations that have taken place behind prison walls. Viewers see what may be considered wasted talent such as Chris "Stretch" Rich in *Bad Boys of Summer.* Stretch was once a promising pitcher, having played in the College World Series of Baseball, but he is serving a twenty-six-year to life sentence for killing his wife. In San Quentin, he is able to follow his passion for baseball. Stretch expresses remorse for his crime: "She deserves to be alive today." The importance of these programs is also central to these documentaries. Earl Smith, the prison chaplain and baseball coach, is featured in *Bad Boys of Summer*. The way that he sees it, the inmates can do time or they can be encouraged to change into someone the public would want released into the community. For many of the inmates who he deals with, the opportunity to play baseball does just that. In many ways, his views echo those of Angola's warden Cain, which are depicted in the documentaries about Angola. According to an inmate participating in the San Quentin baseball program, "Baseball is like nothing else in its ability to make us feel like we are people still. It is a miracle for me." Similar stories are found in the other documentaries of this type; however, not every story is a successful one. There is realism in the images, in that there are inmates who struggle despite being given opportunities for such programming. But considering that viewers see a vast number of hopeless cases and failures in other documentaries, overall these images are refreshing and hopeful.

By showing prison programs and highlighting positive stories of transformation and redemption, these treatment-based documentaries accomplish two things. First, they humanize the people behind bars. Regardless of the crimes committed, the offenders who participate in these programs demonstrate through their stories that they too are human beings. So often we get the picture that the people behind bars are evil and do not want to change; however, these stories often contradict that message. Second, these documentaries convey the message that rehabilitation is a possibility. This view is one that is not often represented by the media, especially in popular crime-related television programming.

Issue-Based Documentaries

Early prison documentaries uncovered critical issues such as abuse, cover-ups, and problematic policies. These films came at a time when prison imagery was limited and, thus, they were considered to be investigative documentaries. Modern prison documentaries continue the quest to expose prison-related issues, but the trend is to document effects of the imprisonment binge and that we have become a prison nation. Many of these films retain an investigative quality but, given the amount of available information today, the impact is not the same. The goal of these films appears to be to educate viewers on issues that are many times overlooked by the media in general. Issue-based documentaries have examined the imprisonment binge and its economic impact, changing policies such as solitary confinement, and how prisons handle inmates with special needs. These issues are not ignored in serialized prison documentaries, but the broader story line renders them incapable of addressing these problems in their entirety.

The imprisonment binge. The imprisonment binge brought with it a host of problems, including some unexpected ones. Incarcerating more and more people meant that new institutions needed to be built. Towns that used to turn away prisons began to embrace the industry as a viable source of employment. Soon people discovered that there was big money in imprisonment, especially with the use of private corrections companies. While some may benefit from this new business venture, it has had many negative effects. Prison documentaries occasionally mention the cost of incarceration, but rarely has this topic been the main focus. Three films that directly tackle the economic impact of the imprisonment binge are *Corrections* (2001), *Prison Town, USA* (2007), and *Prison Valley* (2010). The first focuses on the privatization of corrections while the other two examine the economic impact of prisons on communities. In *Prison Town, USA* (2007), which aired on PBS's *P.O.V.*, the producers investigate the impact of a new prison on the economy of Susanville, California. The prison offered the community a viable source of employment; however, the residents quickly found out that having a prison in their town was not necessarily the solution. The effects on the local community are highlighted throughout the film (*Prison Town, USA* 2007). The prison industrial complex and its effects on society is an important consideration in this age of imprisonment; however, no mainstream documentaries tackle the issue in a critical manner. It is left to the purview of independent documentarians.

The economic impact of mass incarceration is also touched on in documentaries that focus more generally on the imprisonment binge. Surprisingly, this particular issue has received little attention in mainstream imagery, although has not been ignored completely. It is common to provide viewers with statistics on the number of inmates incarcerated and refer to the drastic increases in the prison population since the 1980s, but these facts are only the tip of the iceberg. *Ted Koppel's Breaking Point* (2007) is a documentary that dives headfirst into the issue. It is perhaps the host's years of experience as an investigative journalist that add a more critical eye to these tales of California State Prison Solano. Ted Koppel examines the effects of severe overcrowding in prisons. Typical prison stories are contained within, such as an extensive discussion of gangs, but the complexity of race relations in this particular prison system is connected to the discussion. Koppel also explores the effects of the three strikes law and the importance of education. According to television critic Ed Bark, "*Breaking Point* is exceptional. Real-life looks at prison life generally aren't crowd-pleasers, even if fictional depictions often are. But Mr. Koppel and his longtime executive producer, Tom Bettag, have fought another good fight on behalf of in-depth television journalism about a subject of true import" (Bark 2007, para. 20).

The discussion of the imprisonment binge has continued on PBS. The station aired "two raw, explosive films that explore America's fixation on incarceration" (PBS 2014). The first, *Prison State,* examines the imprisonment binge from a unique perspective. The filmmakers focus on the state of Kentucky and its attempts to reform the use of incarceration in the adult system. The film introduces viewers to a community in which one of every six residents will cycle through the prison system each year. By following the stories of four residents of Beecher Terrace (Louisville), the film demonstrates the complexity of crime and imprisonment. It features the stories of two female juveniles on the road to a lifetime of imprisonment, a Vietnam veteran, and a man who has been in and out of prison so much that it has already cost the state more than a million dollars to incarcerate him. Instead of focusing on prison life, the policies and conditions that contributed to mass incarceration in the United States are laid out for viewers to see.

Together, documentaries such as *Prison Town, USA,* and *Prison Nation* tackle the drastic effects of the imprisonment binge. For years, many have thought that the price was worth it. There has been a general belief that the increasing incarceration rate was a major contributing factor in the drop in crime, despite the fact that criminologists have been arguing to the contrary (see Zimring 2008). The Sentencing Project recently released a report that found the crime rate dropped faster in three states that decreased their prison populations by 25 percent (The Sentencing Project 2014a). This finding was significant enough to be headlined in the news media such as in the *Huffington Post* (O'Conner 2014). Documentaries on the imprisonment binge add important elements to the conversation by digging deeper into the issue and personalizing the story. A person's social construction of prison is incomplete without such knowledge.

Solitary confinement. During the imprisonment binge, the prison system increased its reliance on solitary confinement. Nearly every modern prison documentary on cable television includes images of segregation units in which inmates spend the majority of their time in isolation, yet few of these documentaries offer any critique of the practice. In the era of the imprisonment binge, solitary confinement in administrative segregation units has become commonplace; however, the stories are difficult to tell because the media has had limited access. James Ridgeway (2013) discusses his and other journalists' experiences in trying to cover solitary confinement stories in various states. Ridgeway himself wrote a story on two members of the Angola Three, who have been in solitary confinement for more than forty years. His original article was based on public records but, wanting to explore the issue further, he sought permission to enter Angola Prison to interview these men. Angola Prison appears to be a media-friendly institution, but Ridgeway was denied access at first. When he was finally granted entry, he was given a standard tour and brought nowhere near the confinement area that he wanted to write about. Other journalists have also been unable to gain access to that part of Angola. But as can be seen by the many images of solitary used in programs such as *Lockup* and *Hard Time,* some prison administrators are willing to allow cameras inside. The two most recent films focusing on solitary confinement aired on PBS. *Herman's House* (2013) and "Solitary Nation" (2014) present viewers with stories about the use of solitary confinement in the United States. The techniques used in these two films are vastly different, yet they share a similar critique of solitary confinement.

Just because a filmmaker is unable to gain access to a solitary unit does not mean that the story cannot be told; it just takes a little creativity and a unique story. *Herman's House* is one such film. Herman Wallace is one of the Angola Three, who spent four decades in a six-by-nine-foot cell. Jackie Sumell, an artist from New York, attended a talk on solitary confinement and became interested in Herman's story. She began writing to him and, at one point, asks him to describe his dream house. Through letters, phone calls, and visits, she designs the house for him. Viewers see the process unfold and hear Herman talk about what it is like to be in solitary for so long. Herman is the epitome of an older lifer—having been in the mix early on, he now wants to end the cycle in his community. He asks Jackie to build the house and to create a community center for youth. There is much more to *Herman's House,* including details about Jackie's life and how it changed through the process, and the story of how a man who served seven years in solitary learned valuable lessons from Herman. The only shots of the actual prison that viewers see are the front entrance and an aerial shot at the end. They see a mock cell that Jackie built to understand Herman's environment. And with the exception of old photographs, they never see Herman. Despite not being provided with the visual imagery, the story that unfolds personalizes the practice. While it is a unique story, there are many other inmates who could end up like Herman. Shortly after the film was released, Herman was placed in a prison hospital due to liver cancer. He ultimately won freedom, only to die days later.

While viewers of *Herman's House* do not see footage of an actual isolation unit, those who watch "Solitary Nation" are inundated with thought-provoking images of the unit in Maine State Penitentiary. At times the footage is difficult to watch, with blood-covered cells and feces on walls flashing before the viewers' eyes. These scenes are reminiscent of those used in programs such as *Lockup* and *Hard Time,* but the overall story is much different. "Solitary Nation" explores the overuse of solitary in the United States by focusing on a state that has the goal of decreasing its reliance on isolation. The program shows shocking imagery to demonstrate how solitary confinement negatively affects people and to question its use. As Andrew Cohen (2014) writes, "You need to watch only the first five minutes of 'Solitary Nation'" (par. 1). While acknowledging the purpose of solitary confinement in prison, Cohen thinks that there is a deeper purpose to this film. "The point of the film, I think—and perhaps the best argument against the continued use of solitary—is that regardless of how inmates feel about it, there is no redeemable value to it to the rest of us" (par. 4). By following four inmates who are in solitary confinement over the course of six months, viewers are able to see the connection between isolation, disciplinary problems, and mental illness. For many, prison is out of sight, out of mind. However, most prisoners are released at one point or another; therefore, this practice does affect us all. These documentaries demonstrate the problems with the extended use of solitary confinement.

Special populations. The prison population is a reflection of the free world. Prisons house a diverse group of people with a variety of problems, including mental health issues, terminal illnesses, and aging in general. The institution must find a way to deal with the unique needs of these individuals. Some independent prison documentaries focus on special populations, highlighting their needs, the challenges they present for the system, and how prisons deal with these issues.

Mental illness is a major issue in the prison population, with an estimated 56 percent of the state prison population suffering from one form or another (James and Glaze 2006, 3). *The New Asylums* demonstrates how Ohio's Lucasville Prison cares for this special population of inmates. This prison was also featured in National Geographic Channel's *Hard Time*, but this part of the story was not told. Ohio's Department of Rehabilitation and Correction prides itself in trying to rehabilitate offenders. The advances it has made in the treatment of mentally ill inmates are considered to be the best in the country. Its treatment of these prisoners and the problems that they create for the system are at the heart of this documentary.

Not only do we have more people in prison today than ever before, but these inmates are serving longer sentences than in the past. Mandatory minimum sentencing laws have contributed to the graying of the prison population. Prisons must now provide care for those with dementia and other age-related health issues. Two documentaries tackle this issue by examining the treatment of the terminally ill behind prison walls. In 2011, a documentary titled *Serving Life* aired on the Oprah Winfrey Network. Filmed at Angola Prison, where inmates are more likely to die than be released, it depicts the issues related to housing the elderly in prison. The film follows inmates in the prison infirmary and hospice as well as the inmates who work with the sick and dying. It is a heart-wrenching tale of some of these inmate's last days of life. A similar look is presented in *Prison Terminal: The Last Days of Private Jack Hall* (2013).

Another unique film is *Cruel and Unusual: Transgender Women in Prison* (2006), which is an award-winning documentary that made the circuit at various film festivals. The film examines issues surrounding transgender women in men's prisons, including abuse, isolation, self-mutilation, and struggling without hormone treatments. It also traces the struggles that these women face on the outside, including homelessness and unemployment. What becomes clear in many documentaries of this type is that the prison system is ill-equipped to handle inmates with such significant needs. Other special populations exist, not all of which have programs to help them or have been filmed by documentarians, but these few films bring awareness to the complexity of life behind prison walls. Documentaries on special populations are eye-opening journeys into the complexities of imprisonment.

In general, independent documentaries delve into specific aspects of the prison world that are often ignored or passed over in serial documentaries. These films are no longer inaccessible to the public and each provides an important piece of the puzzle. Both public and cable television stations have opened their doors to the independent documentarian, making it more likely that people are watching this type of prison imagery.

Conclusion

The prison documentary genre may have been slow to develop, but today there are many choices for viewers interested in experiencing a version of life behind bars. Modern prison documentaries have splintered into two groups—cable series reaching masses and independent documentaries with limited viewership. Both types of documentaries have opened the gates and revealed the prison world. What people choose to watch, however, will shape their views on prisons in the United States. There is certainly overlap in many of these documentaries, but there is also a distinction between the types of stories told and the perspective from which they are presented.

Early prison documentaries on cable television tended to be single-episode explorations into a single institution, but this format has limitations. In general, they could provide only an overview of that particular prison and its main issues. In comparison to the multiepisode look at these institutions, little context is provided about the prisons and the inmates. It is no wonder that there was a reliance on the most exciting aspects of prison life and the most shocking inmates. While continuing to rely on these frames to some extent, the prison documentary series evolved by spending more time in these institutions.

To sum up, documentaries are "part record of what exists, part argument why and in what ways it should be changed" (Ellis and McLane 2005, ix). If one follows this definition, *Lockup* and most of the other documentaries airing on cable television in the twenty-first century do not fit this definition in its entirety. Without a doubt, these programs are a record of at least a part of what exists in the prison system. Yet in the modern media marketplace, the end result is shaped by its ability to draw in viewers—to enthrall them enough that they will tune in time and time again. Many of these documentaries also tackle the question of why. For example, in several of the programs that I have discussed, SHU is a popular topic. In their depiction of these units, there is typically an explanation of why they are used in the prison system. They are commonly framed as a necessary evil for a population that continues to be out of control behind bars. Most of the programs that I discussed stop at their consideration of ways that prisons should be changed. If anything, the most popular prison documentaries do not suggest change, but instead support current practices. In the world of infotainment television series, it is not the job of documentarians to spoon-feed viewers the answers; it is their job to create a good reputation with prison administrators and their viewing audience so that they will be welcomed back. Obviously, some viewers will gain insight into the system and be able to deduce that there is a critical need for change, even if they are not completely aware of what these changes ought to be. Other viewers will take away information about the prison system, but will be more entertained than anything. The sensationalistic stories of gangs, violence, the hole, and such are without a doubt entertaining, especially in our culture where crime dramas and other crime-related television shows are a dominant type of programming on the small screen.

Does this mean that documentaries, as defined by Jack C. Ellis and Betsy A. McLane (2005), about prisons are absent from modern television programming? Not at all; they just are not the most common and most widely viewed types of prison imagery consumed by the US public. There are many independent documentaries available that stray from the formula popularized by *Lockup* and other serialized prison documentaries. Documentaries such as *University of Sing Sing, Bad Boys of Summer,* "Prison State," "Solitary Nation," and *Herman's House* offer a much more complex look at the issue of imprisonment in the United States and the people incarcerated. At times, some of the stories contained in these documentaries are reminiscent of prison films. There are inmates in these films whose stories shed light on who these inmates truly are, leaving empathetic viewers rooting for them. Prisons as depicted in serialized documentaries are often supportive of crime control policies that have been in place since the 1980s. Viewers who already agree with these policies are likely reassured by the images presented to them through the television screen.

The truth lies somewhere in between the sensationalized world of monster inmates, gang fights, and SHU and the empathetic view of model inmates participating in extraordinary prison programs. True reflections of most inmates and typical prisons are scarce, perhaps because they have insufficient impact to draw in viewers. Taking students to visit maximum security prisons invokes much excitement on their part and, whatever their beliefs, there is a strong reaction to the experience. However, when students are taken to medium security institutions, the reaction is toned down. Only a few truly take the time to reflect and are touched by the experience. These are the same reactions that viewers are likely to have, their responses being dependent on the type of imagery provided.

7

Women Behind Bars

ONE MIGHT BELIEVE THAT PRISONERS ARE JUST PRISONERS, RE-
gardless of gender, and that prisons are identical no matter who they
hold. There are, however, some major differences between male and
female inmates as well as the history and functioning of institutions in
which they are incarcerated (see Table 7.1). Thus, we should expect
media images of women in prison to be unique. Prison imagery is, in
fact, gendered; however, most are representations based on men's experiences (Britton 2003). In the eyes of many people, "the generic prison
is a men's institution, a site in which brutal inmates and sadistic guards
perpetually battle for dominance" (Britton 2003, 13). Historically, the
most common images of female prisoners have been rooted in tales of
femininity and sexuality, with violence being a secondary frame. Some
modern images of women in prison use a generic representation, relying
on violence and masculinity to tell their stories. To understand modern
media imagery of this incarcerated population, the discussion begins
with the fictional representations found of women in prison films and
televised crime dramas.

Women in Prison Films

Women in prison films follow a pattern similar to movies depicting
imprisoned men, but they are cut from a different fabric. An analysis of
the development of these films offers insight into popular media images
of female prisoners and common misconceptions about this population.
Suzanne Bouclin (2009) classifies women in prison films into two cate-

Table 7.1 History of Women's Prisons and Prison Imagery

■ **1790–1870**

When prisons were first created, separate institutions for women did not exist. Women were incarcerated in men's prisons and were often subjected to isolation and abuse.

Prison Imagery

Popular prison imagery was rare, including that of female prisoners.

■ **1870s–1920s**

Middle-class reformers developed separate institutions for women, the first of which was Indiana's Women's Prison in 1873. Whereas men were sent to prison for felonies, women who committed morality and public order offenses, including promiscuity, were incarcerated. Reflecting popular beliefs of the time, these institutions sought to reform these fallen women through proper female activities—sewing, doing laundry, and wearing dresses were common. Unlike male prisoners, women could be held until they were reformed, which for some was indefinitely (Rafter 1985). Women imprisoned in the South had a very different experience. They remained housed in men's prisons, where punishment was the main goal, and women of minorities were overrepresented in this prison population.

Prison Imagery

At the turn of the century, silent films were popularized and on occasion presented melodramatic stories of imprisoned women.

■ **1930s–1970s**

The Great Depression brought with it the end of the reformatory era; women's prisons transformed and, in many ways, began to resemble men's institutions. More of the female prison population were convicted of felonies, leaving less room for minor offenders (Rafter 1985). The purpose became punishment, yet the same types of gender-based programs promoting domesticity were the norm. By the end of this era, every state had a women's prison.

Prison Imagery

During this time, prison films were the main images available. These films began as romantic melodramas and eventually transformed into so-called babes-behind-bars films. Each type of film sent its own messages about proper female behavior.

■ **1980s–present**

The war on drugs contributed to the imprisonment binge and women became the fastest-growing portion of the prison system (Covington and Bloom 2003). From 1977 through 2011, there was an approximately 900 percent increase in the number of women incarcerated (Drug Policy Alliance 2014). The work of feminist criminologists flourished and culminated in gender-responsive programming in women's prisons, yet women's prisons continue to be more neglected than those of men.

Prison Imagery

Sexualized images of female prisoners continued; however, more diverse imagery developed. Women's prisons were depicted in documentary series and independent films. The first successful US drama series on female prisoners debuted.

gories. The first category appeared in the 1930s: these films were guided by the Hays Code, which restricted the content of Hollywood movies, and were essentially romantic melodramas. The second category appeared in the 1960s within the genre of exploitation filmmaking. These B feature films were aimed at drawing in young heterosexual male audiences. Despite what appears to be two distinct types of films, there are many overlapping elements (Bouclin 2009). Both types of women in prison films send viewers specific messages about proper behavior and punishment while also feeding male fantasies.

Even before the prison film genre was truly born, silent films began introducing theater audiences to women behind bars. An example is Cecil B. DeMille's *Manslaughter* (1922), which depicts the story of Lydia Thorne, a party girl who kills a police officer while driving recklessly. District Attorney Daniel Bannon prosecutes her even though he is in love with her. Most of the film takes place outside prison walls, but eventually Lydia is sentenced to prison. The film uses scenes that became typical of those in many prison movies. Lydia is fingerprinted and given a checkup by the prison doctor. She is brought to her cell where an inmate gives her a uniform and quickly puts her in her place. She is told, "You are whining because you're going to give up a few French dresses and limousines! But suppose you had to leave an old mother and a sick child, as I did!" Once Lydia is left in her cell alone, reality sets in and she begins to unravel. She eventually ends up in the prison hospital sick with a fever, where she dreams of killing Bannon and has an awakening—she wants to live life again. She leaves prison miraculously reformed, wanting to help those who helped her. Her main beneficiary is Bannon, who has become an alcoholic and ruined his career but ends up running for the office of governor thanks to the help of the newly reformed Lydia. While the prison itself is not responsible for Lydia's transformation, it is her time there that allows her to help the man she comes to love. Essentially, this film is a tale of a nonconforming woman who is punished, thereby allowing her to be reformed and fall into the proper role of supporting her man. It is not truly a lesson about prison; instead, it provides viewers with the fantasy of love and redemption behind prison walls. This formula is repeated often in future women in prison films.

Romantic Melodramas

As the prison film genre developed in the 1930s through the 1950s, more filmmakers delved into the world of women behind bars. Early women in prison films include *Ladies of the Big House* (1932), *Hold Your Man* (1933), *Ladies They Talk About* (1933), *Condemned Women* (1938), *Women in Prison* (1939), *Convicted Woman* (1940), *Lady Gangster* (1942), *Girls in Chains* (1943), *Lady in the Death House* (1944), *Girls of the Big House* (1945), *Caged* (1950), *Women in Prison* (1955), *Girls in Prison* (1956), and *I Want to Live!* (1958). These films and others borrow heavily from movies about men in prison while interweaving tales of being proper women and finding the love of a man.

Many of the earliest women in prison films also draw from other genres in their storytelling. *Ladies They Talk About* and *Women in Prison* borrow elements from gangster films, as both begin with a female accomplice to a bank robbery committed by her gangster boyfriend. Execution films draw from legal dramas, in trying to find the true culprit before time runs out. While some of the scenes in *Lady in the Death House* and *I Want to Live!* occur within the prison, much of the story in both films takes place outside of the prison.

Characters, plot twists, and themes popularized in prison films beginning in the 1930s are also found in women in prison films. First there is the hero, or in this case the heroine, who either is innocent of the crime that has resulted in her imprisonment or at the very least the offense does not warrant such harsh punishment. In these early films, it is sometimes the man in her life who is the true culprit. It is his influence and her love for him that lands her behind bars. For example, in *Ladies They Talk About* (1933), Nan Taylor is an accomplice in her gangster boyfriend's plan to rob a bank. At first, she is the only one caught and is eventually sent to the female wing at San Quentin Prison. While Nan is a somewhat willing accomplice, the audience recognizes the influence of her boyfriend and does not hold her completely culpable, thereby allowing them to side with her. An even more sympathetic character is Marie in *Caged* (1950), who is a nineteen-year-old incarcerated for armed robbery. In times of economic strife, her husband cannot find a job and in desperation commits armed robbery while she is in the car. He is shot and Marie runs to the side of her dying husband, only to be arrested and sent to prison. One feels sympathy for this young widow as she enters prison, discovers she is pregnant, and goes through a transformation that most do not foresee. Nan and Marie are just two of many sympathetic protagonists at the heart of these films. This character is often contrasted with other inmates who appear to be more deserving of punishment.

Traditional prison films also contain paternalistic wardens, cruel guards, and prison doctors. In women in prison films, there are maternal superintendents, horrific matrons, doctors, and teachers. These characters enable the reform-punishment debate to be highlighted. In *Caged* (1950), Superintendent Ruth Benton is a reformist who wants what is best for her wards. She believes that the women need education and to prepare for release; however, she loses every battle. In response to her requests for reform, the lieutenant governor mocks her by asking if she wants swimming pools and other luxuries. This exchange is an example of a debate that commonly appears in dramatic portrayals of both men's and women's prisons. In some cases it is an outsider of sorts, a doctor, psychiatrist, or teacher who questions the purpose of the institution and, thus, the treatment of the women. For example, in *Girls in Chains* (1943), the teacher, Miss Helen Martin, exclaims, "You can't keep them in there. This isn't a penitentiary; it's a house of correction. They'll be worse!" While many of the superintendents fit the persona of a reformist, Amelia Van Zandt in *Women in Prison* (1955) is anything but maternal. She is a rendition of the wardens to come in future prison films. Each and every abuse and punishment given out is ordered by her. She even beats an inmate named Joan to death in an effort to elicit information from her. In the end, she does not get away with it. When a riot erupts in the prison, Joan's husband hunts her down. She is eventually found hiding in a padded cell where she is put into a straightjacket. Her cruelty results in insanity and a cell of her own.

Whether good or bad, the superintendents in these films are aided by matrons who oversee the daily grind of the institution. Like the cruel guards in films about men's prisons, these matrons are typically heartless, mean, and abusive. These characters include Mrs. Lowry in *Ladies of the Big House* (1932), Mrs. Clara Glover in *Condemned Women* (1938), Mrs. Brackett in *Convicted Woman* (1940), and Mrs. Peters in *Girls in Chains* (1943). In *Caged* (1950), this character is Matron Evelyn Harper, who is in sharp contrast to Superintendent Ruth Benton. She hands out privileges for a price; those who can provide her with candy, clothing, and, of course, money can live a somewhat peaceful existence behind bars. While Superintendent Benton assigns Marie light duty in the laundry due to her delicate condition, Harper immediately makes her clean the bull pen floors, a strenuous task for a pregnant woman. She yells at and slaps Marie frequently. She even ignores the girls' pleas to help June, who finally kills herself. The breaking point for Marie is when Harper shaves her head and throws her into solitary. After this incident, she is never the same. The abuse and neglect at the hands of the prison staff provide the backdrop for the inmate's fight against injustice that is found in many of these films. In most cases, these evil matrons get their due by being fired, attacked by inmates, or locked in a padded cell. In *Caged* (1950), Harper is stabbed with a fork and dies. After all the torture she put the inmates through, justice is achieved through her death.

Traditional prison films rely on escapes and riots to demonstrate that justice has been restored or authority reasserted. Many women in prison films also use these standard elements. For example, prison escapes are seen in *Ladies of the Big House* (1932), *Ladies They Talk About* (1933), *Condemned Women* (1938), *Women in Prison* (1955), *Convicted Woman* (1940), *Girls of the Big House* (1945), and *Girls in Prison* (1956). A riot in *Women in Prison* (1955) is the pivotal end to Van Zandt's reign of terror while in *Girls in Chains* (1943) it erupts when a guard beats an inmate after the girls refuse to eat. In *Caged* (1950), a riot breaks out when a cat that Marie found is discovered by the matrons. Regardless of how the escapes and riots occur, there is nothing unique about the way these plot devices are used in prison films about women. There is, however, another major plot device used in these films that is not common in films about men—help from the outside. In several films, a man on the outside works feverishly to clear to the protagonist's name. This particular story line ties into a larger theme in these films, which centers on women's relationships with men.

The relationships that these women have, or dream of having, are seen in different ways in these films; some are pivotal to the plots while others are just flashing glimpses of their desires. In *Ladies They Talk About* (1933), *Women in Prison* (1955), and *Girls in Chains* (1943), the women commit crimes for, or are framed by, the men they love. Other characters in some of these films dream about the men waiting for them. Linda in *Ladies They Talk About* (1933) sums it up when she says, "I don't like being teased . . . out here within a few feet are the two things you want the most, but you're always a few feet away—freedom and men." In *Women in Prison* (1955), Helene has a husband waiting for her; the film ends as she runs out the prison gates and into his arms. Her cellmate Gracie is shown talking in her sleep, dreaming of her man; Carol is about to be released and has been up since 3:00 A.M. getting ready to see her boyfriend; and Joan's husband sneaks over from the male side of the prison to visit her. Finally, in several of these films it is a man who is able to clear the woman's name, culminating in her release and their impending marriage. Versions of this plot are seen in *Hold Your Man* (1933), *Condemned Women* (1938), *Prison Farm* (1938), *Women in Prison* (1955), *Convicted Woman* (1940), *Lady Gangster* (1942), *Lady in the Death House* (1944), and *Girls of the Big*

House (1945). Nan, in *Ladies They Talk About,* is far from innocent, yet she is able to get a reputable man to stand by her side and protect her from further imprisonment. David Slade, a radio evangelist, attempts to help Nan before she goes to prison. Once she admits that she was involved in the crime, he allows her to be incarcerated; however, he cannot forget her. He stays in touch with her, and she continues to use him in her plot to escape. When her accomplices are killed, she seeks revenge against David and shoots him. But when the police show up, he tells them everything is fine and they are getting married. In each of these examples, the man is essentially responsible for justice being achieved—he is the epitome of a knight in shining armor.

In many ways, these early women in prison films are similar to their male counterparts with their plots, characters, and messages about justice and authority. However, there are more prominent messages in these films that reflect common beliefs about female offenders and femininity. The first prison scene in *Ladies They Talk About* (1933) contrasts the male and female sides of San Quentin. The men's side is orderly and regimented while the women's side is brimming with excitement as if in a sorority house. These films reveal a common belief that female offenders are emotional, hysterical, and even crazy. The characters in each of these films is seen to be unraveling, presumably because of their weaker state. These women in prison films also provide commentary on proper female behavior. Many of the women are nonconforming women who are punished for their actions. The characters that stray the furthest from the conventions of proper womanly behavior remain in prison or meet some other end. The typical protagonist, however, may have broken some rules of femininity, but is reigned in and saved by her relationship with a man. Thus, when she is released, she is no longer a threat to the social order.

Two films diverge from this formula, *Caged* (1950) and *I Want to Live!* (1958). Viewers watch as Marie endures unbelievable hardships in *Caged* (1950). She comes to prison a widow, finds out she is pregnant, is abused by prison staff, and must give up her baby for adoption. She resists the invitation to become a booster, which would earn her early release from a corrupt system and enable her to support herself on the outside. Throughout the film, viewers believe that she will be redeemed; however, the tables turn when her head is shaved and she is placed in solitary. She begins to fight prison staff and eventually decides to become a prostitute on release. As she leaves the prison, she says to Superintendent Benton, "For the $40 that Tom and I heisted, I sure got an education." She walks out the gates and steps into the back of a car filled with men. Marie is far from being saved. Rather, it is the system that made her into a nonconforming female. In *I Want to Live!* (1958) Barbara Graham, a jazz-loving petty criminal is innocent of the murder for which she is sentenced to die. She is a defiant inmate, constantly challenging the prison's procedures and the execution process. Much of the latter portion of the film is spent watching Barbara endure several stays of execution. A lawyer and a journalist attempt to save her life, but they are unsuccessful. In the end, viewers watch Barbara take her last breath in the gas chamber as a room full of men looks on. While she is not as innocent as Marie, viewers know that justice has not been served. She essentially has been punished for her wild ways. (This film is based on a true story; therefore, the ending could not have been any different.)

Exploitation-Style Films

As films began to change, so too did those about women in prison. From the late 1950s through the 1960s, these films struggled to find their footing. In the 1970s, the genre emerged in a very different format—exploitation style, which is commonly referred to as babes-behind-bars films. Exploitation-style films had been around for several decades, but they did not feature women in prison until the late 1960s. While some prison films purport to expose the realities of life behind bars, these new films were pure fantasies meant to titillate male audiences. According to Anna Clark (2005, 37–38), "These tales of vulnerable things navigating a harsh prison are largely vehicles for money-shot-style images that are the films' raison d'être: a roomful of women being hosed down by their sadistic warden as punishment (1971's *The Big Doll House*), say, or a young reform school inmate gang-raped with a plunger by her roommates (1974's *Born Innocent*)." Unfortunately, this type of women in prison film has become the most well-known format.

The first true babes-behind-bars film was Jess Franco's *99 Women* (1969). Franco, a Spanish filmmaker, was known for producing exploitation films. Originally released in Spain, *99 Women* became a box office hit in the United States and many other countries. This film depicts the story of Marie, prisoner number 99, who is incarcerated for murder. She was gang-raped and one of her attackers was killed but it was believed that she was selling her body, and when the man refused to pay she murdered him. Marie is sent to an isolated island prison. She and the other inmates on the transport boat are immediately greeted by Thelma Diaz, the head matron. What follows is a tale of extreme cruelty, exploitation, sex, gang rape, and murder. Marie is used as a sexual pawn by fellow prisoner Zoie, Matron Diaz, and even Matron Leonie Carroll, who is the one glimmer of hope. Matron Carroll has been sent to the prison by the Ministry of Justice after the death of three inmates. However, when an escape and a riot ensue following her abandonment of strict discipline, she hands the prison back to Matron Diaz and the island's governor. Before leaving she tells them, "I seem to be a victim of a disease that does not flourish behind prison walls. I suffer from excess humanity" (*99 Women* 1969). Similar to Superintendent Burton in *Caged,* she has lost her battle against an abusive system.

Franco's film is considered an important one. According to Danny Shipka (2011, 191), the impact of *99 Women* "cannot be overestimated, as it was the first successful 'women in prison' movie, a cinematic staple in the exploitation genre." Franco modernized the stories from the melodramatic films by adding nudity, lesbian relationships, and sadomasochism (Shipka 2011), all of which became staples of the babes-behind-bars films to follow. This movie was released worldwide but, due to censorship issues, it appeared in many different forms. Additional sex scenes were included in some countries and, according to Franco, there is even a version containing pornographic scenes that he did not film or approve (Franco 2005). Reflecting on this film and his others, Franco says, "In a prison film, naturally one is disturbed by defenseless women at the mercy of a group of bastards. It's something that afterwards you may think 'oh shit, they went too far.' But while you are watching it you're watching something beautiful" (Franco 2005). Some find this type of filmmaking intriguing while others find it disturbing. Although the film is filled with scenes of abuse, gang rape, death, and sex, it is considered tame in comparison to films that were to follow. This formula worked well for Franco and he made several other babes-behind-bars films, but none were as successful as *99 Women.*

Filmmakers worldwide were influenced by Franco's film, but the work of Roger Corman was probably the most influential in the development of US women in prison films in the 1970s. Corman has made approximately 400 films over the course of his career. He has been referred to as the "B-Movie King" and is known for filming these low-budget movies in just a matter of days (Nashawaty 2009). He had already produced and directed many exploitation-style films before delving into the world of incarcerated women. In all, he has produced or directed ten women in prison films, including *The Big Doll House* (1971), *Women in Cages* (1971), *The Big Bird Cage* (1972), and *Caged Heat* (1974). The stories are all similar: they draw some elements from early melodramas, combine it with Franco's method of storytelling, and add a Hollywood exploitation-style spin. Other films of this genre include *10 Violent Women* (1982), *The Concrete Jungle* (1982), *Chained Heat* (1983), *Caged Fury* (1989), *Prison Heat* (1993), *Bikini Chain Gang* (2005), and *Sugar Boxx* (2009). Slight variations on the genre have also been made, including musicals, science fiction, and horror films. Babes-behind-bars films have unfortunately become the most well-known type of women in prison movies, depicting perhaps the most damaging imagery of these women.

Just like their melodramatic counterparts, babes-behind-bars films follow a pretty standard formula. These films feature a protagonist, who is an innocent inmate, brought into the prison at the beginning of the film (e.g., Marnie Collier in *The Big Doll House* and Carol Jefferies in *Women in Cages*). In prison, Marnie is searched "inside and out" (*The Big Doll House* 1971) and checked by the doctor. Even before entering her cell, she sees what is to come, with scenes of bodies being carried out. In her cell she meets her cellmates, a variety of beautiful women of varying hair color and ethnicity (thereby appealing to all young men's tastes). Her place in the cell hierarchy is quickly established and what follows is a tale of sex, torture, death, riots, and escape.

The young heroine is joined by other standard characters, some of which were identified by Marsha Clowers (2001) after examining a small sample of these films. One of these characters is the violent and sex-crazed prisoner, who typically works with the prison administration to further her goals. Another is "the innocent victimized limpet" (Clowers 2001, 23), who is taken advantage of by other inmates, which often incites the heroine and her accomplices to take action against the prison. The earlier women in prison melodramas used similar characters, but the violence was downplayed in comparison to these exploitation films. The biggest difference between these types of women in prison films is the sexual nature of the characters. Femininity was highlighted in the earlier films, but now it is sexuality. The women are scantily clad, with nudity a common feature, and they are crazed because their sexual desires are pent up. In *The Big Bird Cage* (1972) an inmate gets upset, proclaiming, "She has no right not to tell us. She is the only one around here that gets any and she won't even talk about it!" Movie posters include taglines such as "Women's prison U.S.A.—Rape, Riot, Revenge! White hot desires melting cold prison steel" (*Caged Heat* 1974); and "Their bodies were caged, not their desires. They would do anything for a man—or to him" (*The Big Doll House* 1971). The message is that these women cannot live without men.

Whether sending messages about proper female behavior or feeding male fantasies about women in prison, both types of films are potentially damaging. However, given the life experiences of incarcerated women, which typically includes sexual victimization, the latter is more detrimental. Clowers (2001, 28) comments that "these films reinforce society's stereotypes about female prisoners: that they are violent, worthless, sex crazed monsters totally unworthy of humane treatment." Whether emphasizing femininity or sexuality, women in prison films serve as a commentary about the nonconforming woman and the need to punish women who break these rules.

Modern Women in Prison Films

After the onslaught of these exploitation-style films, women in prison films became less common, but the impact of the babes-behind-bars films continues to be seen in many images of women in prison. In the 1990s, there were several made-for-TV women in prison movies such as *Prison Stories: Women on the Inside* (1991), *Better Off Dead* (1993), *Against Their Will: Women in Prison* (1994), *Getting Out* (1994), *Girls in Prison* (1994), *Prison of Secrets* (1997), and *Time Served* (1999). *Prison Stories: Women on the Inside* features three vignettes tackling the issue of women in prison and their families. It is one of the few made-for-TV movies to stray from the sex-in-prison formula. The others borrow from the popular babes-behind-bars films, toning them down, however, to be aired on television. The tagline for *Girls in Prison* is "Two sexy rebels . . . in the wildest lockup yet," while in *Time Served* the inmates participate in a work release program that requires them to become tabletop dancers. For the most part, these made-for-TV movies continue to feed male fantasies of female prisoners and sex.

The women in prison film genre does not have a modern identity. Some films spoof or copy the exploitation films while others use stories depicted in men's prison films but use female leads. For example, *Brokedown Palace* (1999) is the story of two young women who are convicted of drug crimes in Thailand and must endure the tortuous treatment they receive while in prison. This film could be considered a tamed-down female version of *Midnight Express* (1978). In addition, while *Brokedown Palace* is cited as a prison film, it is similar to early women in prison films in that much of the story takes place outside of the institution. Similar to legal dramas, the fight for justice takes place mostly in the courtroom.

Occasionally, a film is released that attempts to tackle critical issues facing women in prison, but they often fall short by presenting additional stereotypes and making these institutions seem identical to men's prisons. One such film, *Stranger Inside* (2001), aired on HBO. This drama follows Treasure, a young girl who is transferred from juvenile detention to prison. Treasure deliberately stabs a girl to be transferred to an adult institution where she believes her mother is incarcerated. The creator of this film lent authenticity by delving into research on women in prison and using former prisoners as actors. The end result does contain some realism; however, once again, sensationalistic scenes win in the final cut.

Stranger Inside features a cast of mostly minority women, thereby reflecting the overrepresentation of minorities in the prison system. These women are all violent and more masculine than typically seen in women in prison films. They play basketball, lift weights, and fight just like one would expect men to do—gone is the hair pulling and ripping off of clothing. The masculinization of minority women, especially offenders, is common in the media (Chesney-Lind and Irwin 2008), and this film replicates that representation. The typical story of an innocent heroine fighting for justice against the system is absent. Instead, the film focuses on the relationship between Treasure and her mother, Brownie, as well as the inner world of a women's prison. The film features many elements of these institutions, including the inmate economy, pseudofamilies and other relationships, drugs, motherhood, and treatment programs. It depicts inmates like Treasure and Brownie, who are in the mix, and inmates like Shadow, who decided not to play the prison game. Ultimately, while attempting to raise awareness on issues, such as overrepresentation of minorities and the effects of having an incarcerated parent, *Stranger Inside* is reduced to a tale of violence, relationships, and sex. Thus, while this film offers a more realistic representation of women in prison than babes-behind-bars films have ever done, it has some serious flaws.

A similar representation is found in *Civil Brand* (Cirigliano 2002), which is an award-winning film that tackles the issue of prison through the eyes of African American prisoners in the fictional Whitehead Correctional Institution (aka "the plantation"). The story is a noble attempt to bring two major issues—prison labor and abuse—to the attention of viewers. In the opening scene, Sabrina is interviewed by a journalist while reading a newspaper with a front-page story about abused female prisoners winning a lawsuit. What unfolds is a tale of abuse, violence, and revolution. The women want to be treated fairly while working in the prison factory, but are instead physically beaten by a guard after they make demands. A pregnant inmate is raped by a correctional officer and, as a result, she and her unborn child die. This death further incites these women and an inmate kills the abusive guard. In the end, all of the main female inmate characters are killed, but in a way justice is achieved when the prison is shut down. *Civil Brand* is successful in bringing up issues critical to our prison system. However, like *Stranger Inside,* it draws heavily from the images of men in prison, presenting this population as equally brutal as its male counterparts.

Both *Stranger Inside* and *Civil Brand* follow the trend of filmmakers in changing the face of the imprisoned. Each sets out to tackle the issue of the number of African American women behind bars. While doing so, however, the films repeat popular masculine and violent images of these women. In their own way, these two films repeat the lessons on proper female behavior. The popular construct of women is based on white middle-class standards of what it means to be female. In every sense, the actions of the African American female characters in these films go against this expectation, thereby justifying the severe treatment of this correctional population. Given that African American women are significantly overrepresented in the prison population, this imagery potentially is doing more damage than good.

Women in prison films struggle to truly represent life behind bars for female prisoners in the United States. Fantasy trumps reality. Most of the modern films rely on sex to titillate viewers and violence to further entertain them. The influence of this imagery can be seen in other media images of this population, but the genre most likely to repeat these messages is televised prison dramas.

Women in Prison on the Small Screen

Given that US crime dramas have rarely embraced the prison world, it is not surprising that women in prison dramas have been almost nonexistent. Prison shows such as *Oz* and *Prison Break* focus on men's institutions, although from time to time a female inmate character is included in the story line. In *Oz* viewers meet Shirley Bellinger, a death row inmate temporarily housed in the prison. But this character serves as a plot device rather than a reflection of the true nature of women in prison. Other countries have successfully created fictional television programs about women in prison, some of which have developed worldwide cult followings. Shows like *Prisoner: Cell Block H* and *Bad Girls* entertained audiences with soap operas set behind bars, but attempts to remake these programs for US television have not been successful.

Early Representations of Women in Prison on US Television

While no US-made women in prison drama has been successful on television, viewers have been entertained by televised images of the female prison population. This imagery is seen on dramas, sitcoms, and soap operas. Many of the representations are fairly predictable, drawing from Hollywood predecessors. For example, a 1970s episode of *Charlie's Angels* called "Angels in Chains" (1976) featured the private detectives going undercover in a women's prison to find out what happened to one of the inmates. The inmates are brutalized by the guards and forced into prostitution. In the primetime dramedy *Ugly Betty* (Hayek and Silvio 2006), one of the recurring characters, Claire Meade, goes to and eventually escapes from prison. Reminiscent of more recent representations of women's prisons, a highly masculinized environment is presented with tough women lifting weights in the yard. Endless examples of these different types of scenes have been incorporated into television shows.

With the increasing popularity of crime dramas in the 1990s, one would expect to see even more images of incarcerated women on television. Similar to the depiction of male prisons, crime dramas most often use brief scenes of female prisoners as a plot device. In many cases, there is just a fleeting glimpse into prison life. A 2009 episode of *NCIS* titled "Caged" (Moreno 2009) begins like many crime dramas, with one of the investigators going to a women's prison to interview a suspect. However, the women take control of part of that prison after a guard is killed. It becomes the team's task to investigate the crime. The prison is simply a unique setting for a typical story line. On occasion there have been more extensive scenes, most often found on some of the alternative crime dramas on cable television, including *Weeds* (Kohan 2005) and *Burn Notice* (Nix 2012). In telling the prison-related story line, the creators often borrow elements from their film predecessors. A main character is typically the heroine that viewers do not believe should be in prison or one they can relate to. The most threatening inmates are masculine: there are cruel guards and, of course, there are lesbian relationships (see Box 7.1).

Even if viewers have not realized it, they have been seeing similar representations of women in prison repeated time and again on television. Most of this imagery has sexual undertones or is an outright sexu-

---

Box 7.1 The Women's Prison on *Burn Notice*

The prison sequence in *Burn Notice* (Nix 2012) provides a good example of the modern representation of women's prisons on television. For five seasons viewers watched Fiona, the love interest of the protagonist, Michael, on the show. She fights alongside him in his quest to clear his name and to find justice for people who have been wronged. Despite the fact that she is an expert in explosives and high-powered weapons, the audience roots for her; after all, the end justifies the means. Justice is achieved at the end of each episode; however, at the end of the fifth season, Fiona is framed for murder. This story line sets the stage for a fairly typical prison tale that is told in season six.

The audience knows that Fiona is at least innocent of the crime for which she goes to prison. While there are hints of sexual imagery, the main images mimic those of the generic men's prison. From the moment Fiona enters the prison, it is a battleground. Predatory inmates are everywhere. Fiona is attacked several times, once by two switchblade-wielding inmates. Ayn, the merchant inmate who can get anyone anything for a price, becomes Fiona's confidant and helper by exploiting Fiona. When Fiona wonders how these women were able to get switchblades into the prison, Ayn replies, "They're lifers. They do contract hits to pass the time, the same way some girls knit" ("Last Rites" 2012). Finally, there is a fake escape attempt that ultimately leads to Fiona's freedom. Highlighting the brutal nature of this prison environment and the corrupt guards who do not search the lifers' cells, this story line presents the quintessential characteristics of recent stories about women in prison.

---

alization of the female prison population. These frames began in women in prison films and were easily carried over to the small screen for their entertainment value. Yet this imagery alone is not enough to sustain a show about women in prison on US television.

Every Inmate Has a Story: Orange Is the New Black

The world of women's prisons burst open when a new series debuted in 2013 after Netflix, which offered digital streaming of films and television shows, began to air original series. One of these series is a women's prison dramedy titled *Orange Is the New Black* (Kohan 2013). The program is based on a *New York Times* best-selling book by Piper Kerman (2010) and was co-created by Jenji Kohan (the creator of *Weeds*). Piper served a year in federal prison for a ten-year-old drug charge and documented the experience in her memoir. Through scenes of prison and flashbacks, the series introduces viewers to Piper's entrance into the inmate subculture and the stories of the women imprisoned in the fictional Litchfield Prison. While there is overlap between the book and the series, more dramatic license is employed in the latter, which at times means drawing from women in prison stereotypes. *Orange Is the New Black* has been met with unprecedented popularity and media attention. It serves as an example of the impact that popular culture can make on people's understanding of the female prison population.

Orange Is the New Black presents a fresh take on women in prison; however, it does not completely diverge from its infamous predecessors. The similarity to prison films is immediately seen. The series starts with a standard element from babes-behind-bars flicks—a shower scene. The sequence begins with Piper in the shower with her lesbian lover, flashes to her and her fiancé in a bathtub, and ends with Piper in the prison shower. An inmate rips away Piper's towel and touches her breasts because she likes their perkiness. While there is nothing overtly sexual about this scene, it may leave one wondering whether this program is just a reincarnation of exploitation films. Yet the show's tagline suggests a very different take on women in prison: "Every sentence is a story" indicates the complexity of what unfolds throughout this series.

Orange Is the New Black presents its audience with daily life behind bars. To do so, it must rely on scenes standardized in many prison films. Many prison representations follow a new inmate being processed into the institution and indoctrinated into the inmate subculture. This new inmate often makes mistakes, learning the rules the hard way. In *Orange Is the New Black* viewers watch as Piper goes through this process, making mistake after mistake until she finds her place in the inmate social system. It is not anything that viewers have not seen before, but the serial format of the story allows for a more in-depth look at the process and issues commonly found in women's prisons.

Prison issues. *Orange Is the New Black* tackles many different issues, including substance abuse, motherhood, health problems, insufficient programming, and the effects of isolation. Drugs and other contraband are smuggled into the prison by a corrupt guard and inmates. The issue of substance abuse is highlighted when an inmate dies from an overdose and later when viewers watch one of the recurring characters, Nichols, struggle with temptation. The challenges of motherhood behind bars are touched on throughout the series. Medical care is incorporated into the series in several ways. There are a terminally ill inmate, pregnant inmates, and even a transgender inmate who struggles when there is an arbitrary change to her medication. Mental illness is seen in varying degrees, from the odd behavior of Suzanne "Crazy Eyes" to Pennsatucky being sent to the psych unit for evaluation. Freedom of religion and other inmate rights are integrated into the story lines, as is the issue of insufficient programming. The use and effects of solitary confinement are also incorporated when Piper and others are sent to solitary. Viewers see how this form of punishment is arbitrarily used and the effects that it has on the individuals who spend time in isolation. The series uses the stories of the women in Litchfield to personalize these real issues found in women's prisons.

The complexity with which *Orange Is the New Black* tackles prison issues is seen throughout the series. A story line in the first season, featuring Taystee, is a poignant example of the storytelling involved and its reflection of real issues faced by female prisoners. Taystee is a young inmate who is excited to be released, only to be reincarcerated shortly thereafter. Her story depicts the difficulties of reentry and the effects of institutionalization. Her friend Poussey wants to know what happened, but Taystee brushes it off, saying probation officers are like the KGB. "Curfew every night; piss in a cup whenever they say; you gotta do three job interviews a week for jobs you're never gonna get. . . . Man, at least in jail you get dinner" ("Fool Me Once" 2013). But this reaction is a facade. The exchange that follows highlights many critical issues faced by women in prison:

> POUSSEY: Man, there's bitches up in here doing fifteen years for letting their boyfriends do deals in the kitchen because they was afraid of getting beat if they say no. And, these bitches ain't seen their kids since they were babies and them kids got their own babies or they're running around the streets carrying guns and shit. . . . So I know you aren't telling me in my face right now that you walked back in this place 'cause freedom was inconvenient.
>
> TAYSTEE: It ain't like that P. Minimum wage is some kind of joke. I got part time working at Pizza Hut and I still owe the prison $900 in fees I gotta pay back. I got no place to stay. . . . Everyone I know is poor, in jail or gone. . . . I know how to play it here. I know where to be and what rules to follow. I got a bed and I got you. ("Fool Me Once" 2013)

Institutionalization and barriers to reentry are real problems faced by many prisoners. Taystee so eloquently captures these challenges. Rarely does fictional prison imagery present the issue in such a way.

Some of the issues found in women's institutions are unique while others are also found in men's prisons. *Orange Is the New Black* does a good job of touching on many of these issues. Although, due to the fact that it is a fictional program, it is never quite able to delve deep enough to offer a complete understanding. An example is found in the story of Maria Ruiz. In the first season, Maria is pregnant, gives birth, and immediately must give her child up. In the second season, viewers see her visiting with the father of her child and the baby. This story line does not include some of the main issues related to pregnant inmates, including shackling the women and the need for many to find someone to take care of their child. It is these sorts of details that are critical to understanding the issues surrounding pregnant inmates.

Diversity and complexity. The diversity of the prison environment is also reflected throughout *Orange Is the New Black*. Women from all walks of life are incarcerated in Litchfield. Piper is a fairly well off, college-educated, white female, who people do not expect to see in prison. While she is the story's protagonist, the series also follows the women with whom she is incarcerated. It is their stories that enable viewers to get an idea of the wide range of people in US prisons. Each episode provides a glimpse into the background of an inmate through flashbacks of her life before prison. These women come from a variety of circumstances and are in prison for anything from theft to murder. Viewers see that there are many different factors that influenced their criminal behavior, including family, love, religion, need, greed, and even adrenaline. Gloria's story highlights abuse. Although it is not the main reason for her criminal behavior, it is an influential factor in her life. Too often, a one-dimensional picture of offenders is presented. Offenders are either psychotic or just plain evil and many female offenders are emotionally unbalanced. While some of these depictions are found in this series, they are not the main reasons that most of the women are incarcerated. The complicated backgrounds of these characters demonstrate that there is much more to the story.

It is not only their personal stories that are wrought with complexities, so too are their interactions behind bars. Pseudofamilies, lovers, and even friendships bring support and challenges for the women, and these relationships form the nexus of many story lines. Viewers witness the women trying to maintain relationships with their children, parents, significant others, and friends. The challenges of communication and visitation are clearly demonstrated. Even more complicated are their relationships on the inside. Prison lovers, friends, and family provide comfort and support, but also betrayal and pain. These interactions are a reflection of the complex social system that exists in women's prisons, one that is very different from that seen in *Oz* and other representations of men's prisons.

Personal relationships are not the only social complications presented. Modern prison imagery tends to highlight the role of race in the social interactions that occur behind prison walls. According to many depictions of men's institutions, race and ethnicity are a dividing force by which many, if not all, interactions are dictated. It is the basis of much of the conflict that takes place, particularly physical altercations. Race and ethnicity are also at the core of *Orange Is the New Black*. The racial divide is depicted early in the series, but it is different from that seen in imagery of men's prisons. There is a clear break between the whites, blacks, and Hispanics in this series, but it is more social than conflict based. Piper is greeted by other white prisoners and learns that she can eat only with them. Morello advises Piper, "Just pretend it's the 1950s—it makes it easier to understand" ("I Wasn't Ready" 2013). She is then reassured that this practice is tribal, not racist. The groups are essentially race-based cliques whereas in men's prisons they are often represented as gangs. The women come together when needed and appear to show compassion for one another. Piper herself seems to be one of the few inmates to break through the racial barriers, befriending many different inmates, which is perhaps a way to further the plot.

Sexual relationships and abuse. Sex has been at the heart of countless representations of women behind bars. Given that there is a tendency to repeat popular frames, it is almost expected that the sexual behavior of Litchfield's prison population would be highlighted. The first episode of the series goes beyond the usual shower scene in establishing this particular story line. After Piper has been processed into the prison, she begins to learn both the formal and informal institutional rules. Her counselor, Mr. Healy, gives her a piece of advice,

> Miss Chapman, no one's going to mess with you here, unless you let them. This isn't *Oz*. Women fight with gossip and rumors. They might peg you for rich and try to hit you up for commissary. And, there are lesbians. They're not going to bother you. They'll try to be your friend; just stay away from them. I want you to understand, you do not have to have lesbian sex" ("I Wasn't Ready" 2013).

Ultimately, his advice is lost on her. She does not give in to the advances made by Suzanne ("Crazy Eyes"), who believes Piper is her prison wife. But when her old girlfriend Alex is incarcerated with her in

Litchfield, the two eventually resume their relationship. Piper's sex life is not the only one featured. Sexual conquests and relationships are a regular part of the series. Sometimes sex is simply alluded to, but it is also shown. Full frontal nudity and sex scenes are used throughout, including sexual encounters in the shower, the chapel, and the housing units.

Viewers have taken notice of the depiction of sex on this program. A search on the Internet will uncover lists of the best sex scenes in *Orange Is the New Black*. Interviews with cast members often include questions about shooting sex scenes. The fascination with sex on this series does go beyond mere titillation. A review in *The Advocate* proclaims that *Orange Is the New Black* "is not just a fantastic female-centric series that could shift the cultural landscape of television—it could turn out to be TV's best lesbian series ever" (Anderson-Minshall 2013). *Slate* examines the complexity of the lesbian relationships and sex in this program, and applauds the program for not pandering to male desires and for depicting a more realistic version of the relationships between these women (Thomas and Fernando 2014). *Orange Is the New Black* ties a lot of the sex to relationships. Viewers are able to see that there is more to it than caged women in need of sexual fulfillment. Yet in many ways it feeds the same stereotype, especially in the second season when viewers see a sex contest between Big Boo and Nichols.

The series' depiction of sex behind bars is vastly different from the book on which it is based. In her memoir, Piper writes about the warden advising her to tell if she is pressured sexually or threatened. According to Piper (Kerman 2010, 55), "She was talking about prison guards, not marauding lesbians." Sexual victimization is a real issue in women's prisons. Often people fail to think about it, given the constant references to dropping the soap in men's prison. In reality, half of all substantiated incidents of sexual victimization in prison involve staff (Beck, Rantala, and Rexroat 2014). Sexual victimization is touched on in the series, but not in a way to truly bring awareness to the issue.

Many different types of sexual victimization exist behind prison walls. Similar to the free world, it runs the gamut between harassment and rape. The most common form of sexual misconduct by officers is suggestive comments and inappropriate touching (Owen et al. 2008). *Orange Is the New Black* includes examples of these transgressions throughout the series, but the importance of what viewers are witnessing is likely lost. They witness guards groping female inmates during pat-downs and inappropriate comments abound, but neither behavior is ever questioned (see Box 7.2 for the depiction of correctional officers on *Orange Is the New Black*). In prison, any type of sexual contact between correctional officers and inmates is classified as victimization. Even what may be considered a consensual relationship in the free world is not when it takes place behind prison walls. The series romanticizes this type of sexual victimization through its story line on Daya and Officer John Bennett. Viewers watch the two flirt and fall in love. Complications arise when Daya finds out that she is pregnant. While it is clear that the relationship is not allowed by the prison system, the story is written in such a way as to have the audience rooting for the couple. Daya also tricks

---

Box 7.2 Correctional Officers in *Orange Is the New Black*

Similar to many other representations of prison life, *Orange Is the New Black* (Kohan 2013) features corrupt and sketchy guards, although they are presented in a much more complex way than simply torturing brutes. Officer George Mendez (aka Pornstache) is the epitome of a smug hack. He uses his position of power to threaten the women, forcing them to smuggle in and sell drugs as well as grant him sexual favors. Officer John Bennett seems to be in sharp contrast to Mendez. He is a new correctional officer who appears to be professional and kind, but he carries on a relationship with an inmate. As his time in Litchfield progresses, Bennett begins to take on characteristics of the other guards; his frustration culminates in harsher treatment of the inmates. Viewers are also introduced to Mr. Sam Healy, the counselor for Piper's unit, and Mr. Joe Caputo, the unit's supervisor. Both of these characters have major flaws and do not always act in the best interests of the women in Litchfield, yet ultimately both try to help the prisoners. Reminiscent of old prison films, Assistant Warden Natalie Figueroa (aka Fig) is uncaring toward her wards. She is a no-nonsense administrator who will do anything to save money and maintain the reputation of the institution. Her real motives are uncovered in the second season when she is caught embezzling money. For the most part, these characters' actions are not as blatant as physical cruelty and abuse contained in smug hack imagery, but they do show the misuse of power. Officers Susan Fischer, Scott O'Neill, and Wanda Bell are also featured throughout the series. Their stories allow viewers to see how policies, procedures, and other prison-related factors influence their jobs. In the end, most are attempting to do their jobs but they occasionally become jaded by the system.

another officer, nicknamed "Pornstache," into thinking she is interested in him so that he will have sex with her. He is then accused of sexual abuse in the second season. As despicable as Pornstache may be, the audience knows that this instance was not sexual assault per se. Given the fact that *Orange Is the New Black* is tackling some important issues related to women's imprisonment, perhaps future seasons will contain a more accurate story line of sexual victimization behind bars. But for the time being, lesbian sex takes center stage.

Representing reality. Ultimately *Orange Is the New Black* offers a comprehensive look at life behind bars for many female prisoners. A reviewer on Netflix wrote, "I have been out of a Woman's State Prison facility for 1 year, no one understands what I have seen or been through. I have attempted to talk about my experience with my friends and my husband and this places the visual to my stay. . . . I do not have to explain any longer" ("Reviewer Comments" 2013). Just days after the release of the series, it was discussed on a Grantland Pop Culture Podcast titled *Hollywood Prospectus* (Greenwald 2013). One of the hosts explains how people have been conditioned to think one way about female prisoners and how this series contradicts that expectation. In particular, he references an episode titled "Imaginary Enemies." Two story lines come together in this episode: Big Boo is a lesbian inmate who is upset that her ex-girlfriend, Mercy, is now with Trish and that Mercy is about to be released. She tells Mercy to watch her back. Piper begins working in the electric shop and accidentally takes a screwdriver. She hides it in her assigned living quarters in the housing unit, but it goes missing after Big Boo and others visit her, and she is scared that someone will use it as a weapon. At the party for Mercy's release, viewers watch Big Boo glaring at Mercy and Trish, but Red tells her to "let it go." Viewers are relieved when she steps in because they have made the same assumption as Red—that Big Boo will retaliate violently. The end of the episode flashes to Big Boo masturbating under the covers in her cube; she used the screwdriver to make a sex toy, not a weapon. Stereotypes may abound, but the episode demonstrates that prison is not always what people expect. A writer for the *Washington Post,* Dylan Matthews (2013), proclaims that it is the best prison show ever created. In his review of the series, he discusses the accuracy of the representation on this show, including a racial breakdown of inmates and various prison policies. Subsequently, many articles have been published in the popular press that discuss the reality of what viewers see on the program. While parts of prison life are left out or dramatized, many things are accurately reflected. *Orange Is the New Black* does a better job than most in representing the reality of life behind bars. However, any imagery is hindered in its ability to offer a completely accurate reflection.

Similar to other prison stories, transformation is at the heart of *Orange Is the New Black*. There are both positive and negative transformations. Many of the women confront issues that existed before their imprisonment as well as those that have become apparent since walking into prison. Perhaps most surprising is Piper's transformation. She is told time and again by her family, friends, and even prison staff that she is not like the others there. With each episode, viewers watch her adapt to the environment, confront who she really is, and ultimately fight for her life. She tells a delinquent who is visiting the prison in a scared straight program, "I'm scared that I'm not myself in here and I'm scared that I am. Other people aren't the scariest part of prison, Deana; it's coming face-to-face with who you really are, because once your behind these walls there's nowhere to run" ("Bora Bora Bora" 2013). Often prison imagery makes a clear distinction between us and them, making sure that the viewer understands that they are in no way like the people behind bars. But Piper's journey demonstrates that even ordinary people are only one bad decision away from a prison cell.

Until recently, there were no fictional programs about the US female prison population. When seen on crime dramas, the women are both sexualized and masculinized. Main characters, such as Fiona on *Burn Notice,* maintain their feminine wiles while in prison. Fiona may have replaced her short skirts and high heels with prison garb but, unlike the other inmates, in the scenes she wears a tight, virtually see-through, tank top. The other prisoners, however, are tough and masculine. By using such images, these dramas are reinforcing the same messages about adhering to society's expectations of proper female behavior. *Orange Is the New Black,* a drama with a comedic twist, is perhaps the best fictional representation of life in a women's prison. It goes beyond the lessons in femininity that are at the heart of many early representations. Even if there are sexual undertones, it does what *Oz* could never do—it humanizes the people behind bars.

Conclusion

While female prisoners historically have been removed further from society than men, people are fascinated with tales of these outlaw women. The fictional images of women in prison have come a long way since the early melodramatic romances about a young beautiful heroine ending up in the cruel prison world, only to be reformed through her love of a man. The inmates in these films challenged conventional notions of femininity, but remained quintessentially female at their core. After all, only female offenders are emotional and mentally unbalanced. These women were not a threat to public safety, but just to the social order achieved by women following their roles in society.

Those images were replaced with male sexual fantasies of women. Instead of pillow fights in lingerie at sleepovers and shenanigans at the sorority house, male viewers can envision what would have happened if these women were locked up in faraway places for long periods of time without them. Given the highly sexualized nature of these images, once again the female prisoner is not a threat. Thus, we do not need to be truly concerned with her. She may be challenging the rules of proper female behavior, but she is locked away feeding male fantasies.

As farfetched as these underlying messages might appear, they are a reflection of the beliefs at the core of the development of women's institutions. Women were commonly punished for nonconforming behavior, especially morality-type offenses related to their sexuality. The ultimate purpose of these institutions was to help these fallen women and to teach them behaviors needed to live a law-abiding life as a wife and mother. Times have changed and so too have views of female offenders and the purpose of the prison system; therefore, this message is no longer the most prominent one.

With the onset of the imprisonment binge, the images took on another dimension—that of the extremely violent and more masculine female inmate. Other than the occasional reference to their sex lives behind bars, which appear more predatory in these new representations, the world of women's prisons does not appear to be different from that of men. The message is clear: this new dangerous breed of female prisoners are women who deserve punishment for their violent ways. *Orange Is the New Black* is an anomaly. While some other fictional representations attempt to tackle issues facing imprisoned women, many times their reliance on preexisting frames limits the stories. *Orange Is the New Black* breaks the mold in many ways. In an at times lighthearted manner, it tackles the complexity of the women—their lives, offenses, and the inmate social structure are examined in depth. The show feeds fantasies of females having sex behind bars, but it does not rely solely on that trick to draw in viewers. It remains to be seen if this particular series will have any effect on altering how this correctional population is depicted, but it has already generated a lot of buzz. In the meantime, interested parties can turn to some nonfictional representations to get a little closer to the truth.

8

Gendered Realities

THE WORLD THAT FEMALE PRISONERS LIVE IN IS NOT TYPICALLY well represented in films and televised dramas. Real-life images of this correctional population have historically been few and far between. Even when documentarians turned their cameras onto men's prisons, women's institutions were left mostly unobserved. Hidden from the public, the real lives of these women and their treatment by the criminal justice system were unknown to most and, thus, they could continue to think of them as sex-crazed violent women deserving of punishment. The same changes that affected the development of prison documentaries in general influenced those about women in prison. The development of feminist criminology brought increased interest in this prison population. During the imprisonment binge, the rate at which women were being imprisoned increased substantially—surpassing the growth in the men's imprisonment rate. It is within this context that women in prison documentaries began to emerge. From cable prison documentary series to independent films, there is some variation in the depiction of these women. Some documentaries repeat elements of babes-behind-bars films with messages about femininity and sexuality while others illuminate the real-life challenges of this correctional population.

Violence, Sex, and Motherhood in Televised Documentaries

Early women in prison documentaries are difficult to find. Occasionally, there were specials on women in prison, such as WBBM-TV's *Cry in*

Darkness, which aired in the 1960s. This program is a thirty-minute piece that looks at female prisoners participating in a sewing program (Museum of Broadcast Communications 2012). In general, however, documentarians did not pay much attention to female prisoners until the 1990s, at which time televised news magazines, such as *Primetime Live* and A&E's *Investigative Reports,* began airing pieces on women's prisons. In 1996, *Primetime Live* aired a segment that featured Diane Sawyer spending a night in a women's maximum security prison in Louisiana (Scott 2015). Several years later, *Primetime Live* aired an entire episode titled, "Inside a Women's Maximum Security Prison" (2004). Again Sawyer dons a prison uniform and spends a day and a night in Georgia's Metro State Prison. While exploring the culture within this institution, sex and violence come to the forefront. *Primetime's* description of the episode begins with: "The Metro State Prison for Women in Atlanta is becoming home to a new kind of female criminal—one more likely to be incarcerated for a violent crime than women in years past" (ABC News 2004, par. 1). As Sawyer interviews inmates, viewers learn a lot about the prison culture, including prison families, but much of the episode focuses on sexual relationships. Sawyer learns all about masculine inmate or "studs" and the more feminine inmates or "femmes" and even how to make a sex toy. Sadly, this look into the incarcerated life of these women perpetuates stereotypes and misunderstandings, a practice that is altogether too common when depicting female prisoners.

Looking Beyond Caged Heat: Media Images of Women in Prison explored televised news magazines and other popular media images of women in prison to determine how the issue was framed. It concluded that these programs offered a limited look into the lives of women in prison and framed the issue much like infamous babes-behind-bars films (Cecil 2007). The programs focus on violent women—the crimes they commit and how they chose to serve their time as well as their sexual relationships behind bars. A few of these representations step outside the sexualized version to explore motherhood; however, in doing so, they draw from early women in prison films and provide lessons on proper female behavior. While showing viewers the challenges of motherhood from behind bars, the issue is framed in such a way as to reinforce the idea that these are bad women who are not doing what they are supposed to do. Good mothers, after all, would not do anything that would take them away from their children. While focusing on violence, sex, and motherhood, the critical issues faced by female offenders are overshadowed. Most of these programs do not delve into addiction, health issues, and abuse. Viewers see the prison world these women live in, but the context and background needed for a complete understanding of the issues at hand are absent. Since that exploration, more real images of women in prison have become readily available. To fully understand the messages being sent by these images, I discuss some of the documentaries examined in Cecil (2007) as well as others that have since been released.

One of the earliest televised prison documentaries to air on cable during the imprisonment binge was HBO's *Prisoners of the War on Drugs* (1992). While most of the documentary features men's institutions, part of the film depicts women incarcerated in New York's Bedford Hills Correctional Facility. As the title suggests, *Prisoners of the War on Drugs* features women in prison for drug offenses. Each featured prisoner discusses her crimes and whether she will use drugs while incarcerated. Within these discussions, however, motherhood and sex are briefly touched on. Since most of this particular documentary focuses on male prisoners, the scenes with the women quickly pass by, barely etching them into the minds of viewers.

Today, people are most likely to see women in prison documentaries on MSNBC, National Geographic, and other cable stations. The original prison documentary series, *Lockup,* contains a few episodes highlighting women's institutions, including "Return to Valley State" (Drachkovitch 2005b), "North Carolina Women's Prison" (Drachkovitch 2007b), and "Tennessee Prison for Women" (Drachkovitch 2010). While the original *Lockup* series includes these women's prisons, *Lockup Extended Stay* has yet to feature one. The other series take a similar approach by limiting their view of women in prison to only an episode or two. For example, National Geographic aired *Lockdown*'s "Women Behind Bars" (2007) and "Female Felons" (2009) as well as *Hard Time*'s "Female Offenders" (2011) and "Women on Lockdown" (2011). Regardless of the specific series from which these episodes originate, each borrows frames from the larger series in their depiction of the female prison population. These programs focus on violence, sex, and motherhood.

Violent Women

Programs such as *Lockup* and *Lockdown* use violence and gangs to tell prison tales. While gangs are not emphasized in the episodes featuring women's prisons, violence most certainly is at the heart of many stories. One way that violence is highlighted is through the women featured in these programs. The majority of inmates highlighted are incarcerated for violent crimes, which is not a true reflection of the female prison population. Their violent nature is further reinforced by the narrator and through interviews with staff and even the prisoners themselves. Examples can be found throughout *Lockdown*'s "Female Felons" (2009) such as the narrator's introduction to the episode: "The most dangerous women in Maryland, they are murderers, dealers, and thieves. From career criminals to first timers all housed in one prison. For many rage and violence are a way of life. Welcome to the world of Maryland's female convicts." The issue of violence is immediately brought to the forefront in *Lockup*'s "Tennessee Prison for Women" (Drachkovitch 2010). The narrator continues the introduction with a comment that the crimes for which the women are there can be "heinous." When the program begins, footage of a fight is the first image presented. The narrator says, "In here, just as in any men's prison, correctional staff can find themselves in a sudden outbreak of violence." Officers respond and the incident is squelched. Transitioning to the next segment, the narrator continues, "This time a potential violent situation is quickly contained, but some of these inmates have committed acts of violence marked by shocking levels of brutality." Viewers are then introduced to Christine, an inmate serving a twelve-year sentence for aggravated robbery and kidnapping. She describes her crime as being a scene out of an Al Pacino movie. Viewers also meet Sandra, who is serving one year for aggravated assault after stabbing someone in a road rage incident. Felicia and Darlene, a daughter and mother, are featured, both serving ten years for soliciting to kill Felicia's husband. And perhaps most memorable is Betty, or "Cornbread," who is serving life for shooting her husband in the head while he was eating cornbread. Each of these offenses is atypical and, therefore, memorable to viewers. This concentration on violence, of course, is not unique to women in prison documentaries; however, women are far less likely than men to be in prison for violent offenses. Whereas over half of the male prison population is incarcerated for violent offenses, more than half of the female prison population is in prison for property and drug offenses (Guerino, Harrison, and Sabol 2011, 29). By focusing on these types of offenses, the images continue to propagate the message that female offenders are more violent than ever before, even though this is not the case.

Lockdown's "Women Behind Bars" (2007), which features California's Valley State Prison for Women, is another good example of how the violence frame is used. The opening scene contains security camera footage of two inmates fighting in the yard and pictures of a bloody cell. The narrator sets the stage: "A brutal fight erupts in an instant; a beating ends in bloodshed and drug trafficking is the main industry. Just what you would expect in a maximum security prison but these inmates aren't men; they're women. And, surviving means navigating a world packed with drugs and danger." He continues, "If you think women are soft, think again. Inside are 3,900 of the most ruthless women in the state's system. They're thieves, drug traffickers, carjackers, and killers; all under one roof." The stories and images that unfold before the viewers' eyes support these opening statements. Most of the featured inmates have extensive histories of imprisonment, including one who committed her first assault at the age of seven by stabbing a boy with a pencil and paralyzing him. Even the pregnant inmates say you cannot be too careful in the infirmary because "you're face ain't pregnant." When images of the blood-spattered cell are revealed, the narrator comments that "this was caused by women using their fists." Ultimately, the violence is attributed to relationships, theft, and drugs. Other women in prison episodes from *Lockup, Lockdown,* and *Hard Time* contain similar statements by the narrator, staff, and inmates. These women are depicted as violent and ruthless; essentially, they are not very different from their male counterparts. But violence in women's institutions is not a daily concern for most prisoners. The main incidents come in the form of verbal conflicts and economic exploitation (Owen et al. 2008). Physical violence itself is typically the result of "escalating conflict over debt or 'disrespect,' or occurred between women in an on-going difficult relationship" (Owen et al. 2008, vii). The stories that unfold in these documentaries make physical violence between the women seem common and senseless.

Luckily, even typical documentary series occasionally step away from the violence frame in their depiction of female prisoners. When the producers of *Lockup* filmed "Return to Valley State,"(Drachkovitch 2005b) they painted a slightly different picture of the women in Valley State Prison for Women, despite their tendency to use the violence frame. *MSNBC Investigates* had filmed "Lockup: Women Inside Valley State" in 2000. Five years later, they returned for a follow-up *Lockup* episode to see if changes made since their visit had made any effect on the overcrowded institution and the women incarcerated there. Violence is treated briefly, but there appears to be more of a focus on how some of the inmates had changed since the first visit. The episode shows the day-to-day process in the prison, touches on segregation and pregnant inmates, and provides updates on prisoners. Violence is not completely left out, but it is framed around the issue of drugs in the institution.

While violence tends to be emphasized in this documentary series, in "Return to Valley State" it is placed on the back burner, allowing the other stories to come to the forefront.

Similar to other documentaries, the issue of control is also covered. Viewers learn how correctional officers control this violent population. In *Hard Time*'s "Women on Lockdown" (2011), the narrator sets the stage for the discussion of control with statements such as, "At the toughest female prison in the state of Georgia maintaining control is an everyday battle." He continues, "It's a battle waged in the dorms, on the walks and in the cells of Metro through daily inspections, regular searches, and a heavy officer presence on the ground." Like the episodes on men's prisons, though, the main control tactic emphasized is the use of solitary confinement. Its use is justified by the actions of the uncontrollable and unpredictable inmate population. In "Women on Lockdown" this discussion continues when the narrator explains, "In a population filled with violent offenders and chronic rule breakers, some inmates become too difficult to handle . . . leaving the prison to take more extreme measures and to serve time in the hole." Similar images of solitary confinement are included in episodes on women's prisons in other series, each ignoring the larger issues related to the use of isolation with this population.

Sex, Relationships, and Motherhood

The women in prison episodes from these series serve to inform viewers about prison life and culture. Viewers can see that there are similarities and differences between the inmate social systems and daily life in men's and women's institutions. They learn about the prison process from intake to release, which is not unique. They are informed about the prison culture, which in some ways differs from that formed in men's prisons. Whereas the documentaries featuring men's prisons discuss gang or at least race affiliations, the episodes on women in prison discuss pseudofamilies and other relationships that the women have while incarcerated. Within this discussion are the emotional and sexual relationships between the women, a topic that is not covered in male prison documentaries.

Lockup's "North Carolina Women's Prison" (Drachkovitch 2007b) highlights the issue of female relationships behind bars. Warden Annie Harvey says that these relationships are "a very interesting, a very unique, a very complex issue that we [prison administrators] have to contend with." She goes on to comment that "in a prison setting these things have to be discouraged. And one of the reasons you have to discourage it is because people are here a long time and some boundaries are bound to get cloudy between women." This episode features inmates Kathy and Devan discussing their prison "marriage" as well as the relationship between Danica and Jennifer. Other episodes from the prison documentary series highlight sex and relationships behind bars, addressing the issue of situational homosexuality in this population. In general, however, stereotypes about lesbians are perpetuated in these images: the more "masculine" inmates are shown as being predatory in their search for sex behind bars. What is absent from the discussion is the very real issue of sexual harassment and abuse that takes place in prison.

Another relationship that these documentaries briefly describe is motherhood. Prisons must be equipped to deal with pregnant inmates as well as the relationships that these women have with their children. The documentaries on Valley State Prison for Women feature stories about pregnant inmates in "Lockup: Women Inside Valley State" (2000) and "Return to Valley State" (Drachkovitch 2005b), as well as "North Carolina Women's Prison (Drachkovitch 2007b) and "Tennessee Prison for Women" (Drachkovitch 2010). The scenes of these women are a small part of the story. They provide enough information to inform viewers that there are pregnant women in prison who must give up their children but, within the context of a single episode, they are unable to truly get at the larger issues related to motherhood behind bars.

Women in Prison Documentary Series

Following the evolution of other televised prison documentaries, after 2005 documentary series about women in prison began to emerge such as *Women on Death Row* (Brockhoff and Brown 2006), *Women Behind Bars* (Burrud and Swindell 2008), *Cellblock 6: Female Lockup* (Bingham, Bishop, and Forman 2010), *Prison Women* (2011), *Prison Diaries* (2011), and *Breaking Down the Bars* (Drachkovitch 2011). This list might suggest that women in prison documentary series have overrun the airwaves, but some of the titles are deceptive. *Cellblock 6* and *Prison Women* are both about county jails, with the latter focusing on female correctional officers. Several of the others are essentially carbon copies of the popular show *Snapped* (2004), which examines crimes committed by out-of-control women. Each of these programs explores these women's crimes in detail, without much attention to actual prison life. *Breaking Down the Bars* is the only series to focus exclusively on daily life in a women's prison.

In 2011 the Oprah Winfrey Network aired *Breaking Down the Bars* (Drachkovitch 2011), which was filmed at Indiana's Rockville Correctional Facility, a medium security prison. The security level of the featured prison is one of the elements that makes this series unique. It moved away from maximum security life, potentially enabling the filmmakers to present a more representative version of life behind bars. The stories of eight inmates are highlighted throughout the series. Adding a unique spin to this series, there are many scenes of the women being counseled during their sentences by Stephanie Covington, a renowned therapist and codirector of the Center for Gender and Justice. Although many other women in prison documentaries on cable television emphasize violence and sex, for the most part these themes are absent in *Breaking Down the Bars*. Some of the women may be incarcerated for violent offenses, but there is no discussion of institutional violence. Furthermore, little attention is paid to any relationship that these women may have on the inside. Instead, viewers are presented with stories of anger, addiction, recovery, and transformation.

The first episode, "You're Not Here to Make Friends" (2011) is like many others. It begins with a new inmate going through the intake process. Through scenes of the prison routine, from meals to group therapy, viewers are privy to how a new inmate settles in, the importance of prison rules, and the consequences of breaking these rules. "The Recovery Process" (2011) continues the lesson in rule breaking by showing a disciplinary hearing, although most of the focus is on recovery. Several of the featured inmates have addiction issues. Working with Covington, getting an education, and being a part of the drug treatment program are some of the ways these women deal with their anger issues and their addictions. The theme of "Walking a Fine Line" (2011) is how these women want to change, but there are challenges as to whether they think they are capable of transforming. Tiffany is an example of this challenge; she is in prison for robbery and criminal confinement. Her mother was a dancer and her dad was a pimp. She was gang-raped at the age of seventeen years old. She became a prostitute, robbing johns at the urging of her pimp boyfriend. Tiffany is clearly angry and struggling in prison. Her mother, who has cancer, is the caregiver of her children, and it is her family that is her motivation for change. She comments, "I'm changing because I have to. I have to grow up now because my mom and my family needs me. . . . It's more important than breathin' right now" ("Walking a Fine Line" 2011). Despite this motivation, she is angry, which plays out in disciplinary issues that threaten her release date.

In "An Offender Mentality," (2011) viewers continue to witness some of the thinking patterns that threaten the recovery and rehabilitation process for these women. Lisa, who killed her abusive husband, struggles with its anniversary date and a mother-in-law who will not forgive her. Nicole, whose child died while unattended in the bathtub, is about to be released. She feels guilty about her addiction and the accident, and gets into trouble just days before the release date. The final three episodes, "A Lot to Be Angry About" (2012), "If I Had a Daughter in Here" (2012), and "Beyond the Bars" (2012) continue with many of these issues. Viewers see Tiffany and others still struggling with anger. Nicole and other inmates are released and discuss the challenges of reentry. Viewers also witness the importance of family support. Hannah, in prison for attempted robbery due to her drug addiction, stays connected with her family and boyfriend. While the family blames the boyfriend for her drug addiction, they work with him and Hannah to understand the issues at hand and to get ready for her release. Viewers even witness a family counseling session held with Covington. They also get to know Larretha, a star basketball player incarcerated for armed robbery. Although she does not have encouragement from her family, her former basketball coach visits her to offer support. And Tiffany is seen on release, working with her mother to take back the caregiving role in her children's lives. While there are challenges, the update at the end of the series says she is living in her own apartment with her children.

Breaking Down the Bars (Drachkovitch 2011) exposes viewers to both typical and unique prison programs as well as detailed stories of the featured inmates. By not emphasizing the violent nature of the prison environment, it is better able to humanize these incarcerated women. It highlights addiction and abuse. In some ways, it is the documentary series equivalent of the dramedy *Orange Is the New Black* (Kohan 2013).

At the time of the last episode of *Breaking Down the Bars,* the released women were doing well considering the challenges of reentry. Unfortunately, what the documentary series is not able to show is what happened after the cameras stopped. At the end of the series, Larretha earned her general equivalency diploma (GED) and was released and living with her grandmother. Her story ends with hope because she is given the promise of a future basketball career by her former coach. With a GED, her grandmother's support, and basketball to look forward to, she has a chance to turn her life around. Viewers are left rooting for her, as is evident by their comments on the program's website. But this was not to be. Old issues resurfaced with a tragic end. In July 2012,

Larretha was killed in a shooting (King, Tuohy, and Neddenriep 2012). Sadly, stories such as this one are altogether too common for prisoners reentering society. Most end up returning to their old neighborhoods and influences, and have the added obstacle of being a felon (as viewers of *Orange Is the New Black* saw in Taystee's story line). Women in particular experience difficulties related to substance abuse, employment, and family reunification. For example, women are two times as likely as men to return to prison within twelve months due to offenses related to drug addiction (La Vigne, Brooks, and Shollenberger 2009). Yet the challenges and realities of release are rarely depicted in televised documentary series, even on one as comprehensive as *Breaking Down the Bars*. Viewers commonly see inmates serving long sentences, so thoughts of release may not even enter their minds. In the few instances when viewers are able to see inmates back in the free world, many of the stories are successful ones despite the reality that a significant portion will return to prison within three years (Petersilia 2009).

In a sea of cable television prison documentary series, *Breaking Down the Bars* is a change of pace, but is an edited version of reality. Because it was filmed at a medium security institution and delves deep into the stories of these women, viewers get the chance to truly understand the main issues facing many female prisoners. The series is perhaps a victim of this type of storytelling. The Oprah Winfrey Network was probably the best venue for this show, but the station struggled to maintain viewers from the beginning (Stelter 2011). The network does not have plans for another season. Interestingly, *Breaking Down the Bars* is a product of 44 Blue Productions, the producers of *Lockup,* but it does not approach the popularity of the shows on MSNBC or National Geographic Channel. Again, it appears that the sensationalistic images of prison life are the best way to draw in viewers.

Abuse, Motherhood, and Treatment in Independent Documentaries

People do not need to rely exclusively on prison documentary series on cable television to get to know the female prison population. Interested parties can tune into alternative images provided by independent documentarians. Similar to films documenting life in men's prisons, these films can be divided into two general categories—issue-based and treatment-based documentaries. Both the issues presented and the treatment programs featured are vastly different from those covered in documentaries on men in prison. These films provide insight into the unique nature of the female prison population. Most issue-based male prison documentaries focus on broader issues affecting the system such as the imprisonment binge and special populations. Those depicting female prisoners highlight issues specific to that population such as the role of abuse and being a mother behind bars. Treatment-based documentaries on female prisoners are less common, although there is overlap between the two types of films. When addressing the issue of motherhood, unique prison programs are often included in the story. These films provide deep insight into the lives of incarcerated women (see Table 8.1).

Abused Women Behind Bars

Abuse is a major issue in the lives of many women involved with the criminal justice system. In order to offer a comprehensive look at women in prison, the role of abuse must be explored. Some end up in prison because they use drugs to self-medicate; others have fought back

Table 8.1 Independent Documentaries on Women in Prison

■ **Treatment-Based**
What I Want My Words to Do to You (2003)
The Grey Area: Feminism Behind Bars (2012)
Sweethearts of the Prison Rodeo (2009)
Freedom Road (2004)

■ **Issue-Based**

Abuse
The Nature of the Beast (1993)
From One Prison (1994)
Defending Our Lives (1994)
Crime After Crime (2011)
Sin by Silence (2010)

Motherhood
Voices from the Inside (1996)
When the Bough Breaks: Children of Women in Prison (2001)
Prison Lullabies (2003)
Troop 1500 (2005)
A Sentence for Two (2008)
War on the Family: Mothers in Prison and the Children They Leave Behind (2010)
Purdy (2010)
Babies Behind Bars (2011)
Mothers of Bedford (2011)

against their abusers and find themselves serving long prison sentences because of that. Documentarians have played an important role in sharing the stories of abused women in general. These prison documentaries add to the genre by addressing victims who have become offenders.

Documentaries about abused women behind bars focus specifically on the stories of the women who have killed their abusers. The images leave viewers with extensive knowledge of the individuals. *From One Prison* (1994) features the stories of four women incarcerated in Michigan for killing their abusive spouses. The main purpose of the documentary is to depict their stories of abuse, the incidents that landed them in prison, the prosecution of their cases, and their sentences. Almost two decades later, *Sin by Silence* (2010) was released. Originally available only on DVD, this documentary aired on cable television in 2012, thereby having the potential to reach a larger audience than many of the other documentaries on this subject. Similar to *From One Prison,* the cases of several women are highlighted. What makes this documentary unique, however, is the focus on activism by the women. Inmates in the California Institution for Women formed Convicted Women Against Abuse (CWAA), which is a support network and an activist group. Their work has contributed to changes in California's laws and, subsequently, has given some of these women the opportunity to reopen their cases. The stories presented are both heartwrenching and heartwarming; they highlight the effects of abuse on the women and their families and the way the system punishes these women with extremely long sentences.

Each of these documentaries on abused women behind bars exposes stories of extreme abuse and a system bent on punishing victims. While highlighting a critical issue, like many other documentaries it is the most sensational examples that are featured. What these stories fail to highlight are the countless numbers of other female prisoners with extensive histories of abuse and the abusive behavior that takes place behind prison walls. These stories are not completely absent from women in prison imagery. Histories of abuse are woven into the stories told by women featured in other documentary films. For example, several of the women in *What I Want My Words to Do to You* (2003) unveil sexual and physical abuse in their lives. Cynthia is one such inmate. She was sexually abused as a child and it is a precursor to the crime that she commits many years later. Abuse at the hands of correctional officers is rarely depicted; however, in *From One Prison* the women talk about either being touched by a correctional officer or witnessing such a violation. To understand women's involvement in crime and their experiences behind bars, it is critical to address the various types of abuse that affect their lives. Not many prison documentaries thoroughly examine this issue.

Mothers Behind Bars

Abuse is not the only factor with which many female offenders must deal. Another major concern related to the imprisonment binge is the number of children who are affected. Nearly two-thirds of the female prison population have minor children. These incarcerated mothers are more likely to have lived with their children than imprisoned fathers (Glaze and Maruschak 2008, 4). For many women, separation from their children is one of the greatest pains of imprisonment. The prison system must be able to deal with the consequences of this stress. In addition, it must be equipped to handle the special needs of pregnant inmates, including prenatal care, childbirth, and placement of children. Pregnancy and motherhood among the female prison population is a topic commonly brought up in the media. More in-depth examinations of the issues and programs can be found in several independent documentaries and the two-part *Babies Behind Bars* (2011). Most of these documentaries, however, feature some of the least common, but most interesting, programs for women and their children.

Prison Lullabies (2003) is an award-winning documentary filmed at the Taconic Correctional Facility in New York. A cinema vérité film, it follows four women who are in the nursery program. Viewers witness these women participate in the program, a mother saying goodbye to her son at the age of one year, all of the women being released, and some being returned to prison. It is a tale of motherhood, the struggles of addiction, and reentry. A similar look at motherhood behind bars is presented in *Babies Behind Bars,* the two episodes of which aired on TLC. This show highlights the Wee Ones Nursery at the Indiana State Women's Prison. It follows women enrolled in the program as well as applicants. Absent from both of these documentaries, and others about motherhood, are prison violence and sex. Instead, both documentaries offer insight into having babies while in prison. However, these nursery programs are not common in the United States, and are available in only five states.

Documentaries on motherhood behind bars are not limited to those highlighting nursery programs. These films tell a variety of stories about imprisoned mothers and their children. *Mothers of Bedford* (2011) follows the stories of five women in Bedford Hills Correctional Facility who struggle with raising their children, while imprisoned, with the help of the Children's Center. A reviewer of the documentary comments that, from watching *Mothers of Bedford,* viewers learn that these children do not grow up motherless simply because their mothers are in prison (Strochlic 2011). An earlier documentary, *When the Bough Breaks: Children of Women in Prison* (2001), offers a slightly different view by following the children, not the mothers. Another film depicting how the experience affects the children is *Troop 1500* (2005). Its filmmakers had the unique opportunity to film mothers and their daughters during Girl Scout troop meetings at the prison. The daughters were given the chance to interview their mothers on camera, which unveils much of the turmoil experienced on both sides. One of the mothers confesses, "I am constantly reminded of the suffering that they are going through because of my bad choice. I don't know my children anymore." In another scene, Kenya's eldest daughter says to her, "Sometimes I think your mistakes are kind of becoming a habit. Do you ever think about that and how I feel?" To which Kenya replies, "I think about it a lot. It hurts that I put myself in that position that they can't count on me. I am not going to let it get the best of me, the guilt and all that. I am just going to lace up my boots and do what I have to do." If Kenya is convicted of another crime, she will be sentenced to twenty-five years to life, a realization that shocks her daughter.

Films such as these highlight the challenges of being a mother behind bars. It is a subject that is at least dealt with briefly in nearly every documentary about women in prison. Women in prison documentaries on cable television series tend to frame these women as bad mothers. However, independent films suggest that, even if they were not good mothers on the outside, many of them are seeking redemption while in prison. The images demonstrate that incarceration does not need to be a complete barrier to being a mother, but that there are challenges that make it difficult for even the most willing. Perhaps more important, it puts a face on the children who are affected by harsh prison sentences.

Treatment-Based Documentaries

Documentaries on mothers in prison highlight parenting and nursery programs, but these are not the only types of programs available in women's institutions. There are a variety of program options, some of which are exclusive to women's prisons. Most independent documentaries do not focus on common treatment programs such as drug treatment and counseling; only *Breaking Down the Bars* (Drachkovitch

2011) with its serial format does that. Instead, they highlight some unique programs available to a small portion of the female prison population. Yet by watching these documentaries, viewers gain insight into the factors that brought these women to prison as well as their struggles both in and out of these institutions and are able to witness some incredible transformations.

Women in Bedford Hills Correctional Facility are highlighted in *What I Want My Words to Do to You* (2003), which aired on PBS. For several years, a group of inmates participated in a writing program led by author and playwright Eve Ensler. This documentary is a compilation of their writing exercises as well as actresses preparing to read their words at a live performance at the prison. The final part of the documentary shows some of the performance and the reactions of inmates in attendance. Ensler puts the women through a series of writing tasks. For example, she asks them to write about the facts of their crime and about a scar they have. The women read their pieces to the group, reflecting on what they have written and as a result confront issues plaguing them. It is a moving documentary that takes an in-depth look into the lives of these women. For the most part, however, these are not typical female prisoners. They include Pamela Smart, a teacher convicted for having her student lover kill her husband, and Judith Clark and Kathy Boudin, both former Weather Underground Organization members. Most of the featured inmates are incarcerated for violent crimes. One tough reality of the New York system is brought to light in ending credits—the harshness of the Rockefeller Drug Laws. Some of the women are serving incredibly long sentences for drug crimes and, at the time of filming, were appealing these sentences. Despite featuring some unique inmates, the stories of their lives are in many ways parallel to those of other women in prison—stories of abandonment, anger, abuse, and drugs. The complexities of their stories become apparent. Cynthia Berry tells her story of being abused as a child and turning to drugs and prostitution. She felt that sex was her only source of power. The effects of the abuse, however, led to far worse acts. She stabbed a seventy-one-year-old customer. She remembers stabbing him three times, when in fact she was in such a rage that she stabbed him twenty-eight times. She later found out that the man had recently been widowed and was presumably looking for some comfort. Cynthia is struggling in prison, wanting to die because of her actions. Many of the women's stories are laced with regret and shame, and occasionally with hope. By listening to these women's voices, viewers begin to see the complexity of their lives.

The Grey Area: Feminism Behind Bars (2012) and *Sweethearts of the Prison Rodeo* (2009) are two other films that present unique prison programs. In 2012 *The Grey Area* began making its rounds at various film festivals. It depicts a unique educational program at the Iowa Correctional Institution for Women in Mitchellville. The Grinnell Liberal Arts Prison Program is a volunteer program run and staffed by students. These volunteers go into prisons and teach a variety of classes, including writing and dance. Similar in some ways to *What I Want My Words to Do to You* (2003), the film captures candid discussions between the inmates and volunteers. In the end, it is essentially a film about feminism behind bars as well as the importance of education. *Sweethearts of the Prison Rodeo* (2009) features a vastly different prison program. The Oklahoma State Prison Rodeo was established in 1940 and is the only rodeo to be held behind prison walls. Before the rodeo shut down in 2010, the prison allowed female inmates from the state to compete. The documentary follows their journey to the 2007 rodeo. Through their stories, viewers see the personal side of these women, each of whom is incarcerated for drug-related offenses in a state that incarcerates women at double the national average. The grip that drugs has on many of these women is apparent, but so too are their transformations within the confines of prison walls and their chance to participate in the rodeo. These stories are similar to the ones told about the men who participate in the Angola Prison Rodeo. One difference is that viewers see some of these women released, and they return to cheer on their teammates from the stands at the 2008 rodeo.

Whether documenting the experiences of incarcerated mothers, uncovering the lives of women who killed their abusers, or demonstrating that female prisoners are willing to work on reforming themselves through prison programming, there are more similarities than differences between these independently produced documentary films. Similar to some of the independent documentaries on men in prison, focusing on these topics allows the filmmakers to convey the complexities of the lives of prisoners. These types of documentaries add important context to viewers' understanding of the female prison population.

Conclusion

In 1980, 13,258 women were incarcerated in US state and federal prisons. In 2012 this number grew to 113,606, which is more than a 700 percent increase (The Sentencing Project 2014b). Some believe that this increase is because women are more likely to commit crimes than in decades past; however, this belief is one that is propagated in large part by the media. Since the 1970s, the media have depicted different versions of the new female offender and bad girls in society. From female revolutionaries to gang members and bullies, viewers are inundated with violent women who presumably deserve to be punished (Chesney-Lind and Irwin 2008). Feeding into this belief are the current popular images of women in prison, especially those provided by documentarians.

As the get-tough era was ushered in and there were increased efforts in the war on drugs, more women were sent to prison. The mandatory minimum sentences and zero-tolerance policies cast a wide net, capturing women who previously escaped imprisonment. Rather than telling tales about the effects of these policies, documentary series on cable television delved into the world of women's prisons. Similar to preceding images of these women, the focus became violence and sex but, instead of cat fights between scantily clad women, viewers watched in shock as these women fought one another like men and in many other ways appeared more masculine.

When I originally examined images of women in prison (Cecil 2007), violence, sex, and motherhood were the main frames used by producers. Since then, women in prison documentaries have become more plentiful and accessible. There are two implications of this growth. First, more people have the opportunity to experience life in a women's prison through this imagery. Second, the programs are telling a variety of stories, thereby hopefully providing a more comprehensive view of this correctional population. Of course, the types of messages that viewers receive about them are highly dependent on the programs they choose to watch.

Serialized programs, such as *Lockup,* continue to present a limited view of women in prison, one that in many ways is the same as its portrayal of male prisoners. The women are incarcerated for violent crimes, and they continue this brutality on the inside. Where these programs diverge is in their depiction of relationships and sex. With a few exceptions, these topics are taboo in documentaries about male prisoners, which is ironic considering the number of jokes about sex in men's prisons. In episodes featuring women's institutions, the inmates' relationships with one another is a common topic. The women talk candidly about these relationships, not all of which are sexual. The prison administrators highlight the problems that such relationships cause for the institutions. While this is a concern in women's institutions, far more critical issues need to be addressed such as abuse, lack of programming, and inadequate medical care. Viewers are entertained more by the thought of women having sex behind bars than by the realities of sexual assault and harassment at the hands of the people who are in charge of watching over them—the sex frame is used simply to titillate viewers.

Overall, programs such as *Lockup, Lockdown,* and *Hard Time* show viewers the dark side of female offenders. These violent and sex-crazed women are an uncontrollable population that is deserving of severe punishment and solitary confinement. This message coincides with the more popular media images of crime and justice, including those in some modern prison films. These show female offenders as being worse than ever before and, at the same time, back current crime control policies. This fits neatly with the messages found in many crime dramas, reality-based shows, and even the news.

Leaving sex and violence frames alone, more complex views of women in prison are depicted in *Breaking Down the Bars* and independently produced documentaries. Similar to the documentaries on men's prisons, when filmmakers are able to hone in on a special program or population the end result is a more humanistic view of incarcerated women. One of the volunteers featured in *The Grey Area* (2012) says it best: "My general thought was that good people are outside prison and bad people are in prison and there's not a lot of grey. Now my whole life is kind of devoted to living in that grey area that I didn't know existed." These documentaries are similar to *Orange Is the New Black* in their overall depiction of the female prison population (with the exception of prison sex) in that they unveil the complexities of the lives of incarcerated women.

Focusing on these programs does have a potential downside of its own. In general, proper and effective programming to deal with the issues that women inmates face is not always accessible in women's prisons. The programs that are highlighted in documentaries and series are exceptional ones at that. Treatment programs of any kind require resources that are already strained in most states. They are dependent not only on money, but also on community resources. Hillsborough Correctional Institution in Florida was a character-based institution for female offenders, and the programming options were vast. The programs were not solely reliant on state funding, but were also made possible by more than 300 volunteers who donated hours and resources. Unfortunately, the abundant opportunities for these incarcerated women came to an end in 2012 when Governor Rick Scott closed the institution. Many other prisons are unable to offer such programming. Watching many of these independent documentaries may leave viewers with the belief that incarcerated women are well taken care of behind bars and the opportunities to receive help are endless. Nothing could be further from the truth.

These documentaries also feature stories of transformation. Viewers learn about the women's lives, their struggles in and out of prison, and how this time has changed them. In many cases, there is a happy ending so to speak. They watch women, such as Tiffany described above in the discussion of *Breaking Down the Bars* (Drachkovitch 2011), and begin to root for them to succeed. When Tiffany is released, the cameras expose viewers to some of the realities of prisoners reintegrating into society and reuniting with their families. The final update on Tiffany given on the documentary is that she was living in her own apartment with her two youngest sons. Unless one is interested enough to investigate further that is the last image of her life with which viewers are left. Based on information that Tiffany previously provided to the show's old website, her life continues to be a struggle but she is managing. Her eldest son passed away, but she is trying to keep the rest of her family together and she was scheduled to be released from parole in September 2012. Stories such as Tiffany's demonstrate that many inmates want to do what they can to better themselves—not every person behind prison walls will be a threat to public safety on release.

The independent documentaries highlight stories that explain the pathways many of these women take to the prison gates. These sources provide the much-needed context to offer a better understanding of women in prison; unfortunately, these are not the most popular documentaries among the masses. Regardless, these sources uncover some of the complexities of the women's lives and crimes. The underlying message, however, is that the system is equipped to help these women and, if they are released, many are successful because of the programs they participated in while incarcerated.

Documentary images of women in prison do not exist in a vacuum. They exist within the realm of all prison imagery. Even with alternative images of this particular prison population available, the most prominent images are likely to leave the biggest impression. In the age of the imprisonment binge, these have been popular documentary series on cable television. Whether depicting men or women, prisoners are represented as others and prisons are necessary to protect the public. But the variety of potential viewers should not be discounted. A number of them will seek out the less sensationalistic and more thought-provoking views. They do not mind being uncomfortable with the realities of this sometimes vulnerable population.

9

Music, Comedy, and Beyond

REPRESENTATIONS OF PRISON LIFE HAVE BECOME INGRAINED IN the broader lexicon of popular culture. References to prison can be found in music, video games, and even smartphone applications. Some of these representations attempt to bring awareness to flaws in the system, while others continue legends of life in the big house or parody it. While more prominent and realistic images of prison are likely to have a greater impact, these other references should not be discounted. Media effects models are applicable to these representations as well. Stereotypes and misunderstandings might be perpetuated and, potentially, undermine the importance of the issue. It would be next to impossible to assess every pop culture reference of prison life. Thus, I selected the most prominent—music and comedy. The impact of these representations is not as strong as the visual images provided by film and television, but their existence says a lot about the role of prison in US culture.

Prison Songs Tell Tales of Life Behind Bars

Music is an important part of most cultures, and popular songs include tales of love, heartbreak, personal experiences, historical events, and lifestyles. At times, songs are a form of protest or they speak of injustice. Incorporated into various genres of music are songs about people's experiences with the criminal justice system. From Elvis Presley's "Jailhouse Rock" (1957) to N.W.A.'s "Fuck tha Police" (1988), there are a variety of ways to tell these tales—some lighthearted, some

159

in your face, and many in between. Prison songs can be found in many genres of music, but country and hip-hop are where they are the most prevalent.

Music and prison have a long history in the United States. The roots can be traced back to work songs of African American inmates in Southern prisons. Carried over from plantation life, these songs were a way to deal with endless hours spent working in the fields. According to Bruce Jackson (1999, xix), these songs "are used so the singers can make it"; that is, make it through the hell of prison life. Sung only by African American inmates while working, few of these songs are known by the public. However, thanks to Alan and John Lomax, who archived folk music of the early twentieth century, recordings do exist. These songs are about "guards, escape, sentence length, geographical places remembered or longed for or heard of, sickness, death, guns, the work itself" (Jackson 1999, xx). The work song tradition ended with the integration of Southern prisons. For those who have explored these songs in depth, they depict a rich tale of prison life; to the rest, they remain relatively unknown. Their influence, however, can be felt in the blues. Paul Oliver (1990) discusses the history of African Americans and imprisonment in the South and connects it to various blues songs recorded in and out of prison. For example, *20 to Life: Prison Blues, Songs from the Angola State Penitentiary* (1960) is a compilation of songs recorded at Angola. Blues songs about chain gangs, life on prison farms, the death penalty, and other imprisonment-related issues are abundant (Oliver 1990). The artists sang from experience, reflecting on how the system was affecting them. The message was clear: the prison system they experienced was not much different from the plantations of the South. Slavery may have ended, but it was replaced with a new repressive regime. But not only prisoners sing about life behind bars, others have told these stories through songs much more accessible to the general population.

Country Music Songs of the Big House Era

While not directly influenced by prison work songs, but still largely drawn from life in the South, country music provides a wealth of songs about prison. This genre is known for telling simple stories about everyday life. There are countless songs about crime, victimization, revenge, and justice. Songs such as Blake Shelton's "Ol' Red" (2001), Loretta Lynn's "Women's Prison" (2004), and Hank Williams III's "Louisiana Stripes" (2006) relay tales of prison life. The most well-known prison songs in this genre were recorded decades before the imprisonment binge by Johnny Cash and Merle Haggard.

Undeniably, the most well-known prison song of all time is Cash's "Folsom Prison Blues" (1955). This song is ingrained in US culture and has been covered by many artists, including Merle Haggard, Keb' Mo', and Everlast. Cash was inspired to write it after seeing *Inside the Walls of Folsom Prison* (1951). The song is a story of an imprisoned man who hears a train and dreams of escaping Folsom on it. Prisoners fantasizing about something other than the walls around them is a common theme in prison songs. Despite having never served time in prison, Cash found a way to convey messages to those serving time, as well as to listeners in the free world, about prison life through "Folsom Prison Blues" and several other songs. Cash did more than just sing these songs; over the course of his career, he held more than thirty performances behind prison walls, including at Huntsville in Texas and Cummins in Arkansas (see Box 9.1). The most well-known performances, however, were at California's Folsom Prison in 1968 and San Quentin in 1969; it was at these performances that he recorded his hit albums *At Folsom Prison* (Cash 1968a) and *At San Quentin* (Cash 1969).

The songs in Cash's repertoire convey the life of many men in prison as well as their experiences and dreams. In "Cocaine Blues" (Cash 1968b) he tells the story of how a man gets a ninety-nine-year sentence because, like many other songs in this genre, he killed his wife for cheating. Several of Cash's songs express life behind bars. "I Got Stripes" (Cash and Williams 1968) is a simple song about a man who gets sentenced to a chain gang and ends up in solitary, living on bread and water, for having been caught with a file. The file is the representation of a plan to escape, which is a prominent part of other songs by Cash. In both "The Wall" (1968f) and "The Walls of a Prison" (1970), Cash sings about prisoners attempting to escape but killed in the attempt. Climbing over the wall is not the only way for inmates to escape. Glen Sherley, an inmate in Folsom Prison, composed "Greystone Chapel" (Cash 1968d), in which he expresses that his belief in God is what provides him freedom though he is locked up. In general, thoughts of freedom are a common theme throughout Cash's prison songs. Many prisoners dream of their families and being reunited with them, even if they might not ever be released. In "Send a Picture of Mother" (1968e), Cash sings to a fellow inmate asking him to tell his family that he will see them soon, though it is not true. And in "Green, Green Grass of Home" (Cash 1968c), a popular country song covered by Cash and others, a man dreams of returning home, only to awaken in his cell.

Box 9.1 Johnny Cash—Prison Activist

Johnny Cash was never a prisoner himself, yet he sang about prison as though he knew exactly what it was like to be incarcerated. Conveying these messages to his audiences via his music was not Cash's only involvement with these institutions. What many listeners do not know is that he was an advocate for prisoners' rights. In 1972, he testified before a US Senate subcommittee on the topic (Robbins 2013). Cash donated money from a concert to the Cummins Prison in Arkansas, one of the most notorious prisons in the South during the 1960s, to build a prison chapel. He even challenged the governor of Arkansas to match his donation. He had specific beliefs about prison reform—keeping minor offenders out of prison, not housing first timers with old convicts, and the importance of rehabilitation (Robbins 2013). His activism came at a tumultuous time in the history of the US prison system. Arkansas and other states had their entire prison systems deemed unconstitutional, followed by the Attica prison riot and other disturbances. Slowly, prisoners were gaining rights; however, at the same time, rehabilitation was deemed a failure. Even if Cash's efforts did not lead to major changes in the prison system, his words did not fall on deaf ears. Robbins writes, "Perhaps Cash's impact is best summed up in the words of Senator Quentin N. Burdick, one of the men he testified before at the US Senate subcommittee. Having heard Cash's testimony, Burdick said, quite simply: 'We need more Johnny Cashs, I guess.'"

Cash's prison songs are neither protests nor critiques of the system; rather, they are tales of prison life. Taken together, these songs transport listeners to the iconic big house. They can picture inmates in striped uniforms, sitting in their cells and the yard, dreaming of freedom. In general, Cash's music plays an iconic role in US culture. His music made people aware of the lives of incarcerated men. According Danny Robbins (2013),

> For the average person, listening to one of Cash's prison albums, with their songs of prison life, interspersed with convicts' shouts, warders' tannoy announcements and rattling keys, was to be transported into a world that was, until then, largely unknown or ignored. . . . Cash suc-

cessfully humanised the prison population and gave them a voice. (par. 46)

When Cash performed at San Quentin, Haggard was a prisoner. Haggard served out the rest of his sentence and went on to become a renowned musical artist. Haggard's "lyrics are deceptively simple, the music exceptionally listenable. Others who have lived through those same situations recognize the truth in the stories he tells. But Haggard's real gift is that anyone who hears his songs recognizes the truth in them" ("The Merle Haggard Bio" 2011). He writes from experience. A life of crime eventually landed Haggard in San Quentin, and, in 1960 when released, he began to seriously pursue his career in music. He did not have the intention of writing about prison life, but Cash encouraged him to own up to it in his music ("The Merle Haggard Bio" 2011). Haggard's prison songs include "Branded Man" (1967a), "Life in Prison" (1967c), "I Made the Prison Band" (1967b), "Sing Me Back Home" (1968c), "Mama Tried" (1968b), "Green, Green Grass of Home" (1968a), "Will You Visit Me on Sundays?" (1968d), and "Huntsville" (1971).

When Haggard sings, he tells stories about life in prison and the death penalty. He sings about missing home and of escaping. In "I Made the Prison Band," he sings the words of a prisoner who realizes how horrible prison is, but he is learning to play the guitar and is a part of the band. This experience means enough to him that he decides not to escape as he had planned. In "Huntsville," an inmate is being transferred to prison to begin serving two life sentences, but he plans on escaping as soon as he can. A few of Haggard's songs are about life sentences. In "Mama Tried," the words of the prisoner in the song are about his mother doing what she could when raising him and how it is his own fault he is now serving life. And in "Life in Prison," the words relay the anguish of thinking of spending the rest of one's life behind bars and the desire to die instead. Overall, like Cash's songs, these were tunes to which listeners both in and out prison could relate.

The prison songs of Cash and Haggard are the epitome of most country songs, and the stories conveyed are straightforward. Modern country songs about prison are mostly reflections of the past. In "Ol' Red" (2001), Shelton sings about a man who killed his cheating wife and is sentenced to ninety-nine years. On the prison farm, he is given the task of looking after the bloodhound and he uses this to his advantage to escape. Both Williams's "Louisiana Stripes" (2006) and Lynn's "Women's Prison" also begin with the killing of a spouse and the subsequent punishment. But none of these songs reflect modern-day prison issues. In a way they are musical interpretations of classic prison films. For songs that do tackle the imprisonment binge, we must turn to other musical genres.

Rap Songs of Imprisonment

For all of their differences, country and hip-hop music have many similarities, including prison songs. Hip-hop emerged in the 1970s, at a time when African American social movements began to wane (Ards 2004). While it seemed that minorities were better represented and their communities had improved, some of it was a facade and there were vast changes on the horizon that would influence hip-hop. "Under the watch of a new establishment of black and Latino elected officials, funding for youth services, art programs, and community centers was cut while juvenile detention centers and prisons grew" (Ards 2004, 312). The communities now faced joblessness, decaying schools, and increasing levels of violence and drugs. "In the tradition of defiance, of 'creating somethin' outta nothin',' they developed artistic expressions that came to be known as hip-hop" (212). There was hope that hip-hop would fuel activism and social change; it was even called "the black CNN" by Chuck D of Public Enemy (313). Among other things, hip-hop conveyed messages about modern issues, including treatment by the justice system.

A part of hip-hop's defiance comes in the form of rap music, which has gone through different stages. In the early 1980s there were message raps, followed by Afrocentricity in the late 1980s that highlighted the black experience in the United States. The 1990s ushered in gangster rap, followed by materialism in the new millennium, which focused on the importance of material wealth (Ards 2004). The early message raps emerged as the seeds were planted for the imprisonment binge. Increasing gun violence and drugs in the inner city and get-tough policies pushed many inner-city youth onto a path toward imprisonment. The experiences of the youth in these neighborhoods influenced the songs they created; therefore, prison became one of the themes. The expansion of the prison system has been a major factor in hip-hop narratives since the late 1980s (Ogbar 2007). What do rappers tell listeners about prison? Rap has a reputation among many for glamorizing violence and the gang lifestyle; thus, some might expect prison to be glamorized as well. Rap, however, is not one homogenous genre, and there is variation in how prison is depicted.

Since the 1980s, many rappers have sung about imprisonment, including Public Enemy, Convicts, Ice-T, Mac Dre, and the Ying Yang

Twins. Rap artists describe imprisonment and its effects. Some songs critique the system while others are protest songs. Overall, this genre of music offers some powerful commentary on the modern prison system. Several of the early artists, such as Tupac, Professor, and Chuck D, were children of black political activists and some of their musical responses to imprisonment were almost militant in nature (Ogbar 2007). Other songs, however, do not send a strong antiprison message. To show the different takes on prison life, Jeffery O. G. Ogbar (2007, 147) contrasts the music of Public Enemy with that of N.W.A.: "For both groups, prisons were an anathema, as a form of political oppression for one and as a threat to street-level criminal enterprise for the other." There are similarities and differences in the stories told in the rap songs of both types. Ultimately, most rap songs about the prison system depict it as a destructive factor in young men's lives and on their communities. Three main subjects are covered by the artists in these songs—doing time, trying to deter others from making the same mistakes, and oppression.

Doing time. Rappers transport their listeners to a very different prison world than the one presented by Cash and Haggard. Gone are the romanticized images of life in the big house. This imagery is replaced with an uncensored look at doing hard time in a penitentiary. Many rappers give detailed accounts of endless days locked behind prison bars. For example, in "Penitentiary Blues" (1991), the Convicts describe everything from solitary confinement and the commissary to mealtime and masturbating. They rap about the inmate hierarchy that places pedophiles on the bottom and allows others to take retribution. As shocking as some people may find the song, the artists provide important lessons about life in prison.

Part of doing time is contending with the pains of imprisonment. In early prison research, Gresham Sykes (1958) identified these pains. He concluded that being locked up comes with many deprivations, which inmates must learn to live with, from lack of security and heterosexual contact to absence of goods and services. These pains are a form of psychological distress, and inmates cope with them in many different ways. One thing that can ease these pains is support from home. Several artists rap about the pains and ask for help from the outside. In "Locked Up" (2004), Akon wants someone to visit him. He also pleads with his girlfriend to accept his calls since he is locked up with no hope of release. Beanie Sigel raps about the environment that contributes to these pains in "What Ya Life Like" (1999) and "What Ya Life Like 2" (2004). From being on lockdown twenty-three hours a day, to eating junk food from the commissary, and to never being able to see your child, the pains seem constant. All the prisoner in the song seems to want is for someone to write to him and to send him things like socks and underwear—the everyday things that might make it a little easier for him. The words in these songs demonstrate the ways in which incarcerated men are isolated from their communities, both physically and emotionally—the pain of which is a large part of doing time.

Deterrence songs. Some prison rap songs send warnings to their listeners. They use descriptions of the harsh environment and lack of support to show the negative side of crime, with the intent of deterring others from following in their footsteps. "Dead Man Walking" (1997) by Body Count is one of these songs, in which Ice-T raps a cautionary tale about a man on death row. The story explains his life, being processed through the system, and how he ended up waiting to be executed. Ironically, the inmate finds himself more educated because he reads everything that he can and is in better shape from working out now that he is in prison, but he questions what good it will do. He advises listeners to not mess up since, if they are poor, they will end up in a cell next to him. Mac Dre's "I've Been Down" (1999) is also a scared straight song. He raps a lengthy verse about typical prison life, including crowded cells, 5:00 A.M. breakfasts, cruel guards, the hole, the mix, drinking pruno, masturbating, shankings, and his woman having sex with other men. His advice is to stay in school.

Critics of this type of music often complain that songs such as these glamorize a life of crime, yet that is not the intended purpose of these specific songs. These artists and others are attempting to use their music to prevent more African American men from entering the prison system.

Oppression. Rap music has gone through many transformations. Many of the earliest songs were message raps (Ards 2004), some addressing social issues affecting the rappers' communities. Crime, drugs, violence, and imprisonment were among the topics commonly found in these songs. Many of the inner-city neighborhoods that these artists were from are known for their young men being incarcerated at an extremely high rate. Several of the prison songs within rap music critique this aspect of the system and, in doing so, provide commentary on the pervasive racism in US society. Tupac's "16 on Death Row" (1997) depicts the tale of a teenager on death row for murder. He identifies the factors that contributed to the path he took, including life in the ghetto, a broken home, and sexual abuse. It is a commentary on the effects of living in these neighborhoods, but it is also a critique of a system of justice that sentences adolescents to death. His cellmate is also sixteen years old and is routinely raped by other inmates. In the end, his buddy hangs himself and he is on his way to the electric chair. Tupac's "16 on Death Row" is also a song of regret; he regrets not going out on his own terms rather than being executed by a system that is trying to keep young black men in prison. Perhaps he views suicide as the only way to have control over the situation in a system that renders men powerless.

Similar to classic blues songs, some of these raps tie the current system to the past. The song "Black Steel in a Time of Chaos" (1988) by Public Enemy is about an inmate who is serving time for dodging the draft. It outlines a violent prison escape. The artists equate the modern prison system to slavery. In "Penitentiary Blues" (1991), the Convicts use the term "bossman" to describe the correctional officers, conjuring up images of plantation life. Ice-T raps about being transported to prison and acclimating to all of the rules in his 1991 song "The Tower," asking who is in power—whites, blacks, or the guns in the guard tower? Similar messages are seen in "Behind Enemy Lines" (dead prez, 2000). Time and time again, the artists rap about this oppressive system that is keeping the men down, even when the inmates are ready to show the world that they have changed, such as in Nelly's "Fly Away" (2005). The message in these songs is clear—the US prison system is another example of racial inequality and, thus, young black men's powerlessness in the United States.

After all of the work by civil rights leaders, these songs demonstrate that the African American community still is not on equal footing. In some of these songs, the artists make reference to some of these leaders, including Martin Luther King Jr. and Malcolm X. In "Behind Enemy Lines" (2000), dead prez rap about Fred Hampton Jr.'s father, who was a Black Panther. Besides referencing activists, some of these songs are protest songs. The Ying Yang Twins' "23 Hour Lockdown" (2005) not only is a commentary on the use of solitary and a word of advice to the youth to gain knowledge, but it is part of a campaign to free Pimp C. Pimp C is a fellow rapper who was sent to prison for eight years on a violation and spent time in solitary. Rappers commonly shouted "Free Pimp C" in their songs and performances and donned Free Pimp C clothing. Taking a step further is the Prison Moratorium Project, a now defunct group working to end the growth of prisons, which created a compilation CD to raise awareness of the prison system and to raise money for activism. Various rappers contributed songs to the CD titled *No More Prisons* (2000).

If one rap song were to be chosen to represent rap music's view on incarceration, it should be "Do Your Time" (2006), which is perhaps the most poignant rap song about imprisonment in US society today. Ludacris is joined by Sigel, Pimp C, and C-Murder to rap what is essentially an anthem of support for all the African American men serving time. The song covers many of the elements discussed above. The artists give shout-outs to their incarcerated relatives and friends. Several important messages are conveyed in this song such as the history of African American men in the United States and comparing the current prison system with slavery.

The birth of hip-hop culture and rap music was an act of defiance (Ards 2004). However, over the years, it has gained quite a reputation for glamorizing gangster life, violence against women, and excessive spending. This discussion of the rappers' take on prison demonstrates that many of these artists are offering powerful commentary on the effects of the imprisonment binge on African American men and their communities (see Ogbar 2007). The audience that these songs have reached, however, may be limited. In particular, the collaborative work of these artists to protest the prison system has seen little radio time (Ogbar 2007). In some ways, their impact may be the same as the old prison work songs: an expression of a problem affecting the community, which is sung to the community that is affected by it. The songs allow them to get through this tough situation.

The Role of Music in the
Social Construction of Prison Life

Both country and rap music prison songs use their lyrics to transport listeners behind the walls. Prison songs can also be found in other genres of music, including System of a Down's "Prison Song" (2001) and Cold War Kids' "St. John" (2006). In the end, the musical genre may have different ways of telling the story, but the content is similar. In the current media landscape that is inundated with visual images of prison, what role do prison songs play? The saying is that a picture is worth a thousand words; thus, one cannot expect as powerful of an impact from musical representations.

Music has been a way for people to express their experiences behind bars and to share them with the masses. Some of the songs are simple tales of the big house. Music also serves as a form of commentary on the problems with the system, highlighting injustice. The question becomes, who is listening? Take hip-hop music as an example. The history discussed above demonstrates that it was originally meant to convey injustice in the community and, to some extent, this purpose exists today; however, it is overshadowed in the mainstream by stereotypical rap music that is linked either to criminality or to living in excess. The population at large, then, is not likely to listen to what is said. However, those who are listening may not be doing any more than that. According to Angela Ards (2004), even when these songs send out powerful messages, listeners do not rally for change.

Laughing at Life Behind Prison Walls

Laughter is said to be the best medicine. Even in times of strife, people seek out the relief provided by a good laugh. Many classic situational comedies have significant underlying messages—from *I Love Lucy*'s stance on women's place in society, to class issues on *The Beverly Hillbillies,* to race, gender, class, and a host of other issues on *All in the Family* (Greene 2008). Comedy is used to tackle serious events such as when *M*A*S*H* made viewers laugh at the Korean War. As Eugene Ionesco put it, "The comic alone is able to give us strength to bear the tragedy of existence" (quoted in Greene 2008, 7). Crime is one of these tragedies and countless laughs have been gained from comedic references to cops eating donuts and prisoners dropping the soap in the communal shower. Numerous films and television shows have provided parodies, satires, and comedic references to prison life. Stereotypes abound in these representations, yet examining some of these depictions can help us understand the infusion of prison in US culture.

One area of entertainment television that has developed tremendously since the 1980s is the cartoon aimed at adult audiences. Programs such as *The Simpsons* (Groening 1989), *Family Guy* (MacFarlane 1998), and *South Park* (Parker and Stone 1997) began airing during primetime or later on network and cable television, and they are vastly different from *The Flintstones* and *The Jetsons*. These adult cartoons essentially are illustrated situational comedies, but the format allows these shows to go even further than regular sitcoms. Just like their real-life counterparts, these shows are known for providing social commentary while entertaining viewers. Although there are several of these series, *The Simpsons* has been a constant presence in the get-tough era of crime and punishment in the United States.

The Simpsons

The Simpsons offers a moral critique of the US family and society. "Taking on politics, cultural mores, familial dysfunctionalism and anything else that gets in the way, the show uses the jester's privilege afforded by cartooning to take itself where no sitcom has dared go before: on a merciless cruise through the winding cul-de-sacs of contemporary suburbia" (Marc 1997, 192). When the Simpson family first appeared in 1989, no one could have imagined that these characters and the town of Springfield would become so ingrained in US culture. *The Simpsons* is currently the longest-running scripted show on television. It is the perfect specimen to demonstrate how humor is used to convey messages about imprisonment.

Crime exists everywhere, even suburbia, so it makes sense that *The Simpsons* commonly refers to crime and the criminal justice system. The police, headed by Chief Wiggum, are often seen, which opens the door for an occasional prison story. In a Simpson-like fashion, every member of the family has been incarcerated, even Baby Maggie. Thirteen correctional institutions have been used in the story lines, including a jail and a juvenile detention center. The prisons include Springfield State Prison, Springfield Penitentiary, Springwood Minimum Security Prison, Campbell's Chunky Soup Maximum Security Prison, Springfield Women's Prison, Montgomery Burns State Prison, Morningwood Penitentiary, and Springfield Elementary School and Prison. In story lines featuring these institutions, *The Simpsons* pays homage to prison films and provides commentary on punishment in the get-tough era (Groening 1989).

"Black Widower" (Groening, Chastain, and Simon 1992) provides a good example of the depiction of prison on *The Simpsons* by highlighting one of Sideshow Bob's prison terms. Marge's sister, Selma, brings her new boyfriend, who she met through a prison pen pal program, to dinner. The first issue that is brought up is people's opinions of ex-cons. Before the guests arrive, Bart is thrilled that the new guest "can teach us how to kill a man with a lunch tray." Marge likes to see the good side of people and therefore responds, "Now, now he is an ex-convict. He's paid his debt to society." Yet her acceptance only goes so far, as she does not use the "good silver" that night. At dinner, Sideshow Bob reflects on his time in prison, which provides several prison-related scenes throughout the episode.

The first flashback pays homage to *Cool Hand Luke,* with the inmates working on a road crew and the man with no eyes watching them. When Bob wins a Daytime Emmy while in prison Krusty advises him, "Don't drop that thing in the shower, Bob," referencing a common prison trope (Groening, Chastain, and Simon 1992). Other typical and stereotypical images are used: inmates crammed into their cells, guards confiscating contraband, Bob making license plates, and conjugal visit trailers. Bob appears to have changed his ways and is released, and, in general, this fits some people's thoughts about reform—that inmates fool the system to get out. Lisa responds to Bob's story, making yet another commentary on the prison system, "What a beautiful story, Sideshow Bob. You are living proof that our revolving door prison system works" (Groening, Chastain, and Simon 1992). Of course, the system is a failure when Bob is returned to prison again for attempting to murder Selma. As he is being taken away he says, "I'll be back. You cannot keep the Democrats out of the White House forever and when they get in I'm back on the streets with all my criminal buddies" (Groening, Chastain, and Simon 1992). Taken together, this episode highlights problems with the prison system and views about ex-cons, as well as reinforcing the belief that Democrats are easy on crime while Republicans are not. *The Simpsons,* however, uses contrasting characters such as Lisa Simpson and Sideshow Bob to show how opposite ends of the spectrum view the failures of the system. The failure of the system is reinforced throughout the series by images of another habitual criminal, Chester "Snake" Turley (aka Snake Jailbird or Professor Jailbird), who is in and out of prison in many episodes.

Another example of the depiction of prisons on *The Simpsons* is "The Seven-Beer Snitch" (Groening and Odenkirk 2005), in which Homer is sentenced to serve time in the Montgomery Burns State Prison. This episode highlights the privatization of prisons, the inmate subculture, and the reputation of prison snitches. Homer is sent to prison for transporting litter, a law that is now being enforced to fill the for-profit institution. In prison, Homer gets a job in the kitchen where he inadvertently tells the guards that Snake is escaping, and his place as a prison snitch is established. In a parody of the perks of being a snitch, Homer gets his own cell, extra dessert, and even a plasma TV. During a visit, Homer tells Marge that he is a snitch.

MARGE: Haven't you seen what happens to people who snitch in prison movies?
HOMER: Yeah, they're on top of the world then there's a big riot scene, then I don't know. I usually doze off.
MARGE: The prison snitch is killed and that would be you. You're the prison snitch! (Groening and Odenkirk 2005)

What unfolds from that point on is straight out of a prison film. The inmates plot to get Homer through a fake escape plan. They riot, chanting "Kill the rat." Homer escapes the initial attack in a way that could only happen on *The Simpsons*—using the Segway he earned as prison snitch. The story with Homer and Marge hiding from rioting inmates in the gas chamber, while the guards take back the prison with tear gas. Additional commentary is included on cruel guards and overcrowding. In the end, this episode is a parody of both the issue of privatization and prison films (Groening and Odenkirk 2005).

For more than two decades, *The Simpsons* has provided commentary on US families, society, history, and current events. The role of crime and punishment has not been lost on the creators. They have introduced viewers to many different types of offenders and tackled several different prison-related issues; however, the show has not been overtly critical of the system. Instead, it satisfies conservative and liberal viewers to avoid alienating audience members. Doyle Greene (2008) argues that, while *The Simpsons* may have started out pushing buttons, it eventually became a product of its parent channel. One of the critical issues missing from the view of the prison system on this show is race. Although there are minority characters on *The Simpsons*, and the show is known to tackle critical issues, in general it ignores race relations and racism. "Instead of reality, *The Simpsons* depicts a utopian vision of ethnic harmony," which suggests that racism is not an important issue in our society (Cascio 2010, par. 6). *The Simpsons* is not the only cartoon to ignore the reality of race, even *South Park* seems to draw the line at this topic (Stanley 2005). Since minorities are overrepresented in the prison population, ignoring race when critiquing the prison system is a major shortcoming. Where *The Simpsons* and other shows stop, *The Boondocks* picks up.

The Boondocks

The Boondocks began as a controversial comic strip and was brought to life in an even more provocative adult cartoon in 2005. People were shocked by the use of the n-word and the in-your-face satire. Every episode of *The Boondocks* confronts the issue of race in US society. It depicts the lives of two young brothers, Huey and Riley, who are sent to live with their grandfather, Robert Freeman, in the suburbs (McGruder 2005). The brothers are in sharp contrast to one another. Huey is older and wiser—a peacekeeper, negotiator, and revolutionary. He relies on words to fight his battles. Riley, on the other hand, thinks he is street smart and tough—essentially a "wannabe gang banger" (McGruder 2005). Crime- and justice-related issues are prevalent throughout the series. It is when these two brothers get in trouble at school that the subject of prison is predominately featured.

In "A Date with the Booty Warrior" (McGruder 2010), Huey and Riley get in trouble at school for fighting. Their granddad is given the choice between expulsion and participation in the Scared Stiff program. Young Riley, playing into his gangster image, pleads with granddad, "Pick jail! Pick jail! Pick jail! Please let me go to jail!" The group of boys in the program is brought to the Willie Horton Maximum Security Prison (a cultural reference to an infamous African American prisoner) led by another main character in the show, Tom Dubois. Tom's greatest fear in life is being raped in prison. One of the first outright statements about prison and race is made by Uncle Ruckus, an African American character who is racist against his own race. He informs the group that this trip will be just like going to the zoo, "and for you Negros, this just gonna be like a trip to the future" (McGruder 2010). Between Riley begging to go to prison, presumably because that is what gangsters are supposed to do, and Uncle Ruckus's comment to the boys, Aaron McGruder, the creator of *The Boondocks,* is playing on the belief that most, if not all, young black men will eventually end up in prison.

Unlike the mostly white faces in the prison scenes in *The Simpsons,* the inmates in Willie Horton Maximum Security Prison are predominately black while the warden and guards are white. An inmate leading the Scared Stiff program tells the boys that the system is designed to keep black men in place and that they would not know anything about that. To which, the ever informed Huey replies, "The prison-industrial complex is a system situated at the intersection of government and private interests. It uses prisons as a solution to social, political, and economic problems. It includes human rights violations, the death penalty, slave labor, policing, courts, the media, political prisoners, and the elimination of dissent" (McGruder 2010). Huey's description of prison is perhaps one of the most intelligent and critical statements about the modern prison system seen in popular culture and even in the mainstream media for that matter. The scene is reminiscent of the message in many rap songs about the modern prison system. If one is not listening closely, however, the message may be lost. It passes quickly, although one more reference is made as Huey negotiates the terms for ending the prison riot that erupts. He asks the Executive Riot Committee, the group of inmates who started the riot, "What about the end of outsourcing of prison labor to private companies?" (McGruder 2010). Ultimately, these comments are overshadowed by other elements of the episode.

In the media, African American men are typically depicted as violent and aggressive (Rome 2004). In *The Boondocks* "A Date with the Booty Warrior" (2010), McGruder amps up this stereotypical image of black men. Most of the episode focuses on anal rape. It begins with an unaired scene from *To Catch a Predator* where the host is raped. Following the aforementioned discussion of the prison industrial complex, the program leader determines that every inmate in the room has been raped and has raped someone in prison. He states, "You step in here, you get raped!" It is the desire for "booty" that causes the prison riot because "booty is more important than escaping." And when Huey works with the Executive Riot Committee on their lists of demands, the only thing they really ask for is "bitches," especially "white bitches." Even when asked about ending prison labor, an inmate says, "what if we keep doing the work but they pay us in white bitches?" McGruder appears to play up the stereotype that black men are violent sex-crazed monsters who are after white women. At the end of the episode, one inmate is left talking to Huey. He reflects, "You know, I spent a lot of time you know, thinking about all the shit I could've done. I mean I wake up in the morning and I think I could've been the motherfucking President. Shit. Nigga, I wish things had've been different. I mean, I'd do anything in the motherfucking world just for things to be different." He has given in to the realization that the situation will never change, but in typical McGruder fashion, he finishes with "I guess I just gonna be raping niggas' asses for the rest of my motherfucking life." Despite its focus on rape and violence, in the end "A Date with the Booty Warrior" covers a variety of prison issues in a way that most viewers have never seen. While using overdetermined stereotypes of African American men in prison, McGruder tackles the issue of race in the imprisonment binge, problems with the system, and the effects of mass incarceration on the African American community.

The Role of Comedy in the Social Construction of Prison

The Simpsons and *The Boondocks* could not be any more different in their depiction of prison in US society. These two cartoons are not the only ones to depict prison, but others, including *South Park, Family Guy,* and *American Dad,* are more in line with *The Simpsons*'s representation. Whether in the realm of these shows or that of *The Boondocks,* each of these cartoons provides important commentary on modern society. Chris Danies (2006) believes that, in today's media landscape, this type of observation is difficult to find and these cartoons fill the niche: "The satirical nature of cartoons allows them to point out idiosyncrasies avoided or ignored by most serious social commentators. The removal of physical reality allows writers and thinkers to grapple with the most poignant subjects that demand attention in our society."

When providing this commentary, some of these primetime cartoons push the boundaries more than others. People have been critical of many of these shows. *The Simpsons* has been criticized since it first aired, with President George H. W. Bush and his wife Barbara being two of the strongest critics. Barbara Bush said it was one of the dumbest things she had ever seen and President Bush urged people to be less like the Simpsons and more like the Waltons (Waltenon 2009). While not transitioning completely into *The Waltons,* Greene (2008) argues that the creators tempered the show somewhat to appease Fox's desire to please myriad viewers. Boundaries were further pushed on *South Park* and *The Boondocks,* thereby receiving some of the harshest condemnations. Since both of these programs aired on cable, the producers had more freedom, which led to more shocking images. In a discussion of politics and the US sitcom, Greene (2008, 219) addresses the humor of *South Park:* "The humor deliberately sickens, and becomes more sickening because the rampant horror and absurdity is rooted in the fact that *South Park*'s inhuman and inhumane characters routinely do what the moral and ethical viewer would shudder to think, let alone speak out loud." The same could be said about *The Boondocks*. Like the creators of the other shows, McGruder is intentionally provocative—he wants people to talk about issues they usually ignore. In an interview, McGruder said, "I just hope to expand the dialogue and hope the show will challenge people to think about things they wouldn't normally think about, or think about it in a very different way" (Robinson 2005). Perhaps it is this kind of attention that is needed to bring light to the issue of imprisonment in the United States; however, McGruder's attempts may be the most alienating of them all. "A Date with the Booty Warrior" offers important insight into the prison industrial complex, the disproportionate effect on the black community, and the issue of violence within the institution, but its focus on anal rape may further feed stereotypes and put some people off.

Comedy plays an important role in US culture. According to Greene (2008, 210), "The myth of satire and comedy is that it is inherently subversive, oppositional, or anti-establishment." Regardless of the venue of these comedic representations of prison, many are simply meant to use everyday material to entertain (See Box 9.2). On *Seinfeld* ("The Little Jerry" 1997), viewers laugh when George Costanza sets out to have conjugal visit sex, only to discover that there is something better when his inmate girlfriend escapes from prison—fugitive sex. There is nothing inherently challenging about this representation of prison. This type of imagery, however, can influence the way people think about the issue of imprisonment. Most of these depictions play on common stereotypes, thereby further reinforcing them.

Laughing at Prison Rape

An element of prison life that one can count on being referenced in parodies of prison life is anal rape. The issue of prison rape is a serious one, yet it has become perhaps the most recognizable prison trope in

---

Box 9.2 Comedic Representations of Prison

Laughing at prison life is not exclusive to adult cartoons. Comedy sketch shows, such as *Saturday Night Live* (Michaels 1975) and *Mad TV* (Gaines, Bahr, and Small 1995), have turned to prison to offer entertaining material. It has also been a subject for standup comedians like George Carlin and Chris Rock. Chris Rock (1996) even uses material from HBO's *Prisoners of the War on Drugs* (1992) in one of his stand-up routines. Real-life situational comedies also poke fun at prison life. The iconic sitcom *Seinfeld* ended with all of the main characters being sentenced to prison and Jerry doing stand-up in the cafeteria ("The Finale, Part 2" 1998). In the third season of *My Name is Earl,* the main character is sentenced to prison (Garcia 2007). And in *Trailer Park Boys* (Clattenburg 2001), a Canadian sitcom popular with many US viewers, the main characters begin nearly every season getting out of prison, only to be returned by the end. Hollywood has also parodied life behind bars with *Stir Crazy* (1980), *Let's Go to Prison* (2006), *Big Stan* (2007), and even *The Longest Yard* (1974, 2005). While not as common as police parodies, spoofs of prison films also garner laughs. Comedy of all types seems to find humor from potentially one of the darkest places in US society.

popular culture. "Don't drop the soap" conjures up the image of groups of male prisoners showering, the soap slowly falling out of the hand of one of the inmates, and a look of panic and horror appearing on his face as he awaits his fate. One does not even need to spell it out; simple visuals and suggestions are all that are needed. For example, the movie poster for *Let's Go to Prison* (2006) is a bar of soap on a shower floor. References to dropping the soap can be found in anything from music (e.g., Stan Ridgway's 1998 song "Don't Drop the Soap [For Anyone Else but Me]" and Bob and Tom's 2000 song "Prisoner of Love") to children's cartoons (e.g., *The Looney Tunes* and *SpongeBob Squarepants*).

While most adult cartoons depict prison, most on network television do not directly bring up prison rape; rather, it is alluded to. For example, in *The Simpsons,* Krusty advises the imprisoned Sideshow Bob to not drop his Emmy. *The Boondocks,* on the other hand, addresses prison rape head on in two episodes, both of which address Tom's crippling fear of being raped in prison. The opening scene of "A Date with the Health Inspector" (McGruder and Barnes 2005) is a steamy shower filled with naked men and in the midst of this group is Tom. Viewers watch as the soap slips out of his hand and in slow motion falls onto the floor. The look of fright on Tom's face is undeniable. He awakes in a sweat with his wife asking, "You dropped the soap, again?" In a series of flashbacks, viewers learn that Tom saw a violent prison film as a child, which scared him so much that it caused him to lead a straight-laced life. In a self-fulfilling prophecy of sorts, Tom is accused of a crime and sent to jail. When he calls the Freemans for help, Riley advises him, "Don't drop the soap." In "A Date with the Booty Warrior," viewers learn that Tom dreams of being a defense attorney so he can save "people from anal rape instead of sending them to it." During the prison riot, Tom tries to escape the prisoner who is after his booty and finds himself in the shower. The inmate finds him and, while throwing bars of soap at him, tells him not to drop the soap. Luckily for Tom, his attacker slips on a bar of soap, which saves Tom from his greatest fear in life. This show may use humor, but it is a very different take from that seen in other comedic representations of rape in prison. Just like every other controversial issue addressed on *The Boondocks,* shocking images are utilized to get a reaction from the viewers.

The pop culture references to prison rape are endless. From games available for download to smartphones and a board game called Don't Drop the Soap, to comic strips, posters, and tee shirts, the references are endless. Even 7UP based a commercial on this old adage: "Captive

Audience" (2002) depicts a delivery guy passing out cans of soda to prisoners and, when he drops one, he refuses to bend over and pick it up. This particular reference, however, was considered too controversial and the company pulled the ad, thereby suggesting that occasionally people think the joke goes too far. This begs the question—why does this serious aspect of prison life garner so many laughs? Perhaps it is because of the retributive roots of some people's beliefs and misconceptions of who is incarcerated in this country. The frame of other that is commonly used in the depiction of offenders allows people to distance themselves from the horror of the event: if prison is filled with murderers and rapists, why should anyone care if they are harming one another? This exact point is brought up by John Oliver on his show *Last Week Tonight,* which presents a satirical look at the news:

> It is so easy not to care about prisoners, perhaps because by definition they are convicted criminals. It is so easy not to care that we are really comfortable making jokes about the most horrifying things that can potentially happen to them. . . . We are somehow collectively able to laugh at references to the fact that four percent of prisoners reported being sexually victimized in the past year. (Oliver 2014)

He then reverts back to his satirical nature and uses two dozen donuts to show how many prisoners that would be and to mock the audience for caring more about donuts than people. Occasionally, prison rape humor is used to bring awareness to the situation. However, more often than not, no matter how shocking the don't drop the soap trope may be, it provides a wealth of comedic material. And obviously, there is an audience for this type of humor.

Conclusion

Music and comedy are used by people to convey emotions and social issues, and even to relive specific events. People connect to both by the way they make them feel. Songs and comedies teach their audiences something about the world they live in, including lessons about prison. On the one hand, songs by artists such as Cash almost romanticize life in the big house while also conveying the pain of incarcerated men. Rap music, on the other hand, criticizes an unjust system while providing detailed accounts about life behind bars.

Comedy provides its own lessons on prison life. Popular comedies such as *The Simpsons* show prison as a part of any society while at times providing subtle critiques of, or jabs at, the system. In the end, however, the show does not make it appear as if there is anything truly wrong with the system. Viewers can envision inmates making license plates, earning privileges for snitching, and plotting their escapes. The much less mainstream show *The Boondocks* overexaggerates the stereotypes to push people's buttons. Like rap music, it presents a much darker side and offers a critique of the injustice underlying the use of imprisonment in the United States. In the end, neither music nor comedy will teach people all about prison, but, when they are listening to a song or watching a show, elements from these will become integrated into their larger perception of these social institutions.

10

Popular Culture's Legacy

BAD GUYS WILL ALWAYS MAKE GOOD ENTERTAINMENT, AND prisoners have become a large part of the amusement. Today, prison images are readily available, allowing more people than ever before to become "experts" on prison life despite never setting foot in one of these institutions. Some unique imagery is available but, given the nature of the environment of a closed institution bound by walls and fences, overlap in the way prisons are depicted is inevitable. By examining films, television programming, and other aspects of popular culture in this book, I have unlocked the meanings underlying these representations of prison life, thereby allowing for a comprehension of how people come to understand prison in a media culture. People have the option to tune into available imagery to further their understanding of this complex social institution. What they learn is particularly important because, despite recent decreases in the prison population, we are still a prison nation and remain the world's leader in incarcerating our citizens.

Instead of turning citizens into penal experts, in many ways popular prison imagery continues to rot their perceptions of this social institution. Since prison films gave the masses their first true look at the secrets of life behind the impenetrable walls of the big house in the 1930s, significant changes have taken place to the use of imprisonment in the United States and the depiction of prisons. We went from incarcerating less than 130,000 to imprisoning more than 1.5 million people (Carson and Golinelli 2013; Lynch 2007). In the early part of the twentieth century, other than an occasional newsreel, prison films were the only choice for those curious about prison life. But today there are other options. The fantasy of the big house era provided in those early films has not been forgotten: it is recycled in some modern images of imprisonment. Many films and dramatic television programming continue to rely on tales of inmate heroes, cruel guards, and fighting for justice. These are nostalgic representations that create an emotional tie to the past. Similar connections to bygone years of the US prison system are also commonly found in popular culture, including prison songs by Johnny Cash and others, wine and beer bottles, and prison tours, restaurants, and hotels. Using easily recognizable images, these sources offer a link to the past that was decades before the imprisonment binge. If this type of imagery is the sole basis of the social construction of prison, people can remain at a safe distance from the problem of living in a prison nation. It leaves them with an understanding of some standard elements of serving hard time, but these prison fantasies do not dissect issues created by mass imprisonment.

Nostalgia is only a part of the pop culture equation. Another aspect is spectacle, and nothing describes modern popular prison imagery more appropriately. Whereas punishment itself used to be a public spectacle, imagery has taken the place of what people used to witness firsthand and thereby offers a mediated experience rather than a personal one.

Modern Prison Imagery

While prison images were available throughout much of the twentieth century, the seeds planted in the latter part of the century created the perfect setting for more imagery to emerge. People's appetite for crime-related TV programming of all sorts became insatiable in the 1990s. It is within this context that representations of prison life became more popular and sensationalistic than ever. The media landscape of the new millennium is filled with a variety of media depictions of prison life. Television and streaming devices (the contemporary stand-in for TV) have become the primary storytellers, providing a wealth of imagery depicting what takes place inside prison gates. It is an important form of communication that is accessible to all and easy to devour (Dant 2012). Viewers are spectators who gaze at imagery that stimulates their minds and emotions (Dant 2012). The stories are repeated time and again cultivating a specific view of the world (Morgan, Shanahan, and Signorielli 2008). In terms of crime and justice, viewers are continually fed images and messages that reinforce specific beliefs about the prevalence of crime and the most effective ways to deal with the problem. Luckily, in this vast media scene, there are alternatives.

Modern prison imagery can be placed on a continuum (see Figure 10.1). This placement is dictated by storytelling techniques, frames, and messages. Most of the representations fall into the category of mainstream imagery, which has the ability to support, if not invoke, punitive attitudes. On the other end of the spectrum are the alternative images that lean toward a more humanistic view. In some instances, they borrow elements from one another yet manage to maintain their original view of prison life.

Mainstream Imagery Showing Spectacle and Punitiveness

A large portion of the prison representations throughout this book can be classified as mainstream imagery. It is easily accessible, popular, and uses messages commonly employed in other crime-related media. As viewers observe the inner workings of the US prison system presented in this imagery, many of the stories invoke fear and disgust instead of empathy and concern. They lull viewers into believing that incarceration is the best and perhaps only option, instead of questioning the issues that surround a prison nation. Whether fictional or nonfictional representations, prison is commonly depicted as a battleground, in which predatory inmates manipulate and fight one another to survive. The inmates are the performers in the spectacle that is prison, and their behavior is such that the audience cannot look away as they are simultaneously shocked, entertained, and satisfied by what unfolds before their eyes.

Figure 10.1 Continuum of Modern Prison Imagery

Punitive		**Humanizing**
Oz	*Lockup Extended Stay*	*Louisiana Lockdown*
Lockup	*Hard Time*	*The Farm*
Inside		*Breaking Down the Bars*
Prisoners of the War on Drugs		*Orange Is the New Black*

Most of the televised imagery of prison, both dramatic and documentary, provides a commodified message of imprisonment in the United States while generally downplaying the root issues. *Oz* (Fontana 1997) planted the seeds for many of the televised images of prison in the twenty-first century. The predatory environment created by the men imprisoned in Emerald City is repeated. Although *Oz* laid the groundwork, *Lockup* (Drachkovitch 2005a) became the blueprint. While unlocking the gates and presenting the reality of prison life, the producers of this series created a format that would be employed by many to follow. Documentary series, such as *Lockup* and *Hard Time* (2009; 2011), strayed from the more critical lens taken by early documentarians. The popular cable shows present avid viewers with a constant spectacle of scary inmates, convicted of violent crimes, fighting one another in the brutal battleground of maximum security. It becomes clear that the prison administration and the correctional officers must focus on controlling this unruly population and be prepared for anything; thus, providing enough tension and potential plot twists to entertain.

Many of the basic procedures employed in prisons across the country are represented, but this information is background. It provides the set for the drama to unfold. The representation of the "actors" is another story. Viewers are inundated with a one-dimensional representation of people behind bars. The inmates become defined by their crimes, which are typically violent, and their out-of-control institutional behavior. The underlying message is that prisoners are different from most viewers. Using the frame of other establishes a safe distance between the law-abiding good viewer and the predatory evil inmate, making it easier to justify the methods used. Depicting inmates in such a way provides moral amnesty for the viewers, allowing them to enjoy the images that unfold before their eyes.

Occasionally, these documentary series (particularly the extended ones) borrow from alternative imagery by delving further into the lives of some prisoners, thereby providing context and presumably a deeper understanding of these individuals. Such series demonstrate that these are not simply bad people—the story is much more complicated. It would be easy to hate inmates such as Angel featured in *Lockup Extended Stay: San Quentin* but, once he tells his story, viewers can perhaps at least begin to see him as what he is—a human, not an animal. *Louisiana Lockdown* goes a step further, which makes it more closely resemble alternative prison imagery. The series looks into the lives of the staff as well prisoners, ultimately demonstrating that people on both sides of the bars have commonalities, and that even one different decision could have landed them on the other side of the cell door.

Many of the televised dramas take a slightly different approach. Similar to film representations, their focus is on the protagonist. But there are many other violent and animalistic inmates in the cellblock who demonstrate that the undeserving inmate is the exception, not the rule. In the end, even when context is provided and the camera allows viewers to see a different side of inmates, the more popular representation takes precedence. It is the repetitive lessons provided by this imagery that form the basis for people's specific beliefs (Morgan, Shanahan, and Signorielli 2008).

Fictional representations offer sensationalistic riots and attacks as well as seemingly impossible escapes, but nonfictional imagery also relies on some of these same events to entertain. It continues the spectacle with CCTV footage of inmates brawling, wounded inmates, out-of-control prisoners being dragged to SHU or pounding on the door and shouting from their cells in solitary, and even an inmate who paints his cell with a combination of feces and mustard (e.g., *Lockup* 2005a). *Hard Time* (2009) features a manhunt for escaped prisoners. Occasionally, regular day-to-day interactions are seen, especially in the extended series, which offers a better depiction of what is happening behind bars. When this aspect of prison life is highlighted, the point is made that you never know what is going to happen in prison. The tension is built by informing the viewer that this is an unpredictable environment, and things can change in an instant. While this is certainly the case, it is the excitement of a volatile, chaotic, and brutal world that brings many viewers back week after week.

Much of this imagery continues to infuse crime control rhetoric into US culture. Crime-based television programming in particular has been known for sending the message that crime is an individual responsibility, so criminals must pay for the damage they have done. The criminal justice system based on incapacitation and deterrence is presented as a highly effective tool in dealing with the crime problem. In nearly every episode of typical crime dramas, justice is achieved by arresting, convicting, or sometimes killing the suspect. It is then assumed that the criminal is sent up the river to do his time. Even before the birth of prison television shows, the message was clear—incarceration is the appropriate solution. The images presented in dramas, documentaries, and some of the films that I examined, reassure viewers that massive imprisonment in the United States is the right choice.

Alternative Imagery that Is
Humanizing and Shows Reform

Michelle Brown (2009) writes that people choose how they wish to experience prison. If they want to see battles behind bars, the choices are endless. Not every viewer, however, wants to partake in that type of spectacle. Alternative representations of prison life are becoming more readily available. Even HBO switched from shocking viewers with *Prisoners of the War on Drugs* (1992) to showing more humanizing documentaries such as *University of Sing Sing* (2011).

Alternative prison imagery has its own set of messages about the modern penal system. In its own way, this imagery adds to the crime control message by providing viewers with additional images of maximum security and people incarcerated for violent offenses, but another version of reality is also presented. If one looks at independently produced documentaries, the series *Breaking Down the Bars* (Drachkovitch 2011) and *Louisiana Lockdown* (Dugger 2012) as well as *Rectify* (McKinnon 2013) and *Orange Is the New Black* (Kohan 2013), the spectacle is most often replaced with comprehensive stories about the people incarcerated in the United States. Depending on the viewer this imagery may invoke empathy and compassion, and perhaps engage them enough so they want to learn more and even try to invoke change. At the least, the sometimes morally ambiguous images do not afford viewers the same moral amnesty that mainstream imagery does.

Alternative prison imagery presents more of the backstory. Viewers learn about addiction, abuse, health issues, family life, and other risk factors in the lives of those incarcerated in this country. For example, documentaries about women who kill their abusers provide a deep understanding as to how these women end up serving extremely long prison terms. Those that focus on inmates who participate in unique correctional programming do the same. The women in *What I Want My Words to Do to You* (2003) unveil an incredible amount of information about themselves in the stories they write for Eve Ensler's writing program. Even with an emphasis on those incarcerated for violent offenses, inmates are not defined by the crime that landed them in prison.

The brutal environment depicted in the other programs is replaced with a quieter, and at times reflective, one by focusing on programming. While fictionalized, *Orange Is the New Black* and *Rectify* show the complexity of punishment, prison life, and relationships with those in and out of prison. Overall, the crime control message is much less prevalent in all of these alternative images; thus, they have the potential to leave viewers questioning a lock them up and throw away the key policy. In general, providing details about offenders and their crimes dampens viewers' level of punitiveness (Johnstone 2000).

None of the imagery goes as far as saying incarceration is not needed; rather it demonstrates that there must be a better way than to let inmates rot away in cells. The viewers watching this type of programming may be receptive to considering other options. Fixing the system is also at the core of some of these alternative images. Recent documentaries are reminiscent of the early ones, presenting a more critical look at the issue. Films such as *Solitary Nation* (2014) and *Prison State* (2014) address current issues that many states are dealing with due to the imprisonment binge. They highlight the crisis at hand, with the help of those working in the prison system.

In the end, alternative imagery is also a representation—the stories are told from a specific perspective. There is an attempt to tug at viewers' heartstrings to evoke the emotional response needed to get people to question the issue at hand. It is a different type of emotional manipulation than that used in *Oz* and cable documentary series that rely on fear and otherness. When the featured inmates share their stories of abuse, addiction, incarcerated parents, and poverty, emotional responses by many viewers are inevitable. Documentaries on abused women and mothers behind bars are masters at generating intense emotional reactions.

While the mainstream images tend to focus on prisoners continuing their violent ways behind bars, the alternative images demonstrate that transformations are possible. Even violent offenders such as Tiger in *Louisiana Lockdown,* Stretch in *Bad Boys of Summer,* and Herman Wallace in *Herman's House* are very different men from who they were when they committed their crimes. After getting to know Tiger, viewers may be happy for him when he is finally reunited with his son after so many years. Or they may be surprised at the reflective man Herman became. This is not to say that every featured inmate in alternative imagery is transformed. For example, several scenes in *What I Want My Words to Do to You* feature Pamela Smart. Her attitude fluctuates from lighthearted to whiny and pessimistic. Viewers can see that she has not yet gone through the transformation that many long-term inmates and lifers go through. She struggles to take responsibility for her part in the crime that left her husband dead. In *Rectify,* sympathy for Daniel Holden is evoked by the emotional journey he takes reentering society after two decades on death row. However, they are left sickened at the end of the first season by the thought that perhaps he is not innocent of the crime after he attacks his step-brother. There is also the manipulative and violent Vee in the second season of *Orange Is the New Black,* who demonstrates that some people will never change. Adding these stories to the mix demonstrates humanity, which is far from perfect. It also allows viewers to relate to what they see and perhaps become emotionally connected.

Overall, modern prison imagery presents either the visual spectacle of predatory inmates, which invokes anger and fear, or a well-orchestrated play on viewers' empathetic side. Of course, to some extent both are true; the reality being a combination, with a lot of that in-between added to the mix. There are violent inmates and prison violence and there are well-adjusted inmates participating in unique treatment programs. There are transformations and there are failures. Popular imagery skips the middle, which may be too ordinary to invoke the desired response. *Breaking Down the Bars* is an example of what happens when the more mundane and typical aspects of imprisonment are highlighted: it is featured on a channel with low ratings and cancelled after one season (Stelter 2011).

Prison Imagery and Attitudes Toward Punishment

The two types of prison imagery send varying messages about the prison system (see Table 10.1). During the imprisonment binge, the more common mainstream imagery had all the essential elements to support punitive penal policies. Imprisonment as an effective crime-fighting tool is justified by presenting violent inmates in maximum security prisons, who are distinctly different from the audience. Thus, one might conclude that this type of prison imagery contributed to punitive attitudes; however, get-tough beliefs were held decades before the barrage of modern prison images. Popular prison imagery cannot be seen as the cause of punitiveness in the United States. What role then do these images play? Katherine Beckett's concept of elite manipulation can help answer this question.

Beckett (1997) argues that, beginning in the 1960s, political elites used representations of crime and justice to manipulate the public into believing that crime was a critical social issue and punitive policies were the answer. People were receptive to the message because it fit well with core beliefs about individualism, which suggests that individuals must be held accountable for their own actions. Most media images of offenders highlight individual responsibility rather than the role of societal factors.

Table 10.1 Comparing Modern Prison Imagery

Mainstream Images	Alternative Images
Prisons are a social necessity.	Prisons have a place in society, but critical flaws need to be fixed.
Prisons are an effective method for dealing with the crime problem.	Prisons are not the most effective way to deal with the crime problem.
Incapacitation and deterrence should be the main goals of the system.	Incapacitation and deterrence should not be the main goals of the system.
Rehabilitation or reformation is not possible.	Rehabilitation or reformation is possible.
Prisoners are defined by their crimes, which are typically violent.	Prisoners are defined by life circumstances, even when they committed violent crimes.
Prisoners are distinctly different from viewers, with a clear line between us and them.	Prisoners are not very different from viewers; they have many commonalities.
Viewers are shocked, which can result in disgust and fear.	Viewers may be shocked, but empathy and concern may be evoked.

In terms of nonfiction representations of crime, this is partially due to the media's use of government sources as primary claimsmakers, who in turn dictate the conversation (Beckett 1997). For years the mainstream media had been passing along the message of fear and crime control, thus helping to establish a certain level of punitiveness needed for the imprisonment binge to begin. Prison imagery beginning in the late 1990s continued that tradition, especially with its focus on violent inmates. These modern images do not directly cause punitive attitudes since they are passing along messages that have been prominent for almost a half-century. Some of the public was already manipulated into believing that prison is the only solution. Then, the media gave the public what they wanted—to witness punishment and learn about the inner workings of the prison system. The spectacle of prison life provided by mainstream imagery reinforced the need for punitive crime fighting policies. Only recently have we seen a change in the underlying messages with alternative imagery becoming more readily available.

According to the conditional media effects model, people choose the images they consume and react to them based on their experiences. The images they select typically reflect preexisting beliefs, thereby reinforcing their opinions (Perse 2001). Given that a large portion of US society has held punitive attitudes toward offenders for quite a while, it is not surprising that the mainstream images have become commodified in the way they have and that they have enjoyed the level of popularity reached in the twenty-first century. Popular imagery reflects the status quo. Those who do not hold the same beliefs potentially can be swayed by the messages they continually receive. The cumulative effect of crime control rhetoric can influence perceptions of prison. When the same messages and content are repeated, the way that the media frame the issue is adopted after people have seen it again and again (Perse 2001). "The public reacts to crime with fear and panic, because they have been led to believe by the media and public officials that thousands of vicious, intractable street criminals menace innocent citizens" (Austin and Irwin 2012, 21). There seems to be no escaping this imagery; thus, it is not surprising that many have not been willing to question the overabundant use of incarceration. People assume it to be the answer to the crime problem because that is what they have been told time and time again.

Of course, this reaction is also dependent on the viewers; one should not expect imagery to impact everyone uniformly. Reception theory argues that viewers' reactions are shaped by their own experiences. For example, it has been found that whites who watch reality-based police shows have significantly higher confidence in the police than African Americans (Eschholz et al. 2002). This finding can be applied to the prison imagery discussed earlier. Seeing the prison system in the way that it is depicted in much of the mainstream imagery may produce confidence in the system for some viewers. White viewers would probably be more likely to have this response while African Americans would have a different perspective on the issue. Some African Americans have seen the effects of incarceration firsthand in their communities or perhaps in their own families; thus, their knowledge base may negate the overt messaging contained within prison imagery. Rather than contributing to punitive attitudes, it may in fact induce further feelings of injustice.

We must not forget that social construction is based on both symbolic and firsthand knowledge. Those who have experience with the system are less likely to rely on the mediated experiences provided by prison imagery (Pickett et al. 2014). Those who have involvement with the prison system—as an employee, an inmate, a prisoner's family member, or even as a victim of crime—may form their own opinions about punishment based on their personal experiences. Even if they turn to prison imagery, what they experience firsthand likely overrides media-based messages.

Representing the Reality of US Prisons

In general, people are not very knowledgeable about punishment (Pickett et al. 2014), and some will turn to the media to become more informed. Research has demonstrated that those who watch a lot of television see more violence, which contributes to distorted ideas about the prevalence of crime as well as other misconceptions about its causes and the system of justice (Gerbner et al. 1979, 1980; Shanahan and Morgan 1999; Holbert, Shah, and Kwak 2004; Holbrook and Hill 2005; Goidel, Freeman, and Procopio 2006). Not surprisingly then, it has also been found that people who rely on the mass media are less knowledgeable about punishment (Pickett et al. 2014). The accuracy of the provided information is a large piece of the puzzle. If spectacle and emotional manipulation are a big part of the equation, how knowledgeable can one actually become when consuming these sensationalistic representations?

Even when viewers watch for entertainment purposes, there is at least some expectation that what they see is a reflection of what prisons are truly like. Although to draw people into the movie theater or get them to turn their televisions to a specific channel, creative licensing must be employed. Negative imagery and emotional manipulation are used to make the prison environment more entertaining. However, when turning to the reality-based imagery of documentaries, viewers are confident in the realism presented. After all, these are images taken in real institutions, featuring the actual people who are incarcerated within. This nonfiction imagery is not actuality, it is a representation. The prison world is reflected through a fun house mirror of sorts since it is impossible to transfer the physical world to a visual image. There is always a certain amount of distortion.

Reality is a social construction; thus, it is open to interpretation. "Something of 'reality' is always lost, and something is always added by the intervention of human action" (Dant 2012, 1). Even when a person tours a functioning correctional institution, the reality of the prison is altered by the event itself. The prison administrator determines what areas the guests will see, the guide infuses the experience with his or her own tales, and the inmates react to the presence of a group of outsiders.

In terms of the depictions discussed throughout this book, viewers may see visual representations of reality, but there are many intervening factors. The storytelling techniques required for films and TV dramas obviously mean that the greatest reshaping of reality occurs within this fictional realm. Documentaries may provide viewers with real images filmed within actual correctional institutions, but these too are representations. In an interview on NPR's *Fresh Air,* Piper Kerman describes what prison was really like in a discussion of the series based on her memoir, *Orange Is the New Black,*

> The thing that is really striking about every prison I've ever set foot in is just the incredible drabness of the physical landscape. So prisons are generally built out of cinder block, they are painted grey or beige and it's just all hard surfaces; linoleum floors, and so, one of things that's so striking is that it is cacophonously loud in prisons everywhere. Sound is just always bouncing off of metal, off of concrete, off of linoleum. (NPR 2013a)

It is not possible to replicate this exact environment in any sort of imagery. Sitting in the comfort of home diminishes sensory responses to being in a prison. From the smells to the unfiltered sounds, the true nature of the institution itself is lost in translation. Several factors affect the ability to truly represent prison, including the environment, editing, and framing as well as the people who provide access and information.

Filming in an Unpredictable Environment

Filming and editing are a part of the process involved in bringing prison images to the masses. It is a part of the equation that viewers may not consider. With all of the technological advances made in filmmaking over the years, it is easier and much less expensive to make documentaries. It is also obvious that prison administrators seem to be a little more willing to allow film crews into their prisons. Filmmakers, however, are still constrained by the environment in which they are filming. The end product is first shaped by what they are able to capture on film. A cameraman is limited by where the camera is situated. "The angle from which he does shoot is limited to angles from which, he cannot shoot, and so a bias" (Goffman 1974, 451). Even with the advances in filming technology, there is a limit to what the camera is able to capture. The presence of the crew itself is a disruption to the mundane day-to-day life of inmates. Any change can cause agitation, excitement, and curiosity. Some inmates become disturbed by the cameras while others act out to get their fifteen minutes of fame. Featured inmates may be better behaved while being filmed. They may appear to make significant progress only to regress once the cameras are turned off, similar to a person on a reality dieting show gaining weight back once the show is over. Ultimately, the filming process changes the actions of the people involved (Doyle 2004).

The prison environment is an unpredictable one that prison administrators and staff attempt to control. Numerous challenges for the film crew exist, which typically do not make the final cut. The producers of *Lockup* have given viewers some insight into these issues. When watching *Lockup* viewers might conclude that the crew films without hindrance, but *Lockup Raw* opens viewers' eyes to some of the challenges. For example, "Never a Dull Moment" (2010) features a segment on the crew's experience filming in the administrative segregation at Limon Correctional Institution in Colorado. Several inmates act out over the course of a couple of days in protest of the crew interviewing a sex offender. Urine is thrown and cells are flooded. The warden steps in and prohibits the crew from filming in the unit. A week later, he permits them to go back and they do so without incident. It is likely that events such as this occur when the camera crew enters any correctional institution. Any change in the routine becomes a disruption to the environment, causing inmates to act out in various ways. Another less sensational example is found in *Vanguard*'s "Prison Power Play" (Yamaguchi 2007), which takes viewers inside California's Corcoran Prison. Correspondent Laura Ling investigates the role of gangs and race in this crowded maximum security prison. As the scenes unfold, viewers also witness how filming is affected by the environment. They see that Ling and the crew are escorted by a public information officer and other staff. Ling is told to move away from an inmate that she is interviewing because they feel that she will be in danger sitting close to him. Several inmates refuse to give consent for on-camera interviews. And while the prison administrators allow the cameras into the SHU, it is only when the cellblock is empty. Ultimately, the decisions made by the prison administration, unbeknown to the viewers, have a hand in determining the images captured on film. I discuss this influence below.

Editing and Media Frames

The technology of today allows filmmakers to capture endless hours of material that is then edited to create the final product. An unknown amount of footage is cast aside in this creative process. If it does not fit the story being shaped, it is not needed. For example, for every sixty minutes of footage captured in the field for *Cops,* one minute makes it to the final cut (Doyle 2004). It is in this process that framing becomes critical. A frame determines what topics will be covered and how, and those that are used are shaped by the media organization itself as well as previously used frames, history, and ideology (Tuchman 1978). "The view through a window depends on whether the window is large or small, has many panes or a few, whether the glass is opaque or clear" and the scenery that the window faces (Tuchman 1978, 1). Frames affect the nature of the coverage, determining "what will be discussed, how it will be discussed, and above all, how it will not be discussed" (Altheide 1997, 651). Thus, frames dictate the outline of the story and the same ones are used again and again in popular media images of prison.

The window through which people view prison is small, with the shades drawn on the darkest parts of the system. Mainstream prison images rely on two main frames—violence and otherness. A lot of alternative imagery uses these frames as well, but they are not the primary ones through which the issue is displayed. Many times these are violent inmates, who are "different" from the majority, but transformation is a key to the stories crafted. One might say the window that these images are seen through is rose colored, given the uniqueness of the programming and the at times optimistic outlook presented. In the end, however, the desired frames are affected by the ability to capture the images. Fictional representations have a freedom of sorts to tell the stories they want. However, to craft nonfictional stories, the creators must rely on gatekeepers and claimsmakers.

Gatekeepers and Claimsmakers

Prison administrators and public information officers are the gatekeepers to this closed world. Even when prison films were first being made, wardens were consulted; thereby, the films represented their views so they were the primary claimsmakers. Today, wardens' control over media access is a major factor in the ability to represent reality; they can literally refuse to open the gates. It also means that some of the most pressing issues may not be the focus because it all depends on how an issue affects the agency. Ultimately, the reality-based imagery of prison is no different from other reality-based programming. It is a result of collaboration between the media and the agency. There is an agreement that, in exchange for access, the producers essentially "cannot or will not exercise independent and cultural judgment" of the agency (Cavender and Fishman 1998, 11).

The relationship between the agency and creators is perhaps best seen in media coverage of supermax housing units. As discussed earlier, many prison administrators have held their cards close to their chests by limiting media access. In the prison images I have described throughout this book, there are many references to these housing units. SHU is a term that avid consumers of this imagery undoubtedly know. They witness countless inmates in these units, many of them angry, yelling at the cameras, and pounding on the doors. What is largely absent from the conversation, however, is the effects of this practice, its inner workings, and the controversy over its use. Some of the documentaries that I examined in this book delve further into the issue, but they have more limited viewership compared to others. They must also rely on prison administrators to help tell the story. *Herman's House* is a good example, with the entire documentary relying on phone calls and letters. The artist highlighted attempts to bring the reality to the forefront by building Herman's cell. Seeing a mock cell in an art exhibit, however, is vastly different from being in an actual solitary cell for four decades. In July 2013 solitary confinement began to garner media attention, but not because prison administrators opened up about the practice. It instead was because nearly 30,000 inmates in the California prison system started a two-month hunger strike to protest the policies and conditions of administrative segregation. This event was deemed newsworthy and made headlines nationwide, including in the *New York Times* (Medina 2013) and *Rolling Stone* (Devereaux 2013). These articles are typical of news media coverage—episodic stories about an extraordinary event. The ability to delve further into the issue remains hindered by accessibility. It is only when the prison administration gives full access, such as in *Solitary Nation* (2014) where the filmmakers were allowed to be embedded in the supermax unit, that a more comprehensive story is told.

Accessibility, filming, framing, and to some extent appeasing gatekeepers and claimsmakers severely affect the ability to truly represent the problems at hand. Instead of being entertained by tales of maximum security battlegrounds, attention needs to be paid to the core issues facing a prison nation, such as the imprisonment binge itself and racial disparities. Some episodic news stories touch on these topics. When included in other representations, the issues are covered at a surface level and in a fairly benign manner, thereby never truly getting to the real problem. The mainstream media representations are not likely to focus exclusively on the imprisonment binge; perhaps, it is more the purview of a televised news magazine and alternative imagery. There is nothing particularly exciting or even emotional about the imprisonment binge itself. Racial disparities, however, would seem to be a topic that could garner interest through sensationalism and emotional manipulation.

Representing Race and Ethnicity in Modern Prison Imagery

Race and ethnicity are ingrained in modern prison imagery. Inmates are a diverse group and recent films, television programming, and other sources have been better at articulating the racial and ethnic makeup of the prison population. Viewers witness a diverse prison environment, one that is divided along racial lines. The underlying message is that, in order to survive, you stick to your own kind. This divide is a reflection of reality, although it is commonly used within these stories to provide the requisite tension, excitement, and emotional manipulation.

There are countless examples of racial segregation throughout the history of the US prison system. Some are imposed by the administration while others are dictated by the inmate social system. For example, in California, inmates are placed in a cell with someone of their own race; the goal of this segregated housing is to prevent gang violence (Trulson et al. 2008). Racial division is also highlighted in *Vanguard*'s "Prison Power Play" (Yamaguchi 2007) after a white inmate discusses the need to self-segregate and to stick up for one's own kind. And of course, there is Morello's advice to Piper in *Orange Is the New Black* to pretend that it is the 1950s. Again and again, viewers see a world in which race becomes a dividing factor. In reality, it is not as simple as this imagery might suggest. Kerman even discusses the complexity of the racial divide in prison. She found, during her time in prison, that there was both separation and integration. For example, all of the women who supported her as a new inmate were white, but, once she was involved in programming and other aspects of prison life, the racial divide was less prominent (NPR 2013a). The story is much more complicated than even Kerman suggests. Racial division is one thing; racial disparity is quite another.

In the United States, 63 percent of the general population is white (US Census Bureau 2013), but 60 percent of those incarcerated are African American or Hispanic (Carson and Sabol 2012). Most modern imagery fails to address the overrepresentation of minorities in the prison system. The plight of African American inmates is depicted in only a subset of the imagery I discuss throughout this book. Other racial and ethnic groups are a part of the larger picture, but in general their stories are not represented in modern depictions of prison life.

The overrepresentation of African Americans in prison is typically conveyed in music, films, and television programs created by African American artists to highlight the disparities in the system and the effect on their communities. Most of the references refer to the male prison experience since African American men have the highest incarceration rate in the country. Rap music in particular equates the modern prison system with slavery. The problem with conveying the information in this manner is that many mainstream people do not listen to this type of music. Violent gangsters who love the lifestyle are the rap music image that receives the most attention. While there are some songs that glorify crime and even prison, there are other messages contained in the music. As discussed, hip-hop in general emerged out of the need to convey the reality of what was going on in African American communities. The issue of racial disparities is also highlighted in African American–made films and *The Boondocks;* however, these images rely on stereotypes to examine the world of African American prisoners. The media inundates viewers with images of menacing African American men and masculine out-of-control women; thus, it is interesting that these stereotypes are used in an effort to push people's buttons and to bring the issue to light. One documentary that leaves stereotypes behind and attempts to delve into the causes of the problem is an episode of *Lisa Ling's Our America* titled "Incarceration Generation" (Ling 2011). Lisa Ling shares the story of African American men who have been to prison. Instead of focusing on prison life as many cable documentaries do, she explores why these men end up in an endless cycle of incarceration. She follows them from the institution to their homes. There are frank discussions with these men and their families about the factors contributing to their numerous incarcerations and the imprisonment of other men in their families. This is the type of inquiry that is greatly needed, but is unlikely to reach the masses.

Orange Is the New Black is generating much discussion about race and imprisonment. It has the potential to address the issue of disparity, although some comment that it only scratches the surface. "The show certainly reflects the disproportionate rates at which black and brown women are incarcerated in the U.S., but it doesn't go far enough in exploring this reality, especially in proportion to the entirely white staff of the facility" (Diaz 2013, par. 6). The story centers on a protagonist who is white, middle class, Ivy League educated, and makes artisanal soaps for Barney's, which is far from the typical woman in prison. According to Jenji Kohan, the show's creator, this character is her Trojan horse (NPR 2013b). Recognizing the reality of US entertainment, highlighting Piper was the way to sell the series, which then serves as the nexus for the depiction of the other women's stories. Although perhaps not the perfect way to tell the story, some recognize this show's ability to bring not only race, but also gender and sexuality, to the forefront of the conversation (e.g., Diaz 2013). Perhaps the most important impact of this show is that people are talking about the issue of race in prison.

Bingeing on Imprisonment and Prison Imagery

In our culture, many come to understand prison through the mediated experiences provide by media imagery and pop culture references. Of course, people in the United States have a reputation for enjoying things in excess; overindulging is a part of the culture. The country is simultaneously bingeing on imprisonment- and crime-related media, yet there are small indications of change on the horizon.

The imprisonment binge continues, despite the fact that there have been some decreases to the prison population. Between 2011 and 2012, the number of adults in state and federal prisons decreased by less than 1.5 percent (Glaze and Heberman 2013, 3). In comparison to the annual increases that occurred until 2009, these changes are miniscule. At this rate, we may never have a true handle on the problem. The recent changes are due to two factors—budgetary constraints and federal intervention. Several states, including Texas, Florida, and New York, have shut down prisons to decrease correctional budgets. Most of the diminishing prison population, however, can be attributed to the court-mandated changes in California's inmate population (Carson and Sabol 2012). Other states overburdened by their prisons have begun the conversations needed to decrease their populations as well. This effort is echoed in the federal government. In 2014, the US Sentencing Commission amended the sentencing guidelines for drug offenses. If passed by Congress, approximately 50,000 prisoners will be eligible to apply for sentence reductions (Markon and Weiner 2014). Next, the commission will examine sentences for economic crimes and address concerns over mandatory sentences (US Sentencing Commission 2014). The effects of the imprisonment binge will be felt for a long time, but these changes suggest that out of necessity we are starting to change the way we look at imprisonment in the United States. Since necessity is the mother of invention, there is hope that positive changes will come out of the current situation.

Interest in gazing into the incarcerated world also continues. People can binge on fictional and nonfictional representations of prison life as well as other pop culture depictions. From prison films to televised dramas and documentary series, interested viewers can be endlessly entertained by tales of maximum security prison life. Images of prison gangs, violence, tattoos, contraband, cell searches, and the SHU present a modern-day spectacle of punishment. Similar to the way that the news media depict prisons, these images have become commodified. The imagery has been "reduced to certain presumably crowd-pleasing categories that serve as easily digestible substitutes for uncomfortable realities and soothing anesthetics for fears of social dislocation" (Sussman 2002, 273).

Despite showing the same things over and over, people cannot seem to get enough. Shows like *Lockup* continue to be popular. The producers may have turned their cameras onto jails instead of prisons, but to many viewers these institutions are one and the same. Tales of uncontrolled inmates continue even when featuring county jails, fitting well with existing prison imagery. Between reruns and streaming videos, people can watch these images multiple times. These days, it stands to reason that as long as there is demand, prison images will only become more readily available. Even though the president of MSBNC, Phil Griffin, commented that he is going to decrease the amount of *Lockup* programming on his station because he feels the shows "undercut the network's brand identity" (Dana 2013), profit may win out in the end. Rachel Maddow commented that the shows make so much money "that it is like having an ATM in the lobby that you don't need a card for" (Dana 2013). So far, Maddow has been correct. In 2014, nearly every weekend of MSNBC programming included marathons of *Lockup* episodes, and the eighteenth season of the show made its debut in September of that year. The issue remains—most of this type imagery demonstrates that the current policies are necessary to ensure public safety. In sending this message, the toll that mass imprisonment is taking on specific communities and on the nation as a whole is ignored. Any large-scale efforts toward decarceration are thwarted, in part, by this popular imagery.

Alternative prison imagery is more supportive of changes to the prison population. Media trends suggest that viewers may have more access to this type of imagery in the future. Changes in technology ensure that independent productions will continue to be created. Cameras and editing software are more easily accessible. Fund-raising websites like Kickstarter allow creators to seek funding for these projects. Videos can be uploaded onto the Internet and reach a large audience. Social media also plays a role. *Herman's House* (2013), *Mothers of Bedford* (2011), and other documentaries have Facebook pages, as do organizations such as Solitary Watch. The numbers of fans pale in comparison to that of *Lockup,* yet it is a way to connect with people who are interested. Finally, websites such as YouTube and Vimeo allow for twenty-four-hour access to prison imagery. The videos placed on these sites tend to be clips and full episodes of popular cable television programs about prison life. But on occasion, one is able to locate an independently produced documentary, such as *Cruel and Unusual: Transgender Women in Prison* (2006) and *Six Seconds of Freedom* (2008). Regardless of the exact source, the Internet itself ensures that people will never again be in the dark about prison life.

The good news is that it really does not take much to begin to understand the issues at hand. On the satirical late night news show *Last Week Tonight,* John Oliver gave a monologue on prisons. In seventeen minutes, viewers are able to learn more about prison issues than watching an entire season of a prison documentary series. He covers the number of prisoners, the increases in the prison population since 1970, the reasons for this binge, the racial disparities, the conditions of prisons, and the issue of privatizing corrections. The song that he sings with a group of puppets at the end sums it up:

> It's a fact that needs to be spoken, America's prisons are broken. It's a hard truth about incarceration, prisons are needed for civilization, but mandatory minimums for heroin and crack stack the system against Hispanics and Blacks. Our prison system is bigger than Slovenia, because we put people in jail instead of treating schizophrenia. . . . Prison conditions are a national disgrace, with violence and maggots and possibly rape. . . . America's broken system is brought to you by—decades of neglect, lack of political courage, and a generous donation by the Geo group [a private prison corporation] and generous viewers like you. (Oliver 2014)

While using comedy to lighten the mood, Oliver sums up the current state of imprisonment in the United States. Viewers will not walk away completely informed, but they will have a better idea of what is currently taking place.

Perhaps nothing demonstrates the changes to prison imagery more than *Orange Is the New Black*. This show was the most-watched original series on Netflix in 2013 (Law 2014). John Oliver (2014) applauded *Sesame Street* for talking about incarceration while the rest of us were content ignoring the issue. *Orange Is the New Black* has done just that—sparked conversations that were not taking place before the series made its debut. Some of the conversations are simply about the show itself, but many others center on prison issues. Sparking much of the talk is Kerman, whose experiences are fictionalized in the series. She has been speaking across the country about the issues facing incarcerated women. According to Victoria Law (2014), *"Orange Is the New Black*—and Kerman's determined attempt to link the peoples' interest in the fictional story to real women's suffering—has helped get Americans talking about prison in a way few pieces of pop culture have" (par. 5). The show itself has opened doors for Kerman to spread her word. In 2014, she was invited to testify at a Senate Judiciary subcommittee that was holding hearings on solitary confinement, which had ignored the issue with regard to female prisoners at its prior hearings in 2012 (Law 2014). While the show itself will not reform the prison system, the conversation has begun.

Why has *Orange Is the New Black* had this type of impact? Communication research suggests that to induce a change in perceptions, emotionally charged personal stories (as opposed to cold hard statistics and facts) are the most effective (Heath 2009; Zillman 2006). Even though *Orange Is the New Black* is a fictionalized account of a women's prison, the personal stories of the characters combined with those of the creator have perhaps sparked a change in the way viewers are thinking about the use of prison.

There is no doubt that people can and will continue to learn about prison from popular representations, and that the spectacle will endure. The key is to find more ways to create representations that engage people. Sensationalistic imagery is not likely to involve viewers in the way that is needed to induce change. It is not enough to just inform; the general public must relate to the problems and be sparked to challenge the conventions of punishment in US society. Given how these depictions fit with countless other representations of crime and justice, this is probably too much to ask. The cumulative message is ingrained in the minds of generations of people in this country. The combination of a prison nation and a media culture has resulted in the infusion of prison into the very fabric of US society and popular culture. It is a system that comes with tremendous costs and, obviously, profit as well. In the meantime, the next generation can learn from *Sesame Street* that "incarceration is when someone breaks the law, a grown up rule, and they have to go to prison" ("Little Children, Big Challenges: Incarceration" 2013).

Bibliography

ABC News. "Inside a Maximum Security Women's Prison." November 4, 2004. http://abcnews.go.com/Primetime/story?id=227295&page=1#.UZEwt1E -pNg (accessed May 13, 2013).

Afro-American Work Songs in a Texas Prison. Directed by Bruce Jackson. Beacon, NY: Folklore Research Films, 1966.

Against Their Will: Women in Prison. Directed by Karen Arthur. Woodland Hills, CA: Allumination FilmWorks, 1994.

Akon. "Locked Up." *Trouble.* Composed by Akon. Santa Monica, CA: Univeral Records, 2004.

"Alaska's Toughest Prison." *Inside.* Atlanta: Court TV Productions, August 10, 2007.

Alcatraz: America's Toughest Prison. Directed by Paul Krasny. Orland Park, IL: MPI Home Video, 1977.

Alcatraz: Island of Hate. Directed by Pat Mitchell. San Francisco: Asteron Productions, 1971.

Alcatraz: Living Hell. Washington, DC: National Geographic Society, 2007.

Alcatraz Reunion. Directed by John Paget. Buffalo, NY: Paget Films, 2008.

"A Lot to Be Angry About." *Breaking Down the Bars.* Studio City, CA: January 5, 2012.

Altheide, David L. "The News Media, the Problem Frame, and the Production of Fear." *Sociological Quarterly* 38, no. 1 (1997): 647–668.

American History X. Directed by Tony Kaye. New York: New Line Cinema, 1998.

American Me. Directed by Edward James Olmos. Universal City, CA: Universal Pictures, 1992.

Anderson, Carolyn, and Thomas W. Benson. *Documentary Dilemmas: Frederick Wiseman's* "Titcut Follies." Carbondale: Southern Illinois University Press, 1991.

Anderson-Minshall, Diane. "Why You Should Watch *Orange Is the New Black:* Did Netflix Just Create the Greatest Lesbian TV Series Ever?" *The Advocate,* July 10, 2013. www.advocate.com/print-issue/current-issue/2013/07

/10/why-you-should-watch-orange-new-black?page=full (accessed July 15, 2013).

"Angels in Chains." *Charlie's Angels.* Directed by Phil Bandell. 20th Century Fox, 1976.

Animal. Directed by David J. Burke. Pasadena, CA: Animal Film LLC, 2005.

Animal Factory. Directed by Steve Buscemi. Los Angeles: Franchise Pictures, 2000.

"An Offender Mentality." *Breaking Down the Bars.* Studio City, CA: 44 Blue Productions, November 24, 2011.

Arax, Mark. "8 Prison Guards Are Acquitted in Cororan Battles." *Los Angeles Times,* June 10, 2000. http://articles.latimes.com/2000/jun/10/news/mn -39555 (accessed January 10, 2013).

Ards, Angela. "Organizing the Hip-Hop Generation." In *That's the Joint! The Hip-Hop Reader,* edited by Murray Forman and Mark Anthony Neal, 311–323. New York: Routledge, 2004.

A Sentence for Two. Directed by Randi Jacobs. Brooklyn, NY: Fanlight Productions, 2008.

Associated Press. "Court TV Adds Reality Shows." *Today,* April 6, 2005. www.today.com/id/7339936#.UYPQUIE-pNg (accessed May 3, 2013).

At Night I Fly: Images from New Folsom Prison. Directed by Wenzer Michel. Sweden: Story AB, 2011.

Attica. Directed by Cinda Finestone. Humacao, Puerto Rico: Shell Castle Film Company, 1974.

Attica: The Bars that Bind Us. Directed by Teresa Miller. Buffalo, NY: forthcoming.

Austin, James, and John Irwin. *It's About Time: America's Imprisonment Binge.* Belmont, CA: Wadsworth, 2012.

Babies Behind Bars. Directed by Amanda Richardson. Hollywood, CA: Firecracker Films, 2011.

"Back on the Streets." *Hard Time.* Washington, DC: National Geographic Television, March 8, 2011.

"Bad Boys, Bad Boys." *Lockup Extended Stay: San Quentin.* Studio City, CA: 44 Blue Productions, September 28, 2007.

Bad Boys of Summer. Directed by Loren Mendell and Tiller Russell. Hollywood: Angry Young Ranch, 2007.

Bad Girls. Created by Maureen Chadwick and Ann McManus. London: Shed Productions, 1999.

Bark, Ed. "Drama, Politics, and Gang Warfare Behind Bars." *New York Times,* October 6, 2007. www.nytimes.com/2007/10/06/arts/06bark.html?_r=0 (accessed May 21, 2013).

Bazelon, Emily. "The Shame of Solitary Confinement." *New York Times,* February 19, 2015. www.nytimes.com/2015/02/19/magazine/the-shame-of -solitary-confinement.html (accessed May 11, 2015).

Beck, Allen J., Ramona R. Rantala, and Jessica Rexroat. *Sexual Victimization Reported by Adult Correctional Authorities, 2009–2011.* Washington, DC: Bureau of Justice Statistics, US Department of Justice, 2014.

Beckett, Katherine. *Making Crime Pay: Law and Order in Contemporary American Politics.* New York: Oxford University Press, 1997.

Behind Prison Gates. Directed by Charles Barton. Culver City, CA: Columbia Pictures, 1939.

Berger, Peter L., and Thomas Luckman. *The Social Construction of Reality.* New York: Anchor Books, 1967.

Better Off Dead. Directed by Neema Barnette. Los Angeles: Viacom Productions, 1993.

"Beyond the Bars." *Breaking Down the Bars.* Studio City, CA: 44 Blue Productions, January 19, 2012.

The Big Bird Cage. Directed by Jack Hill. Atlanta: New World Pictures. 1972.

The Big Doll House. Directed by Jack Hill. Atlanta: New World Pictures, 1971.

The Big House. Directed by George Hill. Los Angeles: Metro-Goldwyn-Mayer, 1930.

Big House Wine Company. "Big House Wine Company." n.d. www.bighouse wines.com/about/ (accessed June 9, 2013).

Big Stan. Directed by Rob Schneider. New Orleans: Big Stan Productions, 2007.

Bikini Chain Gang. Directed by Fred Olen Ray. New York: Showtime Networks, 2005.

Bingham, Josh, Brad Bishop, and Tom Forman. *Cell Block 6: Female Lockup.* Los Angeles: Discovery Studios, 2010.

Birdman of Alcatraz. Directed by John Frankenheimer. Beverly Hills, CA: United Artists Studio, 1962.

Blue Sky Project. *Criminal Injustice: Death and Politics at Attica.* n.d. http://bspfilms.org/films-criminal-injustice-death-and-politics-at-attica.php (accessed July 18, 2014).

Bob and Tom. "Prisoner of Love." *The Bob and Tom Show Greatest Hits, Volume 1.* Las Vegas: DC Ventures, 2000.

Body Count. "Dead Man Walking." *Violent Demise: The Last Days.* Composed by Ice-T. Hollywood, CA: Virgin Records, 1997.

"Bora Bora Bora." *Orange Is the New Black.* North Vancouver, BC: Lionsgate Television, July 11, 2013.

Born Innocent. Directed by David Wrye. Los Angeles: Tomorrow Entertainment, 1974.

Bouclin, Suzanne. "Women in Prison Movies as Feminist Jurisprudence." *Canadian Journal of Women and the Law* 21, no. 1 (2009): 19–34.

Brandt, Spike, Tony Cervone, Matt Danner, and Chris Headrick. "Jailbird, Jailbunny." *The Looney Toons Show.* Burbank, CA: Warner Bros. Animination, May 17, 2011.

Breitbart News. "MSNBC: Best Demo Night in Two Weeks is 'Lockup' Marathon." September 29, 2014. www.breitbart.com/big-journalism/2014 /90/29/msnbc-ratings-collapse-lockup (accessed May 11, 2015).

Brewers Association. "Craft Continues to Brew Growth." March 18, 2013. www.brewersassociation.org/pages/media/press-releases/show?title =brewers-association-craft-continues-to-brew-growth (accessed June 10, 2013).

Britton, Dana. *At Work in the Iron Cage: The Prison as a Gendered Organization.* New York: NYU Press, 2003.

Brockhoff, Michael, and Angie Brown. *Women on Death Row*. Long Beach, CA: Burrud Productions, 2006.

Brokedown Palace. Directed by Jonathan Kaplan. Los Angeles: Fox 2000 Pictures, 1999.

Brown, Angela, Alissa Camber, and Suzanne Agha. "Prisons Within Prisons: The Use of Segregation in the U.S." *Federal Sentencing Reporter* 24, no. 1 (2011): 46–49.

Brown, Michelle. *The Culture of Punishment: Prison, Society, and Spectacle*. New York: NYU Press, 2009.

Brubaker. Directed by Stuart Rosenberg. Los Angeles: 20th Century Fox, 1980.

Brute Force. Directed by Jules Dassin. Universal City, CA: Universal Pictures, 1947.

Burrud, John, and Richard Swindell. *Women Behind Bars*. Directed by Richard Swindell. Long Beach, CA: Burrud Productions, 2008.

Caged. Directed by John Cromwell. Hollywood, CA: Warner Brothers Pictures, 1950.

Caged Fury. Directed by Bill Milling. Los Angeles: 21st Century Film Corporation, 1989.

Caged Heat. Directed by Jonathan Demme. Atlanta: New World Pictures, 1974.

Caldwell, Maggie, and Josh Harkinson. "50 Days Without Food: The California Prison Strike Explained." *Motherjones*, August 27, 2013. www.mother jones.com/politics/2013/08/50-days-california-prisons-hunger-strike -explained (accessed May 11, 2015).

California Department of Corrections and Rehabilitation. *Public Safety Realignment*. December 19, 2013. www.cdcr.ca.gov/realignment/docs /realignment-fact-sheet.pdf (accessed May 11, 2015).

"Captive Audience." New York: Y&R Ad Agency, 2002.

Carson, E. Ann. *Prisoners in 2013*. Washington, DC: Bureau of Justice Statistics, US Department of Justice, 2014.

Carson, E. Ann, and Daniela Golinelli. *Prisoners in 2012: Trends in Admissions and Releases, 1991–2012*. Washington, DC: Bureau of Justice Statistics, US Department of Justice, 2013.

Carson, E. Ann, and William J. Sabol. *Prisoners in 2011*. Washington, DC: Bureau of Justice Statistics, US Department of Justice, December 2012. www.bjs.gov/content/pub/pdf/p11.pdf (accessed July 19, 2013).

Cascio, Ted. "*The Simpsons* and Psychology: What's Wrong with *The Simpsons*." *Psychology Today,* December 10, 2010. www.psychologytoday.com /blog/hollywood-phd/201012/the-simpsons-psychology (accessed June 6, 2013).

Cash, Johnny. "Folsom Prison Blues." Memphis: Sun Studio Records, 1955.

———. *At Folsom Prison*. Washington, DC: Columbia Records, 1968a.

———. "Cocaine Blues." *At Folsom Prison*. Composed by T. J. Arnall. Washington, DC: Columbia Records, 1968b.

———. "Green, Green Grass of Home." *At Folsom Prison*. Composed by Curly Putman. Washington, DC: Columbia Records, 1968c.

———. "Greystone Chapel." *At Folsom Prison*. Composed by Glen Sherley. Washington, DC: Columbia Records, 1968d.

————. "Send a Picture of Mother." *At Folsom Prison.* Composed by Johnny Cash. Wasington, DC: Columbia Records, 1968e.

————. "The Wall." *At Folsom Prison.* Composed by Harlan Howard. Washington, DC: Columbia Records, 1968f.

————. *At San Quentin.* Washington, DC: Columbia Records, 1969.

————. "The Walls of a Prison." *The Walls of a Prison.* Composed by Johnny Cash. Washington, DC: Harmony Records, 1970.

Cash, Johnny, and Charlie Williams. "I Got Stripes." Composed by Charlie Williams. *Heart of Cash.* Washington, DC: Columbia Records, 1968.

Caster, Peter. *Prisons, Race, and Masculinity in Twentieth-Century U.S. Literature and Film.* Columbus: Ohio State University Press, 2008.

————. "'I Learned Prison Is a Bad Place to Be': 25th Hour and Reimagining Incarceration." In *Homer Simpson Marches on Washington: Dissent Through American Popular Culture,* edited by Timothy Dale and Joseph Foy, 111–124. Lexington: University of Kentucky Press, 2010.

Cavender, Gray. "'*Scared Straight*': Ideology and the Media." *Journal of Criminal Justice* 9 no. 6 (1981): 431–439.

Cavender, Gray, and Mark Fishman. "Televised Reality Crime Programs: Context and History." In *Entertaining Crime,* edited by Gray Cavender and Mark Fishman, 3–15. New York: Aldine de Gruyter, 1998.

Cecil, Dawn K. "Looking Beyond *Caged Heat:* Media Images of Women in Prison." *Feminist Criminology* 2, no. 4 (2007): 304–326.

————. "Televised Images of Jail: Lessons in Controlling the Unruly." In *Popular Culture, Crime, and Social Control (Sociology of Crime, Law and Deviance),* edited by Mathieu Deflem, 67–88. Bingley, England: Emerald Group, 2010.

Cecil, Dawn K., and Jennifer L. Leitner. "Unlocking the Gates: An Examination of *MSNBC Investigates Lockup.*" *Howard Journal of Criminal Justice* 48, no. 2 (2009): 184–199.

Chained Heat. Directed by Paul Nicholas. Park City, UT: Jensen Farely Productions, 1983.

Cheatwood, Derral. "Prison Movies: Films About Adult, Male, Civilian Prisons: 1929–1955." In *Popular Culture, Crime, and Justice,* edited by Frankie Bailey and Donna Hale, 209–231. Belmont, CA: Wadsworth, 1998.

Chermak, Steven M. "Police, Courts, and Corrections in the Media." In *Popular Culture, Crime, and Justice,* edited by Frankie Bailey and Donna Hale, 87–99. Belmont, CA: Wadsworth, 1998.

Chesney-Lind, Meda, and Katherine Irwin. *Beyond Bad Girls: Gender, Violence, and Hype.* New York: Routledge, 2008.

The Children of Alcatraz. Directed by Tom Castellano and Scott Cornfield. Silicon Valley, CA: Independent Productions. 2003.

Chu, Betty. "Bites: Louisiana Lockdown." Animal Planet, June 5, 2012. http://blogs.discovery.com/bites-animal-planet/louisiana-lockdown/ (accessed September 15, 2012).

Cirigliano, Jim. *Civil Brand.* Directed by Neema Barnette. Los Angeles: Mandaly Sports Entertainment, 2002.

Clark, Anna. "Jail Bait: Rethinking Images of Incarcerated Women." *Bitch,* Winter 2005.

Clattenburg, Mike. *Trailer Park Boys*. Toronto, ON: Showcase Television, 2001.

Clowers, Marsha. "Dykes, Gangs, and Danger: Debunking Popular Myths of Maximum-Security Life." *Journal of Criminal Justice and Popular Culture* 9, no. 1 (2001): 22–30.

Cohen, Andrew. "Creating Monsters: How Solitary Confinement Hurts the Rest of Us." *The Atlantic,* April 18, 2014.

Cold War Kids. "St. John." *Robbers & Cowards*. New York: Downtown Records, 2006.

Con Air. Directed by Simon West. Burbank, CA: Touchstone Pictures, 1997.

Concrete and Sunshine. Directed by Nicole Cousino. Lanham, MD: National Film Network, 2002.

The Concrete Jungle. Directed by Tom DeSimone. London: Ideal Films, 1982.

Concrete, Steel and Paint. Directed by Cindy Burstein and Tony Heriza. Blooming Grove, NY: New Day Films, 2009.

Condemned Women. Directed by Lew Landers. Los Angeles: RKO Pictures, 1938.

Conducting Hope. Directed by Margie Friedman. Westport, CT: Westport Productions, 2013.

"The Conjugal Visit." *Lockup Extended Stay: San Quentin*. Studio City, CA: 44 Blue Productions, September 21, 2007.

Conrad, Randall, and Stephen Ujlaki. *Three Thousand Years and Life*. Directed by Stephen Ujlaki. South Walpole, MA: National Prisoners Reform Association, 1973.

Convict Air. Produced by John Scheer and Rob Englehardt. Silver Spring, MD: Discovery Channel, 2003.

Convicted Woman. Directed by Nick Grinde. Culver City, CA: Columbia Pictures, 1940.

Convicts. "Penitentiary Blues." *Convicts*. Composed by 3-2 and Big Mike. Hollywood, CA: Virgin Records, 1991.

Cool Hand Luke. Directed by Stuart Rosenberg. Hollywood, CA: Warner Brothers Pictures, 1967.

Conviction. Directed by Kevin Rodney Sullivan. Los Angeles: Paramount Television, 2002.

Corrections. Directed by Ashley Hunt. New York: Third World Newsreel, 2001.

Covington, Stephanie, and Barbara Bloom. "Gendered Justice: Women in the Criminal Justice System." In *Gendered Justice: Addressing Female Offenders,* edited by Barbara Bloom. Durham, NC: Carolina Academic Press, 2003.

Cox, Stephen. *The Big House: Image and Reality of the American Prison*. New Haven, CT: Yale University Press, 2009.

Crime After Crime. Directed by Yoav Potash. Berkeley, CA: Life Sentence Films, 2011.

The Criminal Code. Directed by Howard Hawks. Culver City, CA: Columbia Pictures, 1931.

Criminal Injustice: Death and Politics at Attica. Directed by David Marshall. New York: Filmakers Library, 2012.

Cruel and Unusual: Transgender Women in Prison. Directed by Janet Baus, Dan Hunt, and Reid Williams. New York: Outcast Films, 2006.

Curry, Jack. "MSNBC's *Lockup:* Documentary or Reality TV?" *Washington Post,* July 8, 2011.

Dana, Rebecca. "Slyer than Fox: The Wild Inside Story of How MSNBC Became the Voice of the Left." *New Republic,* March 25, 2013. www.newrepublic.com/article/112733/roger-ailes-msnbc-how-phil-griffin -created-lefts-fox-news# (accessed August 16, 2013).

Danesi, Marcel. *Popular Culture: Introductory Perspectives.* Plymouth, UK: Rowman & Littlefield, 2012.

Dangerous Minds. Directed by John Smith. Burbank, CA: Hollywood Pictures, 1995.

Danies, Chris. "Cartoons Provide Much-Needed Social Commentary." *Daily Sundial,* February 3, 2006. http://sundial.csun.edu/2006/02/cartoons providemuchneededsocialcommentary/ (accessed June 5, 2013).

Dant, Tim. *Television and the Moral Imaginary: Society Through the Small Screen.* New York: Palgrave Macmillan, 2012.

Davis, Lois M., Robert Bozick, Jennifer L. Steele, Jessica Saunders, and Jeremy N. V. Miles. *Evaluating the Effectiveness of Correctional Education: A Meta-Analysis of Programs that Provide Education to Incarcerated Adults.* Santa Monica, CA: RAND, 2013.

dead prez. "Behind Enemy Lines." *let's get free.* Composed by C. Gavin, L. Alford, V. Williams, and A. Mair. Washington, DC: Columbia Records, 2000.

Death Race. Directed by Paul W. S. Anderson. Univeral City, CA: Univeral Pictures, 2008.

"Death Ride." *Louisiana Lockdown.* New York: Original Media LLC, July 13, 2012.

Defending Our Lives. Directed by Margeret Lazarus and Renner Wunderlich. Cambridge, MA: Cambridge Documentary Films, 1994.

Devereaux, Ryan. "Searching for the Truth About California's Hunger Strike." *Rolling Stone,* August 13, 2013. www.rollingstone.com/politics/news /searching-for-the-truth-about-californias-prison-hunger-strike-20130813 (accessed May 11, 2015).

Diaz, Von. "Why '*Orange Is the New Black*' Is So Addictive." *Color Lines: News for Action,* August 2, 2013. http://colorlines.com/archives/2013/08 /orange_is_the_new_black.html (accessed August 16, 2013).

Dirty Harry. Directed by Don Siegel. Hollywood: Warner Brothers Pictures, 1971.

Doing Hard Time. Directed by Preston A. Whitemore II. Culver City, CA: Destination Films, 2004.

Doing Time: Life in the Big House. Directed by Alan Raymond. Los Angeles: Docurama, 1991.

Dorfman, Lori, and Vincent Schiraldi. *Off Balance: Youth, Race, and Crime in the News.* Washington, DC: Justice Policy Institute, 2001.

Dowler, Kenneth, Thomas Fleming, and Stephen Muzzati. "Constructing Crime: Media, Crime, and Popular Culture." *Canadian Journal of Criminology* 48, no. 6 (2006): 837–850.

Doyle, Aaron. *Arresting Images: Crime and Policing in Front of the Telvision Camera*. Toronto, ON: University of Toronto Press, 2004.

Drachkovitch, Rasha. *Cell Dogs*. Studio City, CA: 44 Blue Productions, 2004.

———. *Lockup*. Studio City: CA: 44 Blue Productions, 2005a.

———. "Return to Valley State." *Lockup*. Studio City, CA: 44 Blue Productions, June 25, 2005b.

———. *Lockup Extended Stay: San Quentin*. Studio City, CA: 44 Blue Productions, 2007a.

———. "North Carolina Women's Prison." *Lockup*. Studio City, CA: 44 Blue Productions, September 14, 2007b.

———. "Tennessee Prison for Women." *Lockup*. Studio City, CA: 44 Blue Productions, January 1, 2010.

———. *Breaking Down the Bars*. Studio City, CA: 44 Blue Productions, 2011.

"Drug Bust." *Louisiana Lockdown*. New York: Original Media LLC, June 15, 2012.

Drug Policy Alliance. "Fact Sheet: Women, Prison, and the Drug War." February 2014. www.scribd.com/fullscreen/234695955?access_key=key-cU4q8 einJarhBxSodF0s&allow_share=true&escape=false&view_mode=scroll (accessed August 26, 2014).

Duffy of San Quentin. Directed by Walter Doniger. Hollywood, CA: Warner Brothers Entertainment, 1954.

Dugger, Jamie. *Louisiana Lockdown*. New York: Original Media LLC, 2012.

Dungeons of Alcatraz. Produced by Michael Hoff. Emeryville, CA: Michael Hoff Productions, 2003.

Earll, Robert. "Angels in Chains." *Charlie's Angels*. Los Angeles: Spelling-Goldberg Productions, October 20, 1976.

Eastern State: Living Behind the Walls. Directed by Tony Alosi. Orange, CA: Wayland Productions, 2008.

Eastern State Penitentiary. Directed by Christine Bowditch. Allentown, PA: Verstehen Video Project, 1998.

Editorial Board. "Gov. Cuomo's Bold Step on Prison Education." *New York Times,* February 18, 2014. www.nytimes .com/2014/02/19/opinion/gov-cuomos-bold-step-on-prison-education .html?_r=0 (accessed May 12, 2015).

Ellis, Jack C., and Betsy A. McLane. *A New History of Documentary Film*. London: Bloomsbury Academic, 2005.

Engineering Supermax. Silver Spring, MD: Discovery Communications, 2004.

"Escape!" *Louisiana Lockdown*. New York: Original Media LLC, July 6, 2012.

Escape! Breakout from Alcatraz. Directed by David M. Frank. San Francisco: Indigo Films, 2000.

Escape from Alcatraz. Directed by Don Siegel. Los Angeles: Paramount Pictures, 1979.

Escape from L.A. Directed by John Carpenter. Los Angeles: Paramount Pictures, 1996.

Escape from New York. Directed by John Carpenter. Los Angeles: AVCO Embassy Pictures, 1981.

Eschholz, Sarah, Brenda Sims Blackwell, Marc Gertz, and Ted Chiricos. "Race and Attitudes Toward Police: Assessing the Effects of Watching Reality Police Programs." *Journal of Criminal Justice* 30, no. 4 (2002): 327–341.

"Exeunt Omnes." *Oz*. Directed by Alex Zakrzewski. Balitmore, MD: Levinson/ Fontana Company, February 23, 2003.

The Farm: Life Inside Angola Prison. Directed by Liz Garbus and Wilbert Rideau. New York: Gabriel Films, 1998.

The Farm: 10 Down. Directed by Nancy Novak and Jonathan Stack. Brooklyn, NY: Highest Common Denominator Media Group, 2009.

Felon. Directed by Ric Roman Waugh. Culver City, CA: Sony Pictures, 2008.

"Female Felons." *Lockdown*. Washington, DC: National Geographic Television, June 14, 2009.

"Female Offenders." *Hardtime*. Washington, DC: National Geographic Television, February 15, 2011.

Film Reference. "African American Cinema: New Jack Cinema." n.d. www .filmreference.com/encyclopedia/Academy-Awards-Crime-Films/African -American-Cinema-NEW-JACK-CINEMA.html (accessed July 6, 2013).

"The Finale, Part 2." *Seinfeld*. Directed by Andy Ackerman. Culver City, CA: Columbia Tristar Television, May 14, 1998.

Flamm, Michael W. *Law and Order: Street Crime, Civil Unrest, and the Crisis of Liberalism in the 1960s*. New York: Columbia University Press, 2005.

Flynn, Gillian. "Prison Break." *Entertainment Weekly,* August 26, 2005.

Follow Me Down: Portraits of Louisiana Prison Musicians. Directed by Ben Harbert. New York: Films for the Humanities, 2012.

Fontana, Tom. *Oz*. Baltimore, MD: Levinson/Fontana Company, 1997.

"Fool Me Once." *Orange Is the New Black*. North Vancouver, BC: Lionsgate Television, July 11, 2013.

Fox, Harriet. "'*Orange*' Uncorked: How Did We Become the Bad Guys?" *Corrections One,* September 24, 2013. www.correctionsone.com/corrections /articles/6463916-Orange-uncorked-How-did-we-become-the-bad-guys/ (accessed July 23, 2014).

Fox, Richard L., Robert W. Van Sickel, and Thomas L. Steiger. *Tabloid Justice: Criminal Justice in an Age of Media Frenzy*. Boulder: Lynne Rienner, 2007.

Franco, Jess. "Interview with Jess Franco." *99 Women* [Director's Cut]. West Hollywood, CA: Blue Underground, Inc., 2005.

Freedom Road. Directed by Lorna Ann Johnson. New York: Women Make Movies, 2004.

Freedom Writers. Directed by Richard LaGravenese. Los Angeles: Paramount Pictures, 2007.

Freeman, Robert M. *Popular Culture and Corrections*. Lanham, MD: American Correctional Association, 2000.

From One Prison. Directed by Carol Jacobsen. Los Angeles: Baseline Pictures, 1994.

The Futon Critic. "Friday's Cable Ratings: ESPN Is Tops with NBA Playoffs." *The Futon Critic,* June 4, 2012. www.thefutoncritic.com/ratings/2012/06 /04/fridays-cable-ratings-espn-is-tops-with-nba-playoffs-398212/cable _20120601/ (accessed April 30, 2013).

Gaines, William, Fax Bahr, and Adam Small. *Mad TV*. Burbank, CA: Warner Brothers Television, 1995.

"The Gang's All Here." *Lockup Extended Stay: San Quentin.* Studio City, CA: 44 Blue Productions, September 7, 2007.

"Gangs Behind Bars." *Inside.* Atlanta: Court TV Productions, August 17, 2007.

Garcia, Greg. *My Name Is Earl.* Los Angeles: 20th Century Fox Television, 2007.

Gerbner, George, Larry Gross, Michael Morgan, and Nancy Signorielli. "The 'Mainstreaming' of America: Violence Profile No. 11." *Journal of Communication* 30, no. 3 (1980): 10–29.

Gerbner, George, Larry Gross, Michael Morgan, and Nancy Signorielli. "Growing Up On Television: The Cultivation Perspective." In *Media Effects: Advances in Theory and Research,* edited by Jennings Bryant and Dolf Zillman, 17–41. Hillsdale, NJ: Erlbaum, 1994.

Gerbner, George, Larry Gross, Nancy Signorielli, Michael Morgan, and Marilyn Jackson-Beeck. "The Demonstration of Power: Violence Profile No. 10." *Journal of Communication* 29, no. 3 (1979): 177–196.

Gergen, Kenneth J. *An Invitation to Social Constructionism.* Thousand Oaks, CA: Sage, 2009.

Getting Out. Directed by John Korty. Los Angeles: Dorothea G. Petrie Productions, 1994.

Ghosts of Attica. Directed by Brad Lichtenstein. New York: Luminere Productions, 2001.

Giddens, Anthony. *The Consequences of Modernity.* Palo Alto, CA: Stanford University Press, 1990.

Girls in Chains. Directed by Edgar G. Ulmer. Los Angeles: Atlantis Pictures, 1943.

Girls in Prison. Directed by Edward L. Cahn. Los Angeles: American International Pictures, 1956.

Girls in Prison. Directed by John McNaughton. New York: Showtime Networks, 1994.

Girls of the Big House. Directed by George Archainbaud. Los Angeles: Republic Films, 1945.

Glaze, Lauren E., and Erinn J. Heberman. *Correctional Populations in the United States, 2012.* Washington, DC: Bureau of Justice Statistics, US Department of Justice, 2013.

Glaze, Lauren E., and Laura M. Maruschak. *Parents in Prison and Their Incarcerated Children.* Washington, DC: Bureau of Justice Statistics, US Department of Justice, 2008.

Goffman, Erving. *Frame Analysis: An Essay on the Organization of Experience.* New York: Harper Colophon Books, 1974.

Goidel, Robert, Craig Freeman, and Steven Procopio. "The Impact of Television on Perceptions of Juvenile Crime." *Journal of Broadcasting and Electronic Media* 50, no. 1 (2006): 119–139.

Gonthier, David. *American Prison Films Since 1930: From* The Big House *to* The Shawshank Redemption. Lewiston, NY: Edwin Mellen Press, 2006.

Goodman, Douglas J. *Consumer Culture: A Reference Handbook.* Santa Barbara, CA: ABC-CLIO, 2003.

Goodman, Walter. "Review/Television: An Unhealthy Hospital Stars in '*Titcut Follies.*'" *New York Times,* April 6, 1993. www.nytimes.com/1993/04/06

/movies/review-television-an-unhealthy-hospital-stars-in-titicut-follies
.html?src=pm (accessed March 9, 2012).

Greene, Doyle. *Politics and the American Television Comedy: A Critical Survey from* I Love Lucy *to* South Park. Jefferson, NC: McFarland & Company, 2008.

Greenwald, Andrew. "The Great *Orange Is the New Black* Is Suddenly the Best Netflix Series Yet." *Grantland: Hollywood Prospectus,* July 15, 2013.

The Grey Area: Feminism Behind Bars. Directed by Noga Ashkenazi. Normal, IL: Musical Chairs Productions, 2012.

Groening, Matt. *The Simpsons.* Los Angeles: 20th Century Fox Television, 1989.

Groening, Matt, Thomas Chastain, and Sam Simon. "Black Widower." *The Simpsons.* Los Angeles: 20th Century Fox Television, April 9, 1992.

Groening, Matt, and Bill Odenkirk. "The Seven-Beer Snitch." *The Simpsons.* Los Angeles: 20th Century Fox Television, April 3, 2005.

Guerino, Paul, Paige M. Harrison, and William J. Sabol. *Prisoners in 2010.* Washington, DC: Bureau of Justice Statistics, US Department of Justice, 2011.

Haggard, Merle. "Branded Man." *Branded Man.* Composed by Merle Haggard. Los Angeles: Capitol Records, 1967a.

———. "I Made the Prison Band." *Branded Man.* Composed by Tommy Collins. Los Angeles: Capitol Records, 1967b.

———. "Life in Prison." *I'm a Lonesome Fugitive.* Composed by Merle Haggard. Los Angeles: Capitol Records, 1967c.

———. "Green, Green Grass of Home." *Mama Tried.* Composed by Curly Putman. Los Angeles: Capitol Records, 1968a.

———. "Mama Tried." *Mama Tried.* Composed by Merle Haggard. Los Angeles: Capitol Records, 1968b.

———. "Sing Me Back Home." *Sing Me Back Home.* Composed by Merle Haggard. Los Angeles: Capitol Records, 1968c.

———. "Will You Visit Me on Sundays?" *The Legend of Bonnie and Clyde.* Composed by Dallas Frazier. Los Angeles: Capitol Records, 1968d.

———. "Huntsville." *Someday We'll Look Back.* Composed by Merle Haggard and Red Simpson. Los Angeles: Capitol Records, 1971.

Hard Time. Directed by Gregory Henry, David Shadrock Smith, and Eric Strauss. Washington, DC: National Geopgraphic Channel, 2009.

Hard Time. Directed by Gregory Henry, Peter Hutchens, and Eric Strauss. Washington, DC: National Geographic, 2011.

Hayek, Salma, and Horta Silvio. *Ugly Betty.* Directed by Horta Silvio. Los Angeles: Silent H Productions, 2006.

Heath, Robert. "Emotional Engagement: How Television Builds Big Brands at Low Attention." *Journal of Advertising Research* 49, no. 1 (2009): 62–73.

Herman's House. Directed by Angad Bhalla. New York: First Run Features, 2013.

Higgins, Melissa, and Wednesday Kirwan. *The Night Dad Went to Jail: What to Expect When Someone You Love Goes to Jail.* Chicago: Picture Window Books, 2011.

Holbert, R. Lance, Dhavan Shah, and Nojin Kwak. "Fear, Authority, and Justice: Crime-Related TV Viewing and Endorsements of Capital Punishment and Gun Ownership." *Journalism and Mass Communication Quarterly* 81, no. 2 (2004): 343–363.

Holbrook, R. Andrew, and Timothy Hill. "Agenda-Setting and Priming in Prime Time Television: Crime Dramas as Political Cues." *Political Communication* 22, no. 3 (2005): 277–295.

Holden, Stephen. "The Nightmare Disbelief of a Prisoner Under Siege." *New York Times,* July 18, 2008. http://movies.nytimes.com/2008/07/18/movies/18felo.html?_r=2& (accessed January 10, 2013).

Hold Your Man. Directed by Sam Wood. Hollywood, CA: Metro-Goldwyn-Mayer, 1933.

"The Hustle." *Hard Time.* Washington, DC: National Geographic Television, February 1, 2011.

Ice-T. "The Tower." *O.G. Original Gangster.* Composed by Bilal Basher and Ice-T. Burbank, CA: Sire/Warner Brothers Records, 1991.

"If I Had a Daughter in Here." *Breaking Down the Bars.* Studio City, CA: 44 Blue Productions, January 12, 2012.

I Love You Phillip Morris. Directed by Glenn Ficarra and John Requa. Hollywood, CA: Consolidated Pictures Group, 2009.

"Imaginary Enemies." *Orange Is the New Black.* Directed by Michael Trim. North Vancouver, BC: Lionsgate Television, July 11, 2013.

IMDb (Internet Movie Database). "Oz User Comments." n.d. www.imdb.com/title/tt0118421/reviews?start=0 (accessed March 13, 2013).

In a Day's Time: Songs of the California Men's Colony. Directed by Ben Harbert. 2007.

"Inside Anamosa." *Lockup.* Studio City, CA: 44 Blue Productions, October 15, 2005.

"Inside a Women's Maximum Security Prison." *Primetime Live.* New York: ABC Television, November 4, 2004.

"Inside Riverbend." *Lockup.* Studio City, CA: 44 Blue Productions, June 3, 2005.

"Inside San Quentin." *Lockup.* Studio City, CA: 44 Blue Productions, January 26, 2003.

Inside the Walls of Folsom Prison. Directed by Crane Wilbur. Hollywood, CA: Warner Brothers Entertainment, 1951.

Irwin, John. *Lifers: Seeking Redemption in Prison.* New York: Routledge, 2010.

I Want to Live! Directed by Robert Wise. Beverly Hills, CA: United Artists, 1958.

"I Wasn't Ready." *Orange Is the New Black.* North Vancouver, BC: Lionsgate Television, July 11, 2013.

Iyengar, Shanto. *Is Anyone Responsible? How Television Frames Political Issues.* Chicago: University of Chicago Press, 1991.

Jackson, Bruce. *Wake Up Dead Man: Hard Labor and Southern Blues.* Athens: University of Georgia Press, 1999.

Jailbait. Directed by Brett C. Leonard. New York: Belladonna Productions, 2004.

James, Doris J., and Lauren E. Glaze. *Mental Health Problems of Prison and Jail Inmates.* Washington, DC: Bureau of Justice Statistics, US Department of Justice, 2006.

Jarvis, Brian. *Cruel and Unusual: Punishment and US Culture.* London: Pluto Press, 2004.

———. "The Violence of Images: Inside the Prison TV Drama *Oz*." In *Captured By the Media: Prison Discourse in Popular Culture,* edited by Paul Mason, 154–171. Portland, OR: Willan, 2006.

Jewkes, Yvonne. "Creating a Stir? Prisons, Popular Media and the Power to Reform." In *Captured By the Media: Prison Discourse in Popular Culture,* edited by Paul Mason, 137–153. Portland, OR: Willan, 2006.

Johnstone, Gerry. "Penal Policy Making: Elitist, Populist, or Participatory?" *Punishment and Society* 2, no. 2 (2000): 161–180.

Journalism Fund. "What Is Investigative Journalism." n.d. www.journalism fund.eu/what-investigative-journalism (accessed July 2014).

Joyella, Mark. "Sunday Ratings Reveal U.S. Is More Interested in *Lockdown* Reruns than Egypt (Sigh)." *Mediaite,* February 11, 2011. www.mediaite .com/tv/sunday-ratings-reveal-u-s-is-more-interested-in-lockdown-reruns -than-egypt-sigh/ (accessed May 19, 2011).

Kellner, Douglas. *Media Culture: Cultural Studies, Identity, and Politics Between the Modern and the Postmodern.* New York: Routledge, 1995.

Kerman, Piper. *Orange Is the New Black: My Year in a Women's Prison.* New York: Spiegel & Grau, 2010.

Kilborn, Richard, and John Izod. *Confronting Reality: An Introduction to Television Documentary.* Manchester, UK: Manchester University Press, 1997.

"Killer Road Trip." *Louisiana Lockdown.* New York: Original Media LLC, June 1, 2012.

The Killing. Directed by Veena Sud. Los Angeles: Fox Television Studios, 2013.

"Killing Time." *Lockup Extended Stay: San Quentin.* Studio City, CA: 44 Blue Productions, September 14, 2007.

King, Robert, John Tuohy, and Kyle Neddenriep. "Larretha Draughon: Former Indiana All-Star Killed in Shooting on Indianapolis' Far Westside." *Indy Star,* July 4, 2012. www.indystar.com/article/20120703/NEWS02/20703 0324/Former-Indiana-All-Star-basketball-player-Larretha-Draughon-killed -shooting-Indianapolis-Far-Westside?gcheck=1 (accessed September 22, 2012).

Kirell, Andrew. "Without Prison Docs, MSNBC's 2013 Ratings Were Even Worse." *Mediaite,* January 8, 2014. www.mediaite.com/tv/without-prison -docs-msnbcs-2013-ratings-were-even-worse (accessed May 11, 2015).

Knaggs, Angie. "*Prison Break* General Gabbery: Extra Hyperdiegetic Spaces, Power and Identity in *Prison Break*." *Television and New Media* 12, no. 5 (2011): 395–411.

Knox, Merrill. "Ratings." *Media Bistro,* October 2012. www.mediabistro.com /tvnewser/category/ratings (accessed October 21, 2012).

Kohan, Jenji. *Weeds.* North Vancouver, BC: Lionsgate Television, 2005.

———. *Orange Is the New Black.* North Vancouver, BC: Lionsgate Television, 2013.

Krczmar, Marina, and Yuliya Strizhakoa. "Uses and Gratifiction as Media Choice." In *Media Choice: A Theoretical and Empricial Overview,* edited by Tilo Hartmann, 53–69. New York: Routledge, 2009.

Kurtis, Bill. *Investigative Reports*. New York: A&E Television Networks, 1991.

Kysel, Ian M. "End Solitary Confinement for Teenagers." *New York Times*, December 16, 2014. www.nytimes.com/2014/12/17/opinion/end-solitary -confinement-for-teenagers.html (accessed May 11, 2015).

Ladies of the Big House. Directed by Marion Gering. Los Angeles: Paramount Pictures, 1932.

Ladies They Talk About. Directed by Howard Bretherton and William Keighly. Hollywood, CA: Warner Brothers Pictures, 1933.

Lady Gangster. Directed by Robert Florey. Hollywood, CA: Warner Brothers Pictures, 1942.

Lady in the Death House. Directed by Steve Sekley. Hollywood, CA: Producers Releasing Corporation, 1944.

Langan, Patrick A. "Race of Prisoners Admitted to State and Federal Institutions, 1926–86." Washington, DC: National Criminal Justice Reference Services, May 1991. www.ncjrs.gov/pdffiles1/nij/125618.pdf (accessed July 7, 2013).

The Last Days of Private Jack Hall. Directed by Edgar Barens. New York: Cinema Guild, 2013.

"Last Rites." *Burn Notice*. Directed by Nick Gimez. Los Angeles: Fox TV Studios, June 28, 2012.

La Vigne, Nancy G., Lisa E. Brooks, and Tracey, L. Shollenberger. *Women on the Outside: Understanding the Experiences of Female Prisoners Returning to Houston, Texas*. Washington, DC: Urban Institute, 2009.

Law, Victoria. "Can '*Orange Is the New Black*' Change the Way Congress Thinks About Prison?" *Bitch,* June 5, 2014. http://bitchmagazine.org/post /season-two-of-orange-is-the-new-black-real-life-prison-piper-kerman -advocacy (accessed August 18, 2014).

Let's Go to Prison. Directed by Bob Odenkirk. Universal City, CA: Universal Pictures, 2006.

Let the Doors Be of Iron. Directed by Hal Kirn. Philadelphia: Halkirn & Associates, 1987.

Life After Lockup. Studio City, CA: 44 Blue Productions, 2011.

Life at Stateville: The Wasted Years. Chicago: WBBM-TV, 1960. http://www .museum.tv/archive.htm.

Lilien, Stephen, Elizabeth Sarnoff, and Bryan Wynbrandt. *Alcatraz*. Decatur, GA: Bonanza Productions, 2012.

Ling, Lisa. "Incarceration Generation." *Lisa Ling's Our America*. New York: part2 pictures, November 20, 2011.

Lippmann, Walter. *Public Opinion*. New York: Harcourt, Brace, 1922.

Lipschultz, Jeremy H., and Michael L. Hilt. *Crime and Local Television News: Dramatic, Breaking and Live from the Scene*. New York: Routledge, 2002.

"Little Children, Big Challenges: Incarceration." *Sesame Street,* June 13, 2013. http://www.sesameworkshop.org/incarceration/ (accessed August 12, 2014).

"The Little Jerry." *Seinfeld*. Culver City, CA: Columbia TriStar Television, January 9, 1997.

Lockdown. Directed by John Luessenhop. Culver City, CA: TriStar Pictures, 2000.

Locked Down. Directed by Daniel Zirilli. Winnipeg, ON: Buffalo Gal Pictures, 2010.

Lockout. Directed by James Mather and Stephen St. Leger. Saint-Denis, France: Europacorp, 2012.

Lock Up. Directed by John Flynn. Culver City, CA: Tri-Star Pictures, 1989.

Lockup Extended Stay. Studio City, CA: 44 Blue Productions, 2007.

Lockup Raw. Studio City, CA: 44 Blue Productions, 2008.

Lockup Special Investigation: Lake County Juvenile. Studio City, CA: 44 Blue Productions, 2009.

"Lockup: Women Inside Valley State." *MSNBC Investigates.* Studio City, CA: 44 Blue Productions, November 19, 2000.

Lockup World Tour. Studio City, CA: 44 Blue Productions, 2009.

Lonely Island: Hidden Alcatraz. Directed by Rick Butler. San Francisco: KQED, 2003.

The Longest Yard. Directed by Robert Aldrich. Los Angeles: Paramount, 1974.

The Longest Yard. Directed by Peter Segal. Los Angeles: Paramount Pictures, 2005.

Ludacris. "Do Your Time." *Release Therapy.* Composed by Ludacris. Atlanta: Disturbing the Peace, 2006.

Lynch, Michael. *Big Prisons, Big Dreams: Crime and the Failure of America's Penal System.* New Brunswick, NJ: Rutgers University Press, 2007.

Lynn, Loretta. "Women's Prison." *Van Lear Rose.* Composed by Loretta Lynn. Santa Monica, CA: Interscope Records, 2004.

Mac Dre. "I've Been Down." *Rapper Gone Bad.* Composed by Mac Dre. San Francisco: Romp Records, 1999.

MacFarlane, Seth. *Family Guy.* Los Angeles: 20th Century Fox Television, 1998.

The Mannsfield 12. Directed by Craig Ross Jr. North Hollywood, CA: Asiatic Associates, 2007.

Manslaughter. Directed by Cecil B. DeMille. Los Angeles: Paramount Pictures, 1922.

Marc, David. *Comic Visions: Television Comedy and American Culture.* Malden, MA: Blackwell, 1997.

Markon, Jerry, and Rachel Weiner. "Thousands of Felons Could Have Drug Sentences Lessened." *Washington Post,* July 18, 2014. www.washington post.com/politics/thousands-of-felons-could-have-drug-sentences-less ened/2014/07/18/4876209e-0eb1-11e4-8341-b8072b1e7348_story.html (accessed May 12, 2015).

Martinson, Robert. "What Works? Questions and Answers about Prison Reform." *The Public Interest* 35 (1974): 22–54.

Mason, Paul. "The Screen Machine: Cinematic Representations of Prison." In *Criminal Visions: Media Representations of Crime and Justice,* edited by Paul Mason, 287–297. Portland, OR: Willan, 2003.

———. "Relocating Hollywood's Prison Film Discourse." In *Captured by the Media: Prison Discourse in Popular Culture,* edited by Paul Mason, 191–209. Portland, OR: Willan, 2006.

Matthews, Dylan. "'*Orange Is the New Black*' Is the Best TV Show About Prison Ever Made." *Washington Post,* July 17, 2013. www.washington post.com/blogs/wonkblog/wp/2013/07/17/orange-is-the-new-black-is-the -best-tv-show-about-prison-ever-made/ (accessed July 17, 2013).

McGruder, Aaron. *The Boondocks.* Culver City, CA: Adelaide Productions, 2005.

———. "A Date with the Booty Warrior." *The Boondocks*. Culver City, CA: Adelaide Productions, June 27, 2010.

McGruder, Aaron, and Rodney Barnes. "A Date with the Health Inspector." *The Boondocks*. Culver City, CA: Adelaide Productions, December 5, 2005.

McKinnon, Ray. *Rectify*. Beverly Hills, CA: Gran Via Productions, 2013.

Medina, Jennifer. "Hunger Strike by California Inmates Already Large, Is Expected to Be Long." *New York Times*, July 10, 2013. www.nytimes .com/2013/07/11/us/hunger-strike-by-california-inmates-already-large-is -expected-to-be-a-long-one.html?_r=0 (accessed May 11, 2015).

Men of San Quentin. Directed by William Beaudine. Hollywood, CA: Producers Releasing Corporation, 1942.

"The Merle Haggard Bio." *Merle Haggard Official Website*. 2011. http:// merlehaggard.com/bio/ (accessed June 1, 2013).

Michaels, Lorne. *Saturday Night Live*. New York: NBC Studios, 1975.

Midnight Express. Directed by Alan Parker. Culver City, CA: Columbia Pictures, 1978.

Miranda, Elyse. *The Big House*. Gettysburg, PA: Greystone Productions, 1998.

Mitchell, Gail. *Lockdown*. Washington, DC: National Geographic Television, 2007.

Monster's Ball. Directed by Marc Forster. Santa Monica, CA: Lionsgate Films, 2001.

Moore, Barbara, Marven R. Bensman, and Jim Van Dyke. *Prime-Time Television: A Concise History*. Westport, CT: Praeger, 2006.

Moreno, Alfonso H. "Caged." *NCIS*. Los Angeles: Belisarius Productions, January 6, 2009.

Morgan, Michael, James Shanahan, and Nancy Signorielli. "Growing Up with Television: Cultivation Processes." In *Media Effects: Advances in Theory and Research*, edited by Jennings Bryant and Mary Beth Oliver, 34–48. Hoboken, NJ: Taylor & Francis, 2008.

Mothers of Bedford. Directed by Jenifer McShane. Grapevine, TX: Covey Productions, 2011.

MSNBC. "MSNBC About." n.d. http://tv.msnbc.com/about/#.UHtNv1E8pas (accessed October 18, 2012).

MSNBC Investigates. New York: MSNBC Cable, LLC, 2000.

Muhammad, Bahiiyyah, and Muntaquim Muhammad. *The Prison Alphabet: An Educational Coloring Book for Children of Incarcerated Parents*. Atlanta: Goldest Karrat, 2014.

Murder in the First. Directed by Marc Rocco. Hollywood, CA: Warner Brothers Pictures, 1995.

Museum of Broadcast Communications. 2012. www.museum.tv/archive.htm (accessed August 18, 2012).

Mutiny in the Big House. Directed by William Nigh. Los Angeles: Monogram Pictures, 1939.

My Six Convicts. Directed by Hugo Fregonese. Culver City: Columbia Pictures, 1952.

Nashawaty, Chris. "Roger Corman: The B-Movie King." *Entertainment Weekly*, November 13, 2009. www.ew.com/ew/article/0,,20319462,00.html (accessed September 23, 2012).

National Geographic. *Explorer.* National Geographic Channel, 2012. http://channel.nationalgeographic.com/channel/explorer/ (accessed October 23, 2012).

National Parks Conservation Association. "Alcatraz Island: Challenges and Highlights." 2010. www.npca.org/about-us/center-for-park-research/state oftheparks/alcatraz/ALCA_Report.pdf (accessed May 11, 2015).

The Nature of the Beast. Directed by Ondi Timoner. Watertown, MA: Documentary Educational Resources, 1993.

Nellis, Mike. "British Prison Movies: The Case of 'Now Barabbas.'" *Howard Journal of Criminal Justice* 27, no. 1 (1988): 2–31.

———. "Future Punishment in American Science Fiction Films." In *Captured By the Media: Prison Discourse in Popular Culture,* edited by Paul Mason, 210–228. Portland, OR: Willan, 2006.

Nelly. "Fly Away." *Sweatsuit.* Composed by Nelly. Santa Monica, CA: Universal Music Group, 2005.

"Never a Dull Moment." *Lockup Raw.* Studio City, CA: 44 Blue Productions, March 13, 2010.

The New Asylums. Directed by Miri Navasky and Karen O'Conner. Washington, DC: PBS, 2005.

Nix, Matt. *Burn Notice.* Los Angeles: Fox TV Studios, 2012.

No More Prisons. New York: Raptivism Records, 2000.

NPR. "Behind '*The New Black*': The Real Piper's Prison Story." *Fresh Air,* August 12, 2013a.

———. "'*Orange*' Creator Jenji Kohan: 'Piper Was My Trojan Horse.'" *Fresh Air,* August 14, 2013b.

———. "Solitary Confinement: Punishment or Cruelty?" March 10, 2013c. www.npr.org/2013/03/10/173957675/solitary-confinement-punishment-or -cruelty (accessed June 26, 2013).

Numbered Men. Directed by Mervyn LeRoy. Los Angeles: First National Pictures, 1930.

N.W.A. "Fuck tha Police." Composed by Ice Cube, MC Ren, and The DOC. Los Angeles: Ruthless Records, 1988.

O'Conner, Lydia. "Locking Up Fewer People Doesn't Lead to Increased Crime, Report Says." *Huffington Post,* July 5, 2014.

Ogbar, Jeffery O. G. *Hip-Hop Revolution: The Culture and Politics of Rap.* Lawrence: University of Kansas Press, 2007.

OJJDP (Office of Juvenile Justice and Delinquency Prevention). *OJJDP News at a Glance: Justice Department Discourages Use of "Scared Straight" Programs.* Washington, DC: National Criminal Justice Reference Services, March–April 2011. www.ncjrs.gov/html/ojjdp/news_at_glance/234084/top story.html (accessed July 16, 2014).

Oliver, John. "Prison." *Last Week Tonight.* New York: HBO, July 20, 2014.

Oliver, Paul. *Blues Fell This Morning.* Cambridge: Cambridge University Press, 1990.

Olmstead, Matt, and Nick Santora. *Breakout Kings.* Los Angeles: Matt Olmstead Productions, 2011.

On the Rocks. Directed by John Rich. New York: American Broadcasting Company, 1975.

Ortiz, Erik. "'*Sesame Street*' Introduces First-Ever Muppet with a Parent in

Prison." *New York Daily News,* June 19, 2013. www.nydailynews.com /entertainment/tv-movies/sesame-street-introduces-muppet-dad-jail-article -1.1376845 (accessed June 24, 2013).

Owen, Barbara, James Wells, Jocelyn Pollock, Bernadette Muscat, and Stephanie Torres. *Gendered Violence and Safety: A Contextual Approach to Improving Safety in Women's Facilties.* Washington, DC: Department of Justice, 2008.

Parker, Trey, and Matt Stone. *South Park.* New York: Comedy Central Productions, 1997.

PBS. *Frontline: Locked Up in America.* 2014. www.pbs.org/wgbh/pages/front line/locked-up-in-america/ (accessed July 11, 2014).

Perse, Elizabeth M. *Media Effects and Society.* Mahwah, NJ: Erlbaum, 2001.

Petersilia, Joan. *When Prisoners Come Home: Parole and Prisoner Reentry.* New York: Oxford University Press, 2009.

Pickett, Justin L., Christina Mancini, Daniel P. Mears, and Marc Gertz. "Public (Mis)Understanding of Crime Policy: The Effects of Criminal Justice Experience and Media Reliance." *Criminal Justice Policy Review* (March 19, 2014): 1–23.

Pratt, John. *Penal Populism.* New York: Routledge, 2007.

Presley, Elvis. "Jail House Rock." Composed by Jerome Leiber and Mike Stoller. Hollywood: Radio Recorders, 1957.

Prison Bars. Directed by Walter Barnsdale. Los Angeles: Barnsdale Productions, 1901.

Prison Boot Camp. Silver Spring, MD: Discovery Communications, 2003.

"Prison City." *Hard Time.* Washington, DC: National Geographic Television, February 1, 2011.

"Prison Code." *Inside.* Atlanta: Court TV Productions, August 3, 2007.

Prison Diaries. Directed by Richard Swindell. Silver Spring, MD: TLC, 2011.

Prisoner: Cell Block H. Directed by Kendal Flanagan. Syndey, Australia: Grundy Television Productions, 1979.

Prisoners of the War on Drugs. Directed by Marc Levin. New York: HBO, 1992.

Prison Farm. Directed by Louis King. Los Angeles: Paramount Pictures, 1938.

"Prison Gangs." *Inside.* Atlanta: Court TV Productions, August 28, 2006.

Prison Heat. Directed by Joel Silberg. Detroit: Global Pictures, 1993.

Prison Lullabies. Directed by Odile Isralson and Lina Matta. Bedford, NY: Brown Hats Production, 2003.

Prison Medical. Directed by Craig Leake. Silver Spring, MD: Discovery Communications, 2003.

Prison Nation. Washington, DC: National Geographic Television, November 25, 2007.

Prison of Secrets. Directed by Fred Gerber. Los Angeles: Carroll Newman Productions, 1997.

Prison Song. Directed by Darnell Martin. New York: New Line Cinema, 2001.

"Prison State." *Frontline.* Directed by Dan Edge. Boston: WGBH, April 29, 2014.

Prison Stories: Women on the Inside. Directed by Donna Deitch and Joan Micklin Silver. Beverly Hills, CA: Prism Home Entertainment, 1991.

"Prison Tactical." *Inside.* Atlanta: Court TV Productions, August 31, 2007.

Prison Terminal: The Last Days of Private Jack Hall. Directed by Edgar Barens. New York: The Cinema Guild, Inc., 2013.

Prison Town, USA. Directed by Po Kutchins and Katie Galloway. Washington, DC: PBS, 2007.

Prison Valley. Directed by David Dufresne and Phillipe Brault. Strausburg, France: Arte.TV, 2010.

Prison Women. Produced by David Ross Smith. Washington, DC: National Geographic, 2011.

Profits of Punishment. Directed by Catherine Scott. Brooklyn, NY: Icarus Films, 2001.

Public Enemy. "Black Steel in a Time of Chaos." *It Takes a Nation of Millions to Hold Us Back.* Composed by Chuck D. Washington, DC: Columbia Records, 1988.

Purdy. Directed by Daniel Kopec. Tacoma: KBTC Public Television, 2010.

Raemisch, Rick. "My Night in Solitary." *New York Times*, February 20, 2014. www.nytimes.com/2014/02/21/opinion/my-night-in-solitary.html (accessed May 11, 2015).

Rafter, Nicole. "Gender, Prisons and Prison History." *Social Science History* 9, no. 3 (1985): 233–247.

———. *Shots in the Mirror: Crime Films and Society.* New York: Oxford University Press, 2006.

Raney, Arthur A. "Punishing Media Criminals and Moral Judgement: The Impact on Enjoyment." *Media Psychology* 7, no. 2 (2005): 145–163.

Raney, Arthur A., and Jennings Bryant. "Moral Judgement and Crime Drama: An Integrated Theory of Enjoyment." *Journal of Communication* 52, no. 2 (2002): 402–415.

Rapping, Elayne. *Law and Justice as Seen on TV.* New York: NYU Press, 2003.

"The Recovery Process." *Breaking Down the Bars.* Studio City, CA: 44 Blue Productions, November 3, 2011.

The Redemption Project: Inmates Got Talent. Directed by Johnny Collins. Indianapolis: Doin' Time Entertainment, 2010.

Rehm, Diane. "Judging the Credibility of News in the Digital Age." *The Diane Rehm Show,* August 19, 2014.

Reilly, Kelly. "*Sesame Street* Reaches Out to 2.7 Million Children with an Incarcerated Parent." Pew Research Center, June 21, 2013. www.pew research.org/fact-tank/2013/06/21/sesame-street-reaches-out-to-2-7 -million-american-children-with-an-incarcerated-parent/ (accessed August 11, 2014).

"Return to Corcoran." *Lockup.* Studio City, CA: 44 Blue Productions, November 26, 2005.

"Return to Pelican Bay." *Lockup.* Studio City, CA: 44 Blue Productions, November 19, 2005.

"Reviewer Comments." *Orange Is the New Black.* Netflix, July 2013. http://movies.netflix.com/WiMovie/Orange_Is_the_New_Black/70242311 ?trkid=496624 (accessed July 16, 2013).

Rideway, Stan. "Don't Drop the Soap (For Anyone Else but Me). *Pecker* (Soundtrack). Composed by Stuart Copeland, Judd Miller, and Michael Thompson. New York: RCA Victor, 1998.

Ridgeway, James. "Fortresses of Solitude; Even More Rare: Journalist Access to

Prison Isolation Units." *Columbia Journalism Review* (March/April 2013). www.cjr.org/cover_story/fortresses_of_solitude.php?page=all (accessed May 21, 2013).

Ring of Death. Directed by Bradford May. Grunwald, Denmark: Alpine Medien Productions, 2008.

Riot. Directed by Buzz Kulik. San Franscico, CA: William Castle Productions, 1969.

Riot in Cellblock 11. Directed by Don Siegel. Los Angeles: Allied Artists, 1954.

Robbins, Danny. "Johnny Cash and His Prison Reform Campaign." *BBC News Magazine,* January 22, 2013. www.bbc.co.uk/news/magazine-21084323 (accessed May 30, 2013).

Roberts, Julian V., Loretta J. Stalans, David Indermauer, and Mike Hough. *Penal Populism and Public Opinion: Lessons from Five Countries.* Oxford: Oxford University Press, 2003.

Robinson, Brian. "'The Boondocks': Not the N&#@$%a Show." *ABC News,* November 3, 2005. http://abcnews.go.com/Entertainment/story?id=1270 410#.Ua-W4lE-pNg (accessed June 5, 2013).

Rock, Chris. *Bring the Pain.* Directed by Keith Truesdell. New York: Home Box Office, Inc., 1996.

Rome, Dennis. *Black Demons: The Media's Depiction of the African American Male Stereotype.* Westport, CT: Praeger, 2004.

"The Routine." *Oz.* Directed by Darnell Martin. Baltimore, MD: Levinson/ Fontana Company, July 12, 1997.

San Quentin. Directed by Lloyd Bacon. Hollywood, CA: Warner Brothers Pictures, 1937.

San Quentin Film School. Directed by Bruce Sinofsky. New York: Radical Media, 2009.

San Quentin: Life in the Big House. Directed by Amy Smithee. Princeton, NJ: Discovery Communications, 2011.

Scared Straight. Directed by Arnold Shapiro. Toluca Lake, CA: Arnold Shapiro Productions, 1978.

Scared Straight! 10 Years Later. Directed by Arnold Shapiro. Toluca Lake, CA: Arnold Shapiro Productions, 1987.

Scared Straight! 20 Years Later. Directed by Arnold Shapiro. Toluca Lake, CA: Arnold Shapiro Productions, 1999.

Scheuring, Paul. *Prison Break.* Los Angeles: Adelstein-Parouse Productions, 2005.

Schulz, Bill. "Visiting '*Shawshank*' Sites, 20 Years Later." *New York Times,* August 7, 2014.

Scott, Van. *ABC News Announces "A Nation of Women Behind Bars," a Diane Sawyer "Hidden America" Special*, February 25, 2015. www.abcnews .go.com/blogs/headlines/2015/02/abc-news-announces-a-new-nation-of -women-behind-bars-a-diane-sawyer-hidden-america-special/ (accessed May 13, 2015).

Seidman, Robert. "Breakout Kings Scores Record Audiences for A&E." *zap2it,* March 7, 2011. http://tvbythenumbers.zap2it.com/2011/03/07/breakout -kings-premieres-to-2-8-million-scores-1-1-rating-with-adults-18-49 /84878/ (accessed March 22, 2013).

The Sentencing Project. *Fewer Prisoners, Less Crime: A Tale of Three States.* Research Brief. Washington, DC: The Sentencing Project, 2014a.

———. "Trends in U.S. Corrections." 2014b. http://sentencingproject.org/doc/publications/inc_Trends_in_Corrections_Fact_sheet.pdf (accessed August 8, 2014).

Sepinwall, Alan. *The Revolution Was Televised: The Cops, Crooks, Slingers and Slayers Who Changed TV Drama Forever.* New York: Touchstone Publications, 2012.

Serving Life. Directed by Lisa R. Cohen. New York: Austin Street Productions, 2011.

Shackles. Directed by Charles Winkler. Culver City, CA: Sony Pictures Home Entertainment, 2005.

"Shakedown in Santa Fe." *Frontline.* Austin, TX: Galan Productions, February 23, 1988.

Shakespeare Behind Bars. Directed by Hank Rogerson. Santa Fe, NM: Philomath Films, 2006.

Shanahan, James, and Michael Morgan. *Television and Its Viewers: Cultivation Theory and Research.* Cambridge: Cambridge University Press, 1999.

Shapiro, Arnold, and Paul Coyne. *Beyond Scared Straight.* New York: A&E Television, 2011.

The Shawshank Redemption. Directed by Frank Darabont. Los Angeles: Castle Rock Entertainment, 1994.

Shell Castle Film Corporation. *Attica: A Film by Cinda Finestone.* 2007. www.atticathefilm.com/index.html (accessed September 19, 2012).

Shelton, Blake. "Ol' Red." *Blake Shelton.* Composed by James Bohan, Don Goodman, and Mark Sherrill. Nashville: Warner Brothers Records, 2001.

Shipka, Danny. *Perverse Titillation: The Exploitation Cinema of Italy, Spain and France, 1960–1980.* Jefferson, NC: McFarland & Company, 2011.

Sigel, Beanie. "What Ya Life Like." *The Truth.* Composed by Beanie Sigel. New York: Roc-A-Fella Records, 1999.

———. "What Ya Life Like 2." *The Reason.* Composed by Beanie Sigel. New York: Roc-A-Fella Records, 2004.

Sin by Silence. Directed by Olivia Klaus. Los Angeles: Quiet Little Place Productions, 2010.

Six Seconds of Freedom. Directed by Jeff Smith. Pineville, NC: Oasis Films, 2008.

Slam. Directed by Marc Levin. New York: Offline Entertainment Group, 1998.

"Slammin' in the Slammer." *Lockup Extended Stay: San Quentin.* Studio City, CA: 44 Blue Productions, October 12, 2007.

Smith, Dinitia. "Prison Series Seeks to Shatter Expectations." *New York Times,* July 12, 1999. www.nytimes.com/1999/07/12/arts/prison-series-seeks-to-shatter-expectations.html (accessed May 13, 2015).

Snapped. Knoxville, TN: Jupiter Productions, 2004.

"Solitary Confinement." *Explorer.* Washington, DC: National Geographic, April 11, 2010.

"Solitary Nation." *Frontline.* Directed by Dan Edge. Boston: WGBH, April 22, 2014.

Spragens, William C. *Electronic Magazines: Soft News Programs on Network Television.* Westport, CT: Praeger, 1995.

Squires of San Quentin. Directed by J. Gary Mitchell. San Francisco: J. Gary Mitchell Films, 1978.

Stanley, A. "Two Fictional Families, Neither Colorblind, but Only One Really Sees Black America." *New York Times,* November 4, 2005. www.nytimes .com/2005/11/04/arts/television/04tvwk.html?_r=2&pagewanted=all&ores login& (accessed June 7, 2013).

Stelter, Brian. "Oprah's New Channel Struggles to Pull in Viewers." *New York Times,* February 27, 2011. www.nytimes.com/2011/02/28/business/media /28own.html?_r=1& (accessed September 22, 2012).

Stephan, James J. *Census of State and Federal Correctional Facilities, 2005.* Washington, DC: Bureau of Justice Statistics, US Department of Justice, 2008.

Stir Crazy. Directed by Sidney Poitier. Culver City, CA: Columbia Pictures, 1980.

Stone. Directed by John Curran. Los Angeles: Millennium Films, 2010.

Stranger Inside. Directed by Cheryl Dunye. New York: HBO Films, 2001.

Strochlic, Nina. "'*Mothers of Bedford*': New Documentary on Mothers in Prison." *Daily Beast,* November 12, 2011. www.thedailybeast.com /articles/2011/11/12/mothers-of-bedford-new-documentary-on-mothers-in -prison.html (accessed May 14, 2013).

Sugar Boxx. Directed by Cody Jarrett. New York: Showtime Pictures, 2009.

Supermax. New York: ITV Studios, 2001.

"Supermax." *Inside.* Atlanta: Court TV Productions, May 8, 2006.

Surette, Ray. "Prologue: Some Unpopular Thoughts About Popular Culture." In *Popular Culture, Crime, and Justice,* edited by Frankie Bailey and Donna Hale, xiv–xxiv. Belmont, CA: Wadsworth, 1998.

———. *Media, Crime, and Criminal Justice: Images, Realities, and Policies.* Belmont, CA: Thomson Wadsworth, 2011.

"Surviving Maximum Security." *Explorer.* Directed by David Shadrak Smith. Washington, DC: National Geographic Society, March 25, 2005.

"Surviving Prison." *Inside.* Atlanta: Court TV Productions, May 25, 2008.

Sussman, Peter Y. "Media on Prisons: Censorship and Stereotypes." In *Invisible Punishment: The Collateral Consequences of Mass Imprisonment,* edited by Marc Mauer and Meda Chesney-Lind, 258–278. New York: New York Press, 2002.

Sweethearts of the Prison Rodeo. Directed by Bradley Beesley. Boston: Carnivaleque Films, 2009.

Sykes, Gresham. *The Society of Captives.* Princeton, NJ: Princeton University Press, 1958.

System of a Down. "Prison Song." *Toxicity.* Composed by Serj Tankian and Daron Malakain. Los Angeles: American Recordings, 2001.

Ted Koppel's Breaking Point. Produced by James Blue, Jay LaMonica, Elissa Rubin, and Peter Demchuk. Silver Spring, MD: Discovery Communications, October 7, 2007.

10 Violent Women. Directed by Ted V. Mikels. Philadelphia: Alpha Video, 1982.

Thomas, June, and Joel Fernando. "Raw, Real, and Heartbreaking: Sex and Love in *Orange Is the New Black*." *Slate,* June 13, 2014. www.slate.com

/blogs/outward/2014/06/13/orange_is_the_new_black_lesbian_sex_video .html (accessed July 25, 2014).

Throness, Laurie. *A Protestant Purgatory: Theological Origins of the Penitentiary Act, 1779.* Hampshire, UK: Ashgate Publishing, Ltd., 2008.

Time Served. Directed by Glen Pitre. Chicago: Studio City, 1999.

Titicut Follies. Directed by Frederick Wiseman. Cambridge, MA: Zipporah Films, 1967.

Tonry, Michael. *Thinking About Crime: Sense and Sensibility in American Penal Culture.* Oxford: Oxford University Press, 2004.

———. *Punishing Race.* New York: Oxford University Press, 2011.

Torture: America's Brutal Prisons. Directed by Nick London. Brooklyn, NY: Icarus Films, 2005.

Troop 1500. Directed by Ellen Spiro. San Francisco: Independent Television Services, 2005.

Trulson, Chad R., James W. Marquart, Craig Hemmens, and Leo Carroll. "Racial Desegregation in Prisons." *Prison Journal* 88, no. 2 (2008): 270–299.

Tuchman, Gaye. *Making News: A Study in the Construction of Reality.* New York: Free Press, 1978.

Tupac. "16 on Death Row." *R U Still Down? (Remember Me).* Composed by Tupac. Atlanta: Amaru Entertainment, 1997.

20 to Life: Prison Blues, Songs from the Angola State Penitentiary. Compiled by Harry Oster. Beverly Hills, CA: Varese Sarabande, 1960.

Undisputed. Directed by Walter Hill. Santa Monica, CA: Miramax, 2002.

University of Sing Sing. Directed by Tim Skousen. New York: HBO Pictures, 2011.

Unshackled. Directed by Bart Patton. Atlanta: Creative Media Services, 2000.

US Census Bureau. "Quickfacts." June 27, 2013. http://quickfacts.census.gov /qfd/states/00000.html (accessed July 26, 2013).

US Sentencing Commission. "U.S. Sentencing Commission Selects Policy Priorities for 2014–2015 Guidelines Amendment Cycle." August 14, 2014. www.ussc.gov/sites/default/files/pdf/news/press-releases-and-news-advi sories/press-releases/20140814_Press_Release_Rev.pdf (accessed August 20, 2014).

The Visit. Directed by Jordan Walker-Pearlman. Los Angeles: Urbanworld Films, 2000.

Voices from the Inside. Directed by Karina Epperlein. Blooming Grove, NY: New Day Films, 1996.

Wacquant, Loic. "Deadly Symbiosis: When Ghetto and Prison Meet and Mesh." *Punishment and Society* 3, no. 1 (2001): 91–134.

"Walking a Fine Line." *Breaking Down the Bars.* Studio City, CA: 44 Blue Productions, November 10, 2011.

The Walking Dead. Created by Frank Darabont. New York: AMC Studios, 2012.

Waltenon, Karma. "4 *Simpsons* Controversies that Didn't End in Lawsuits." *Mental Floss,* May 18, 2009. http://mentalfloss.com/article/21750/4-simp sons-controversies-didnt-end-lawsuits (accessed June 5, 2013).

War on the Family: Mothers in Prison and the Children They Leave Behind. Directed by John Lyons and Jackie Rivet-River. Chicago: Peace Productions, 2010.

Weeds. Directed by John Hancock. Wilmington, NC: De Laurentiis Entertainment Group, 1988.

What I Want My Words to Do to You. Directed by Madeleine Gavin, Judith Katz, and Gary Sunshine. Brooklyn, NY: American Documentary, 2003.

When the Bough Breaks: Children of Women in Prison. Directed by Jill Evans Petzall and Deed Rogers. New York: Filmmakers Library, 2001.

Williams, Hank, III. "Louisiana Stripes." *Straight to Hell.* Composed by Hank Williams III. Nashville: Bruc Records, 2006.

Wilson, David, and Sean S. O'Sullivan. *Images of Incarceration: Representations of Prison in Film and Television Drama.* Winchester, UK: Waterside Press, 2004.

Wine Institute. "2012 Wine Sales in U.S. Reach New Record: Record California Winegrape Crop to Meet Surging Demand." April 8, 2013. www.wine institute.org/resources/pressroom/04082013 (accessed June 10, 2013).

Wisely, John, and Ellen Creagar. "Prisons Unlock New Tourist Attractions." *USA Today,* May 18, 2012. http://usatoday30.usatoday.com/news/nation /story/2012-05-17/prison-tourist-attractions/55048870/1 (accessed June 10, 2013).

"Women Behind Bars." *Lockdown.* Washington, DC: National Geographic Television, February 11, 2007.

Women in Cages. Directed by Gerardo De Leon. Atlanta: New World Pictures, 1971.

Women in Prison. Directed by Lambert Hillyer. Culver City, CA: Columbia Pictures, 1939.

Women in Prison. Directed by Lewis Seiler. Culver City, CA: Columbia Pictures, 1955.

"Women on Lockdown." *Hard Time.* Washington, DC: National Geographic Television, July 19, 2011.

"The Worst of the Worst." *Hard Time.* Washington, DC: National Geographic Television, March 15, 2011.

The Wrath of Cain. Directed by Ryan Combs. Las Vegas: PI Pipeline Productions, 2010.

Wright, Kevin. *The Great American Crime Myth.* Westport, CT: Greenwood Press, 1985.

Yamaguchi, Adam. "Prison Power Play (Prison Gangs)." *Vanguard.* San Francisco: Current TV, November 28, 2007.

Ying Yang Twins. "23 Hour Lockdown." *U.S.A. (United States of Atlanta).* Composed by Kaine and D-Roc. New York: TVT Records, 2005.

You Can't Beat the Law. Directed by Phil Rosen. Los Angeles: Monogram Pictures, 1943.

"You're Not Here to Make Friends." *Breaking Down the Bars.* Studio City, CA: 44 Blue Productions, October 13, 2011.

Yousman, Bill. *Prime Time Prisons on U.S. TV: Representation of Incarceration.* New York: Peter Lang, 2009.

Zillman, Dolf. "Exemplification Effects in the Promotion of Safety and Health." *Journal of Communication* 56, Supplement 1 (2006): 221–237.

Zimring, Franklin E. *The Great Crime Decline.* Oxford: Oxford University Press, 2008.

Index

About the Book

THROUGH THE CENTURIES, PRISONS WERE CLOSED INSTITUTIONS full of secrets and shrouded in mystery. But modern media culture has opened the gates. Dawn K. Cecil explores decades of popular culture—from the golden age of Hollywood films to YouTube videos, from newspapers to beer labels, hip-hop music, and children's books—to reveal how prison imagery shapes our understanding of who commits crimes, why they do it, and how the criminal justice system should respond.

Dawn K. Cecil is associate professor of criminology at the University of South Florida St. Petersburg.